MW00769634
TO
PEA RIDGE
AND MARVEL
N
ALDRICH
HOAL CREEK
SEWER
HOLE
Golf Course
College
Lake
DAIRY
BARN
COLLEGE
DAIRY FARM
TO
DOGWOOD
HIGHLAND ST
COLLEGE DRIVE
LIBRARY
BLOCK
KING HOUSE
OAK
BLOCK
KING
CEMETERY
OUR
FOOTBALL FIELD
PLOWMAN
PRESIDENT'S HOUSE
FLOWER HILL
KING STREET
WADSWORTH
NABORS
HEDGEROW
GRAY GABLES
APARTMENTS
CARDINAL CREST DR.
MOODY
HIGHLAND AVE
TO
DOGWOOD
HWY 119
TO
ALABASTER

# NO HILL TOO HIGH FOR A STEPPER

*There ain't no hill too high for a stepper.*

— Red Mahan, 1899–1986

# NO HILL TOO HIGH FOR A STEPPER

*Memories of Montevallo, Alabama*

MIKE MAHAN

WITH NORMAN MCMILLAN

NEWSOUTH BOOKS
Montgomery

PUBLISHED IN COOPERATION WITH
THE CAHABA TRACE COMMISSION

*Voices Along the Trace Series*

NewSouth Books
105 S. Court Street
Montgomery, AL 36104


Published in the United States by NewSouth Books, a division of NewSouth, Inc.,
Montgomery, Alabama.

ISBN 978-1-60306-357-9 (cloth) — ISBN 978-1-60306-358-6 (ebook)
Library of Congress Control Number: 2014933019

Design by Randall Williams
Printed in the United States of America
by Edwards Brothers Malloy

Published in cooperation with
The Cahaba Trace Commission
13728 Montevallo Rd, Brierfield, AL 35035

## To My Family:

To Linda, "Neeno," the smartest, most intellectual, most serious, most beautiful, most understanding, most patient, and most loving wife a guy could have.

To Stann Mahan Garris and Miki Mahan Heaton, my two very successful daughters, both of whom during their lives have resided at my childhood home, 159 Shelby Street. There Stann conceived two of my grandsons, both of whom have lived there. Miki, who was conceived in the basement of the house on Shelby Street, grew up and matured with Big Mama and Poppy upstairs in that house.

To the boys. To my caring, receptive, athletic, and loving grandson Michael, now twenty-five years old, who visited regularly at 159 Shelby Street. To Jacob, now twenty-two years old, a smart, talented, beautiful grandson, who is the phrase "everybody loves Jacob." To grandson Jesse, now eighteen years old, a man of few words, whose academic, athletic, and musical abilities speak for him. Both Jacob and Jesse spent their first night out of the hospital on Shelby Street, and there both shared many of the same experiences of fun, discipline, pain, and pleasure I did when I resided there.

To all of the above, I hope that this narrative will give you something to talk about when I am dead and gone.

# Contents

## Part IV—Getting Out of Town



## Part V—Living the Life

# Preface

In 1983, David Ward, one of my friends from Highland Avenue in Montevallo, Alabama, published a short narrative entitled *Lamar and Me*, which described a special friendship that developed between him and a neighbor, Lamar Appleton, as they grew up in Montevallo. So much of what was in David's book rang true to me that I began to think about how important growing up in a small, diversified, academic community like Montevallo had been to me as well. And many of my contemporaries in Montevallo felt the same way.

With the success of *Lamar and Me*, a group of us—including Ed Givhan, Joy Holcombe, Gene Baldwin, Barbara Belisle, me, and, of course, David Ward and Lamar Appleton—thought it might be fun to write a book on our lives in Montevallo. Each would write a chapter or two, after which David would put his expert editorial skills to work. In 2000, the book, entitled *Time Has Made a Change in Me*, was completed and published, and, judging by the comments of readers, well-received.

My chapter in *Time Has Made a Change in Me* was called "In Praise of Shelby Street." The other authors were from Highland Avenue and other parts of town, but I was the only Shelby Street or Frog Holler contributor. After the book came out, Ed Givhan would tell me repeatedly, "Mahan, you have only just begun. You need to write a *book* about growing up on Shelby Street." Lifelong friends, we shared an interest in Alabama history, and he seldom said anything I didn't listen to seriously. He and I had hoped to do a book on historical homes of the Black Belt of Alabama, along with photographer Chip Cooper and Robert Gamble of the Alabama Historical Commission, but both Ed and Chip Cooper had other books to complete, and Ed and his wife, Peggy, were busy restoring a portion of the old family farm near Browns, Alabama. That project was stalled, however, when Ed became very ill. Still, when we were together he seemed always to bring up a book on Shelby Street. I was in his hospital room two days before he died on November 15, 2004. During that visit, he said in a quiet whisper that I had to get busy writing about Shelby Street. For me that was a great commission, and I have been committed to writing a book on the subject ever since.

Another person who urged me to write a memoir is my close friend Marty Everse, who is also devoted to Alabama history. I want to pay special tribute to Marty, who has always been able to bring my blue-sky projects down to earth and has helped me bring many dreams to fruition. I also owe him many thanks for his many hours scanning and editing the many photographs contained in this book. And to his wonderful wife Helon, better known as "Sweet Pea," thanks for sharing. Marty and I have worked together with the Alabama Historical Commission, the Alabama Historic Ironworks Commission, and the Cahaba Trace Commission, which among other things publishes books on the Cahaba Trace region which is made up of counties that border the Cahaba River system. The Commission established a series of memoirs called "Voices Along the Trace." I have written this book with that series in mind.

If any readers enjoy this manuscript, it is because of my friend and writing partner, Norman McMillan. Without his help, this narrative would not have come to completion. On many mornings, I arrived at Norman and Mama Joan's home at seven o'clock , and Norman and I would spend time talking about the people and events that are included in this memoir or sitting at the computer revising the manuscript. To Norman and Joan, all I can say is thanks, thanks, and more thanks for sharing their home and Norman's talent and time.

I must also pay tribute to Misty Jones, a lady who has helped immeasurably in putting my thoughts on paper. Without her, this book would have been impossible.

The petticoat dynasty at the Brierfield Dental office have tolerated, helped, and put up with me for a combined 126 years. To Margie, Betty, Glenda, Sandy (who for years has said, "Come on, Doc, we got to go to work"), Crystal, Amy, Kristy, and Renee (Muffet), I can only say thanks for your putting up with this and encouraging me. Special thanks go to two dear friends, Steve Huffstutler and Tim Wilson, for lending their editorial skills to this effort.

The many photographs in this book came from family and friends, many of whom are mentioned in the memoir. I want to particularly thank the University of Montevallo and its archivist Carey Weatherly for helping with the photographs.

To my classmate in elementary and high school and lifelong friend Emily Pendleton, I cannot count how many phone calls she answered helping me with dates and names. Thanks and I love you, Emily.

To Katie Johnston, I owe thanks for her many hours of copying, numbering, and ordering the photographs as well as for placing into three-ring binders all the drafts Norman sent.

My chief motivation for writing this memoir has been to pay tribute and say thanks to the many individuals who made Shelby Street and Montevallo a launch pad for my life.

# Part I

# *Family*

*The McKibbon House, where it all started. Since its construction in 1900, this grand Victorian structure has functioned first as a private residence, then as four apartments, back to a home, and now as the McKibbon House Bed and Breakfast Inn.*

I

# Beginnings

When my wife Linda and I celebrated our thirty-ninth anniversary in 2001, I rented a room for the night in the tower of the McKibbon House Bed and Breakfast in Montevallo, Alabama. It somehow seemed appropriate to spend an amorous night there, as it was in that very room that I was conceived during the fall of 1933. My parents, Red and Ethel Mahan, had an apartment in this rambling two-story high Victorian house on the corner of Boundary and Shelby Streets, living there with Tootsie and Sister, Ethel's teen-aged daughters by a previous marriage. My mother was about forty-three—eight years older than Red—when she became pregnant, and as her pregnancy advanced he was quite solicitous of her, becoming increasingly fretful that bearing a child at her age could present dangerous problems. He decided to take what was an unusual step in those days: to send her to Birmingham where she could get the best possible care. There she stayed with members of her family for a few weeks, finally entering the South Highland Infirmary for the delivery.

June 29, 1934, was a dark, threatening day. There was a churning and rumbling in the west as Ethel entered the hospital, and the sky got darker and darker as her labor progressed. High winds began to blow, harder and harder, and in time it became obvious that a cyclone—the then common name for a tornado—was coming. As Ethel was wheeled into the delivery room, lightning flashed and thunder cracked, wind rattled the window frames, and heavy rains pelted against the panes. Then, just as I was being delivered, it happened: a cyclone hit South Highland Infirmary with force. When I was finally taken to the nursery, a janitor was still sweeping up broken glass from blown-out nursery windows and workers were tacking up a tarpaulin to keep the rain out.

So I was told in family lore.

I was of course blissfully unaware of all this, lying snug in my bunting, but everyone in Montevallo knew the story soon: Stanley Michael Mahan Jr. had been born in a whirlwind. Later on, some of my friends would say that I have lived in a whirlwind ever since, and I'm bound to say that they have a point.

The Great Depression was ravaging the nation at the time of my birth. Because times were so hard, my father had been forced to sell his Ford coupe. When my mother and I were released from South Highland, he got Mr. Robert Holcombe, who ran the local Independent Grocers Association (IGA) store, to bring us back to Montevallo in his large black sedan. Our route to Montevallo was south on Highway 31 to Calera and west on Highway 25 to Montevallo. Although the road from Alabaster to Montevallo was more direct, it was not paved, and we, like most people, shunned it. Mother thought I needed a soft, smooth ride on a paved road since I had arrived in a cyclone.

In Montevallo, Mr. Holcombe turned off Highway 25 at Shelby Street, crossed over the railroad track, went past the cotton gin and ice plant, crossed the little red bridge over Shoal Creek, came up out of Frog Holler, and proceeded up Shelby Street past the Presbyterian Church on the right, turning to the left into the driveway of what would be my home until I went off to college. Daddy had rented this brand-new small white bungalow from Mr. Pete Givhan, landlord for several families on Shelby Street.

By all reports, my parents were doting, and I came to love them very much. My father, a barber by trade, had brilliant red hair, thereby gaining his nickname. I always associated him with rhythm. He walked in a loose, rhythmic way, and he stropped his razor and clicked his scissors in a rhythmic pattern. A compulsive key and coin rattler, he could never sit still. Every time he made the walk between the shop and our house, which was two blocks down Shelby Street, he invariably took two steps between the marked sections of the concrete sidewalk, always in exactly the same tempo.

If anyone ever relished life more than Red Mahan, I don't know it. School was a drag, he thought, so he stopped going after the ninth grade. There were many pleasant activities he would much rather give his time to, and

*My father, Stanley "Red" Mahan, making music and trying to make time with an unknown Brierfield beauty under the watchful eyes of her father.*

in many ways his ending of his formal education was only the beginning of his real passion to learn.

As a young boy Red developed a great love of music, and when he was a teenager he took up the mandolin and guitar. Before he married, he played off and on with several bands in Montevallo or Bibb County. Many years later, one of his fellow musicians, banjo player Cody Battle, lived near me in Brierfield. By then he was pretty much a hopeless drunk, but he remembered fondly the fun they had playing for both square dancing and round dancing. At some point Dad bought Battle's banjo for me. Dad also developed quite a reputation for his square dance calling and continued to call throughout his life.

Once Dad told me that it was a wonder his Martin guitar had survived those years, as once when the guitar was new a fight had broken out and he had been forced to crown one of the combatants with it. Luckily, his brother-in-law, Jim Splawn, a noted carpenter, glued and screwed it back together, and he played that guitar when Dad was courting Ethel, he played it with

*Red Mahan courting on the Thomas Mill bridge in Bibb County.*

his buddies after work in his barbershop, he played it at church. He even played that Martin guitar when courting his second wife, Miss Opal, whom he married when he was eighty years old.

In addition to Cody Battle's banjo, I still have Dad's Martin guitar, which I still play on occasion. To hold both these instruments in my hands is thrilling to me, as it puts me in touch with the musical traditions that inspired in me my great love of music.

Growing into manhood, Dad became a champion dancer, equally at home with a buck and wing, which was a complicated fast dance, or with a waltz. He entered dancing contests throughout central Alabama and became well known as a high-spirited young man. Some called him a confirmed bachelor; others called him a rounder. He chased women shamelessly, and he was seldom refused. Women and music went together for him, and many photographs were taken of him playing the mandolin with an adoring beauty by his side.

Besides women, Red loved the trains of his day, the ones propelled by steam engines. On numerous occasions he was heard to say, "If it don't have iron wheels and blow smoke, it ain't worth a damn." His brother-in-law Vernon Hubbard, his brother Allen, and his sister Lois were all telegraphers for the railroad, and that was what he aspired to. But since no telegrapher job was available, at the age of seventeen he took a job as a brakeman for the GM&O Railroad, working the Selma to Meridian, Mississippi, line.

Red quickly grew weary of his job as a brakeman, which kept him away from home most of the time. Living in dusty boarding houses in Meridian became too much for him, and he decided to quit the railroad. The Wilton Barbershop was across the tracks from the train depot in Wilton, two miles southwest of Montevallo, and when he was home he would go in and watch the barbers, learning to cut hair by observation. He asked for a job, and he was lucky enough to get it. The location of the shop made it accessible to railroad personnel, locals, and travelers. Dad told me that he could do a haircut in the time it took the engineer to load the tender with water and coal and for the conductor to board the new passengers.

It was the Roaring Twenties when Dad got into the barbering business. At that time, girls were all getting feather bobs in barbershops, and Dad always had an eye out for opportunity. He determined that he should relocate to Montevallo, where there were numerous female students at Alabama College, a women's liberal arts school, who might use his services, tonsorial or otherwise. In 1923, he bought a small barbershop on Main Street from Mr. R. A. Tatum, who had cut hair there for many years. Dad cleverly advertised his new business in the newspaper as "Red's Bobher Shop," and business was quite good, both male and female.

*Following in the footsteps of his older sister Lois and brothers Cary, Jesse, and Allen, Dad got on with the railroad. He is standing on the right side of the cowcatcher with unidentified co-workers on a Georgia, Mobile, and Ohio steam engine.*

In time, Red decided what he really needed was a beauty parlor in the back of his shop. The only problem was that there was not an available beautician in Montevallo to work for him. So he went to the Magic City Beauty School in Birmingham to inquire about a graduate to hire, and there he found a divorcee named Mary Ethel Wood. The next week he drove up to get her in his coupe, taking along one of his girlfriends. Poor Ethel had to ride back to Montevallo in the rumble seat of his two-door, five-window coupe with all her luggage crammed around her, but she didn't complain. She had two teen-aged daughters to support.

Red had a room in the McKibbon House, and he managed to get quarters for Ethel and the girls there, too. Ethel was a real looker with a wonderful smile, excellent anatomy, and a great personality, and before long Red came to look on Ethel as more than an employee. Soon their working relationship became a love affair, and within a year the two were married. Red embraced Tootsie and Sister, who were teenagers, as his own daughters, though he never officially adopted them. They called him Daddy Red, and he grew to love them and happily supported them.

I was well into my teens when I discovered they were not my real sisters. One day when Gene Baldwin, an older neighbor who lived two houses up the street, and I were walking down by the creek behind our houses, somehow I made him mad, and he blurted out that Red was not Sister and Tootsie's father. I was thunderstruck. I accused him of making it up and started running toward my house, tears streaming down my face. I found my maternal grandmother, whom we called Momma, sitting in her bedroom sewing, and I told her what Gene had told me. She took me into her arms and held me and patted my back, then told me to sit down on her bed. "Honey, I've been expecting this for some time. It was inevitable that you would find out so I guess I'm as good as anyone to explain it to you." She told me that Mother had been married to a Mr. Peters, but that he was not a good husband. He was a bad drinker, and when he was drunk he was unkind to both Mother and the girls. She supported Mother totally in her decision to divorce him. Then when Mother married Red and I came along, it just didn't seem worth it to bring the matter up.

That didn't make sense to me. Why couldn't they tell me? All the times

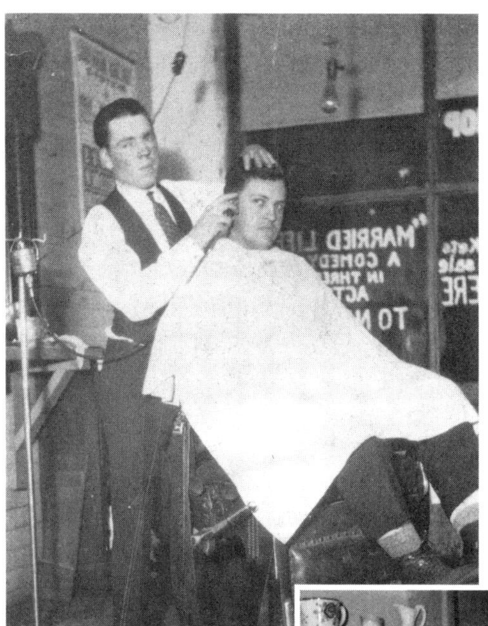

*Tired of life on the railroad, Dad first started cutting hair in a shop in Wilton.*

*My mother, Ethel. Beautiful, talented, caring, and always ready to help, she is standing by her post-World War II General Electric stove in our home on Shelby Street.*

I had seen Dad hug the girls and tell them he loved them became sour memories. He told me the same thing, but I was *his* and the girls were not, and he acted like he loved them as much as me. Plus, as a teenaged boy, it seemed to me that a father should love his son more than his daughters anyway. Luckily, this line of thinking didn't continue long, but I did resent the fact that Sister and Tootsie still went to see Mr. Peters and even considered him their father, even though he did not contribute a nickel to their support. What surprised me most was that Mother didn't seem to object at all to their having a relationship with their father. I couldn't hold anything against my mother for very long, though, and any uncertainty about Sister and Tootsie was forgotten.

If Red was in perpetual motion, my mother Ethel was as steady as the North Star. Although she had only a high school education, she held herself high. She had beautiful manners, and she knew how things were to be done properly. Despite the stereotype of the beauty shop as a mecca for gossip, Ethel did not engage in it. She heard a great deal, no doubt, but she didn't repeat it. Before long she had amassed a clientele of teachers from Alabama College as well as prominent business ladies in town and the surrounding communities. Everyone thought of hers as a high-class operation, despite the fact that the beauty parlor was located in the rear of the "bobher" shop, separated by only a half wall with a swinging saloon door. Her customers did not even seem to mind having to pass by a group of barbershop patrons sitting on a wooden bench against the left wall, some of whom were not subtle in giving Mother's clients the once-over.

As a small boy, I would sit and watch my mother at her daily routine of applying cold cream to her beautiful skin, and when she finished cleaning her face and applying makeup, I thought she looked like an angel. She never washed her face with soap and water, as she thought that in time it would leave her skin dry and hard.

Mother usually worked in a white uniform, but when she would go to the regular Wednesday afternoon teas at Reynolds Hall, the most beautiful building on the campus of Alabama College, she would change out of her uniform and into her very best clothes. I was especially proud of her then. In her white cotton gloves, she held her own quite well among the faculty members, who were the chief guests at these events. Mother took great pride in being asked to "pour" at these Wednesday afternoon teas, especially when she was matched with Dr. Josephine Eddy, the imposing head of the home economics department. Only a little less special was being selected to pour with the librarian, Miss Abi Russell, or Dr. Katherine Vickery, prominent member of the psychology department. At the weekly teas, the college's gleaming sterling silver tea service, flanked by silver candleholders, was placed on a white linen tablecloth alongside a colorful flower arrangement, usually gathered from Flower Hill, the home of the college's president. The group took their tea in delicate pink Wedgwood cups and ate their cakes from Wedgwood plates depicting campus buildings. Mother was in heaven at these events. Just to think that a high school graduate was a valued member of such a sophisticated and classy event.

Like Red, Ethel was a good dancer, but she lacked his enthusiasm. Often at events they attended he would wind up dancing more with Tootsie and Sister than with her. As she aged, Ethel developed arthritis and had to give up dancing. She also developed some anatomical changes that probably didn't please Dad. He always liked shapely women, and his eyes were always open to the comeliness of the female anatomy. So his dance partners became his beautiful daughters, especially Sister.

Red and Ethel would work in the same shop on Main Street for thirty plus years. In the back she would be curling hair; in the front he would be snipping away, and the testosterone and the progesterone seemed to find a nice balance in the barber and beauty sections. But I quickly observed that the tone of the barbershop changed radically when Mother left. There seemed to be an unwritten law that the male customers would not use profanity or vulgarity while the beauty parlor was operating, but when the coast was clear the talk turned almost immediately to more manly stories of wine, women, and song.

So these, then, were my parents, Red and Ethel, who conceived me on Shelby Street and brought me to my home on Shelby Street. This street became the hub of my universe, a magical place that I felt extremely lucky to inhabit. There might have been more fashionable addresses in Montevallo, but I was well-pleased to live at 159 Shelby Street.

*Top: Looking southeast from Main Street down Shelby Street. Rogan's Store was on the left. Mr. Rogan's truck and Pete Givhan's Coca-Cola truck are parked nose to nose. The white building behind Rogan's once housed the town newspaper. Directly across the street sat Mr. Givhan's Coca-Cola warehouse. Barely visible down the street, on the left, is the white-brick Presbyterian Church.*
*Bottom: 159 Shelby Street, my home and the home of Ethel's tree, about 1940.*

2

# 159 Shelby Street

Pete Givhan was an excellent landlord, and he and his wife Sassy seemed more like friends than landlords. Although they might have been seen as Highland Avenue aristocrats, there was never any class distinction that I was aware of. Dad really wanted to own his own house, though, and after World War II he bought the bungalow from Pete as well as the house next door. From then on we lived in what was called the Mahan house. Later it would be numbered 159 Shelby Street, but in those days directions were given in a much more personal way. If I told someone how to get to my house, I would say, "Coming south on Main Street, you turn left onto Shelby Street at Rat Scott's Chevrolet place and Rogan's Store. Then come on down toward the little red bridge to the third house on the right, just two houses this side of Mr. Robert DeSear's. And, hey, it's just antigoglin from the Presbyterian Church." Antigoglin was our word for catty-cornered or, more precisely, cater-cornered.

Our house might have been small and modest, but it was ours and we were proud of it. Except for Mrs. Craig's huge brick house directly across the street, we thought it the finest on Shelby Street. Next to us was the Bloomer Wilson house. It was older, and its one-by-six pine siding was not painted very well. Its drab brown color was trimmed in peeling and dirty white paint, and it smelled of creosote. Inside, however, Bloomer's wife, Miss Lucille, kept everything very, very clean. The Hartley house, down the street from us also needed to be painted at times, and the DeSear house was not very attractive either and needed paint badly.

Our house, with eight-inch clapboard siding, had four gables, and each gable had a louvered vent to let the hot air out. No other house on Shelby had them.

Our house had hardwood floors, which Mother kept waxed to a high shine. Twice a year, in the spring and shortly before Christmas, she would have Harry Miller, who worked for Dad in the barbershop, come down and wax the floors. To begin with, he had the difficult task of removing all the old wax with mineral spirits on a rag, working on his knees. After that, he applied Johnson's Paste Wax to the floor with rags. Then he tied rags to the mop and buffed the floors to a high shine, back and forth, up and down, over and over again. Occasionally, if Ethel planned a big event three or four months later he would give the floors a second waxing— "same song, second verse," to quote my dad.

There were six rooms in our house—a living room and dining room, which we could close off from the rest of the house, leaving only a kitchen and three bedrooms to heat and for our maid to clean. We had two fireplaces, but we heated with coal stoves. We were especially proud of the shiny black pot-bellied stove with brass trim that sat in the living room, which we used only on Sundays and special days. Daddy would arrange some kindling on the grate and put some coal atop that. Then he would roll up a sheet of newspaper and light it and put it under the starter and coal, and in no time a fire was blazing. The heater had isinglass windows behind which there was a cloudy red glow. When Dad would open the heater to add more coal, a blast of extreme heat could be felt half-way across the room.

In the kitchen there was a coal water heater. This little black monster was hot almost 24/7. The silver gray tank held enough water for cooking, washing, and bathing, and when the heater was fired with Aldrich red-ash coal, it would begin talking to you—clicking, popping, thumping, grinding. It was almost as if it were saying, "Oh, no, you're going to heat me up again. Don't I ever get any rest?" Knowing that Dad had started a fire at six o'clock in the morning, I would often run into the kitchen and place my hands on the water heater to see if it was getting about ready for my bath.

Every summer Mother would tell Dad it was time to black the stove. She would not have an ashy-looking stove in her house. After he had applied the special black stove paint and made a fire, there was a caustic smell in the house that faded away after the initial fire. Mother also got the idea of painting the water heater silver, and Dad dutifully got some paint and set to work. He apparently got bad paint, because when the heater got hot, all the paint popped off and Mother's dream of a gleaming silver water heater had to be put on indefinite hold.

For years my job was to bring in scuttles of coal and to cut splinters from the huge hunks of fat lighter wood in the backyard. Dad would go out into the countryside to get these knots of pine, which were the taproots of the long-leaf pine trees that were so plentiful in our part of the world. The wood was so rich that red and yellow resin oozed from it. Dad's job was to cut the knots into six to eight inch lengths, and mine was to take my hatchet and split the pine into splinters. On the back porch was a splinter box, and I was told to make sure that it never was empty. At times I felt a little put upon, but I also took some pride in contributing to the operation of the household.

My parents were not stingy when it came to coal, and I really appreciated that when I would occasionally visit neighbors and find their houses chilly. However, the acquisition of coal was a very complex maneuver. First Dad would call Mr. Day, who had a dump truck, to go to the Aldrich, Dogwood, or Boothton mine to get a load of coal for us. The Aldrich red-ash coal was the preferred coal by far, as it would light quick, burn hot, and leave little ash.

Sometimes I was allowed to go with Mr. Day, and I was excited to watch him pull his truck up under an overhead bin and tell the mine worker atop the bin how much coal he wanted—a quarter ton, half ton, full ton, or so-and-so many cubic feet. He also had to tell him the size—stove coal, fireplace coal, or stoker coal. Then the bin operator would pull a lever and the coal would be released, slide down a trough, and pour into the truck bed. Occasionally the size coal we wanted was not available, and we would have to get big black chunks of glistening coal, some of the pieces so large I couldn't lift them. They would have to be broken up into smaller pieces, using a five or ten pound "blue Monday"—the name my colored friends called a sledgehammer weighing five or ten pounds. It was so called because nobody wanted to start the week wielding such a heavy hammer.

Once Mr. Day's truck was loaded, he took the coal to my house and dumped it in front of the coal shed. Then Dad would shovel it under the shed to keep it dry. So the process of providing heat with coal was a complex matter, and it was an important part of my childhood routine.

When I was in middle school, natural gas arrived in Montevallo, and I felt liberated. The whole town watched with excitement as the pipe was being laid all around the city. Mother, though, was unhappy, as she feared that the laying of the line might injure the majestic water oak tree that stood in the front yard between the sidewalk and curb. It turned out the tree was safe, as the city took jackhammers and cut the concrete in the street to lay the lines so as not to get in the way of water lines that were buried between the sidewalk and curb.

Ethel's tree, as my mother's water oak was known in the neighborhood, was her pride, and she would not have one inch cut from the limbs or let its leaves to be bothered in any way. She had a continuous battle with Mr. Davis and other Alabama Power Company officials as well as with people from the telephone company, and for all her life she came out victorious. But after the house was sold in 2009, Ethel's tree was finally cut down. It took them over half a century, but the utilities finally won.

About the time we moved up to natural gas from coal, Dad also replaced the old electric stove, a G.E. with four burners and an oven at eye level that stood on four white spindly legs. The new electric stove had a nice big oven and three eyes on the cooking surface, and with drawers, not legs, supporting it. But at that time electrical power was quite unreliable, and when it went out Momma would have to cook simple meals on the little black monster in the kitchen, which we had kept to heat our water.

That little black monster could become dangerously hot. In fact, when I was around five years old, it got so hot that the wall behind it caught on fire. Momma calmly called the volunteer fire department. I was afraid the house would burn down. As several firemen, including Dad, rushed in, I held on to Momma's coat tails and watched in fear as they doused the flames with a hand-held extinguisher. We had not bought the house at that time, and Pete Givhan had Dad install asbestos board behind the stove and water heater, and I was happy we were then safe from fire. That asbestos board was still in the kitchen at 159 Shelby Street when my daughter Stann moved into the house in 2003.

Mother was proud of every aspect of our house. She bragged, quite naturally, about the oak floors in the front of the house and the pine ones in the back. She was also fond of saying our front porch, paved with red ten-inch tiles, was much preferable to the wooden porches of most of our neighbors. You couldn't scratch it, and you didn't have to paint it. Her pride in the home was confirmed when my Dad's sister, Aunt Kate, who lived out in the country, followed our house-plan when she and her husband built their new house.

Our porch was the gathering place for neighbors like Mrs. Craig, Mildred Doyle, and the Hartleys, and sometimes, to catch the breeze, we would take the glider and chairs out in the yard and sit there. On some nights when we could see a red glow in the sky to the north, Dad would tell us that that was the Tennessee Coal and Iron open-hearth furnaces all the way up in Ensley, which was forty or more miles away. He explained that we could only see it when low clouds hung over the furnaces, reflecting their glow downward.

For many years Mother had open house for the trick-or-treaters on Halloween, and the house would be flooded with kids, some from outlying areas like Pea Ridge and Dogwood. Everybody else gave out candy at the door, but at our house the ghouls and goblins were brought into the dining room, where Mother ladled red fruit punch into paper cups for them and offered them cookies on Halloween napkins. I felt proud that our house was so popular with the kids in the area.

As a boy, I especially loved sitting in the swing on the front porch at night when the wind was blowing and watching the streetlight on Main blow back and forth, first in my line of vision, then out. Hanging in the middle of Main and Shelby on a wire from corner to corner, the streetlight had a shining green reflector, which cast eerie shades on the buildings and pavement. I would count the seconds the light swung out of sight as the wind blew it, and occasionally I would even get the kitchen clock to measure it. I don't know what value that knowledge had, but as a boy I was constantly gathering information that had little practical value. I began then a lifelong obsession with quantifying, counting, and measuring. Later, along with the white streetlight, a stoplight was installed at the corner of Shelby and Main. It had only two colored lights, red and green—there was no amber in those days—and as it blew in the breeze it was even more eerie than the white streetlight alone.

Daddy kept the yard in first-class condition, and he was extremely pleased when Mrs. Craig across the street complimented him on it. He regularly raked the lawn with a yard broom, which he prized and didn't like for me to use. That was quite all right with me. In the fall when the leaves fell, he would rake the yard carefully, placing the leaves in a long line next to the curbing. He would light the pile at one end, and the fire would crawl slowly along the street from one end to the other. I would take a stick when the fire would die down and stir around until I made the leaves flare up again. I felt like a magician.

Mother and Dad kept White Leghorn chickens in a pen next to the coal shed in the backyard. There was a running debate in our neighborhood over whether our pale white eggs were as good as the brown ones laid by the Domineckers. I could tell no difference in taste myself, but once a year, when we dyed Easter eggs, I preferred our white eggs. It was a great ritual, and brought out our creative talents. Having boiled a dozen eggs the night before, I would get out five or six coffee cups, fill them almost full of water and add different colors of cake coloring. Then we would drop in the eggs, let them sit for a while, then lift them out with a strainer. Voila: those white Leghorn eggs had become Easter eggs. The neighborhood girls, Martha and Kacky Cox and Laura Ann Hicks, greatly outdid us boys, using wax pencils to draw patterns on the eggs before dying them. We boys settled for solid colors, though occasionally we would dye a two-toned egg.

I never think of Easter eggs without thinking of our dog Tag, a little short-legged mixed breed who found all the eggs we couldn't, cracked them open, and slurped out the meat. I swear there was a smile on Tag's face as he pranced around the yard after finding an egg, his tail turned up in a perfect semicircle.

There were five regular occupants in our house: Mother, Dad, Sister, Tootsie, and me. But Momma spent long periods with us, and in the summers my blind Aunt Lucille, who taught at the Talladega School for the Deaf and Blind, would come for extended visits. It became clear to me very early on that Dad and I were outnumbered. We were surrounded by strong, assertive women, and I began my life in a world that would be controlled by a series of petticoat dynasties. But I adored the women in my

*Left: Tag was the best dog that ever lived. He tagged behind me wherever I went for over twelve years, and he was welcomed into the homes of all my Frog Holler and Shelby Street friends. Tag was buried in the back yard of our home on Shelby Street.*

*Below: Many things occurred in my back yard including my sixth birthday party.*

household and did not find their rule oppressive at all.

It was not to be denied that Mother was the dominant one in our household. She was a quite sincere, devoted Christian, and she tried to make her children follow suit. Every morning she conducted family devotionals taken from the Methodist publication, *The Upper Room*, but I didn't cotton to it much. Plus, she made sure we got to Sunday School every week. A teacher in the youth department herself, she had a constant battle with me over preparing my Sunday School lesson every week. She did not want me to embarrass her by being unprepared when I went to Mrs. Kelly's class. The truth was that I could not stand the lessons. I had liked Sunday School as long as we were coloring and drawing pictures, but when it came to memorizing Bible verses and studying the Sunday School lesson book, I quickly lost interest. On many occasions I conveniently "lost" my lesson book. But Mother would make sure I got another, and the battle over preparing my lessons would begin again.

When I was bad, it was Mother who outlined what punishment I would receive. A proponent of progressive education, she was not much for corporal punishment. Occasionally, though, she might cut a little switch from the privet hedge and half-heartedly go through the motions of switching me. But her usual choice of punishment was to make me sit in the bathroom with no form of entertainment. I found that very oppressive, until I discovered that I could keep a rope under the claw foot bathtub and use it for an escape out the window. All I had to do was tie the rope to one leg of the tub, step up onto the commode seat, and lift myself onto the lower window sash. From there it was an easy drop by rope to the yard.

I can't deny that I was always a free spirit. I just didn't have the constitutional makeup to stay where I was supposed to be. "Mike, I'm telling you, stay in the backyard or you're going to be in trouble," Mama would say to me, but in no time I was down at the creek or over at the Presbyterian churchyard. Anywhere but where I was supposed to be.

If my infraction was bad enough, then Mother would turn me over to Dad. "You are going to have to take Mike to the coalhouse, Red." If she said "Red," it wasn't too bad, but if she said "Stanley," then I could be assured it was "Katie bar the door" for me. She would say to Dad, "He sassed me three times this afternoon, Stanley, and after I explicitly told him he could not go down to the creek he went anyway." It seemed to me that Dad looked rather forlorn as he motioned for me to follow him. It was like he too was being punished. As we approached the open doorway of the dirty coalhouse, he would remove his leather belt, and when we entered the dark, dusty room I would brace myself. The truth was that Dad never hit very hard, but still I would always dance the coal room shuffle as he administered the whipping. As the licks became weaker and weaker, he would warn me that I would get

*Mother, Dad, and me in the early spring about 1941. Mother had the kudzu vine behind us planted to block her view of the two-story Hartley house next door.*

more where that came from if I didn't mend my ways. "Do what your mother says," he would always say. "She's the boss."

When I had been particularly bad, Dad would go in the house and come out to the coalhouse with his razor strop, which was four inches wide and thirty inches long. The strop was double, with a thin white leather one used for fine sharpening and a rough dark leather one used for the rougher work. It was the fine side that hit you, followed immediately by the popping of the rough piece. "Flap, clap," it sang out. Dad assumed somehow that this was worse than the belt, but, though it made a great racket, it really hurt much less.

I remember feeling the true blaze of Dad's anger only once, and that hurt me to the quick. This time he didn't need to take off his belt. He wounded me with his words. I was about twelve and had gotten quite interested in mechanical things, spending a lot of time in the garage working on my bicycle. When I got tools from Dad's toolbox, I was careful to put them back, but one day I figured out that it would be much better if his tools were arranged in a more orderly fashion. I found some old black paint and a brush and painted an outline for all of his tools on the wall, taking special pleasure when I drew in places for his prized box-end wrenches—all in graduated order. When I finished hammering in the nails the tools would hang on and putting the tools in their proper places, I stood back and proudly observed my handiwork. Dad was going to love this. I ran in the house and got Mother, who said she was extremely impressed with what a good job I had done. Then I sat on the porch awaiting Dad, who always worked an hour or two longer than Mother.

"Come see, come see," I yelled as he approached the house. I motioned for him to follow me to the garage. I approached the workbench with great pride and a sense of accomplishment. "Ta da," I said dramatically, motioning to the display of tools.

Dad did not smile. As he surveyed the tools, a sour look came over his face, and when he finally said something, he spoke through his teeth: "This is the biggest bunch of shit I've ever seen."

I was crushed. I was heartbroken. I felt tears coming to my eyes. I watched as he yanked the tools from the wall and threw them back in the toolbox. "From now on, you can just leave my tools alone," he said loudly. With those words, he stomped out of the garage, not waiting for a response.

That was probably just as well, as my hurt was fast turning to anger. Even if he didn't like the job I had done, he didn't have to act like a fool. I sat on the floor of the garage for a while and cried, and I couldn't help thinking how much I hated that man. But if I have a virtue, it may be that I do not hold grudges. I just get on to something else. But for the moment I felt an intense resentment the likes of which I had never known.

I suppose Mother and Dad got along as well or better than most married couples. They were partners at work and partners at home. Whiskey was about the only thing I remember ever coming between them. Dad liked a drink, especially on Saturday nights. It would usually begin when Hoot Lucas drove up in front of the shop in his dump truck a little before closing time every Saturday. He was invariably the last customer of the day, getting a shave every week and a haircut every other week. At six foot two, Hoot cut an imposing figure. His black hair, which he liberally applied pink hair tonic to, glistened. His white shirt and dark overalls, bought across the street at Mr. Sam Klotzman's store, were very clean and nicely pressed.

Hoot always wanted his black brogans with their brass eyes and shiny laces spit shined, and when I was there I would spend at least ten minutes on each shoe. When I finished, he would fish a nickel tip out of his pocket and hand it to me with a nod. The ten cents for the shine was added by Dad to the price of the shave, which was six bits.

Hoot always carried a paper sack which he would hand to Dad when he entered the shop. I learned quickly that it held a pint of clear liquid moonshine. When Dad finished shaving Hoot, he would pick up the paper sack and disappear through the swinging saloon doors of the beauty shop. I knew he would walk through Mother's empty beauty shop and go into the back room where the toilet was. When he returned, I could always smell the moonshine. Afterwards, he and Hoot would joke around a little. Then, when Hoot drove off, we'd lock up the shop and walk home.

Mother could smell the moonshine too, and, as a teetotaler, she couldn't help but complain. Sometimes he would ignore her, but more often Dad would get mad and leave the house, with Mother calling out behind him, "Go on and get loaded. See if I care." But she did care.

Dad would sometimes go off with his drinking buddies—P. C. Wilson, Mr. Cunningham, Mr. DeSear, and Bloomer Wilson. Often they would go

*The Man: Stanley M. Mahan Senior, my dad. There never was a hill too high for this stepper. Circa 1920.*

to Mr. Reggie Lawley's house for a drink. Other times, since Dad had no car, someone would pick him up to go out to Randolph to buy more moonshine or illegal labeled whiskey from Burley Jackson. Burley had a garage where he worked on cars, but he also had a room in the back where he conducted his more lucrative business. There he kept pints of bootleg moonshine, and he would also sell you a shot of whiskey for two bits. Everybody drank from the same little glass, and no one ever knew of the glass being washed.

Where Dad went after he left Burley's place was anyone's guess. He liked to party and have a good time, and once he got that on his mind, there was no stopping him. I found myself quite sympathetic with Mother when she and Dad argued, because I had been taught at Sunday School that drinking whiskey was a sin and that it could break up a home. I certainly didn't want it to break our family apart.

The real truth was that this wasn't going to break up our home. I knew that intuitively. Dad would always come home, and as far as I could see there were no major repercussions. Mother would say how crazy it was that he would pay Burley Jackson two bits for a shot when that was all he got for a haircut. She thought it was a terrible use of his hard-earned money. But Dad paid little attention and sometimes walked out of the room singing, "Shave and a haircut, two bits, I've got a gal with two tits." Mother would just shake her head.

I realize how much I am my parents' son. Like my mother, in my profession of dentistry I often think of expenditures in terms of how many crowns or implants I will have to do to pay for the item. And, like Dad, I have a real attraction to a woman's first measurement.

For whatever small failures Dad had, he was in so many ways a model father, looking out for his family and treating Mother with respect. He just had to adjust to the efforts to domesticate him, a man who had lived a free life until he was over thirty years old.

3

# Momma and Aunt Lucille

It seemed to me that Momma set the tone for our family in many ways when she was with us. This short, chunky lady, her gray hair knotted on the back of her head, lived with us off and on for years, occupying the right bedroom in the back of the house. For a while I slept in the big double bed with her, and that always gave me a good, secure feeling. She never read me stories, but she told me about her early life in Carbon Hill and how her newly built home was destroyed in 1926 by a cyclone. Her husband, Samuel Hobert Wood, had run the commissary at the Carbon Hill mine and afterwards opened his own general store. But after the cyclone, he made the difficult decision to leave Carbon Hill and move to West End, in Birmingham, and start all over again. He opened a neighborhood grocery store that he operated until his death, which happened shortly before I was born. One of my regrets in life is that I never got to know this grandfather.

Though Momma never raised her voice and was always gracious, she wielded great power, the power of example. And she was always diplomatic, never siding with either Mother or Dad when they disagreed over something. Because Mother worked, the running of the house, when she was there, was left up to Momma, who had very high standards of housekeeping.

When I think of Momma, I always see the beautiful dining table she set. The main meal of the day, which we called dinner, was served around noon, and it was a formal affair. Even on weekdays, when the silver and fine china were not used, there was a starched white tablecloth and the table was formally laid. Momma thought the cloth had to be white, and I remember a bit of disagreement between her and Mother, who had bought a red tablecloth. She suggested that they use it one day at lunch, but Momma demurred, finally agreeing that it might be all right for breakfast or even supper, but never for the main meal of the day.

*With Momma, my grandmother, the class act of my early life on Shelby Street.*

On Sunday everything really had to be perfect. Emily Post herself would have been envious of the table Momma set. When we sat down to Sunday dinner, we always found linen napkins at each place as well as Momma's fine sterling—a salad fork, a dinner fork, a spoon, and a knife. Also on the table was Mother's fine white china with pink roses around the edges. Later, Tootsie thought Mother needed a better set of dishes, and she presented her with an eight-place setting of more modern design.

If we had soup, there would be a silver soup spoon. Everybody also had their own bread plate, with a little knife for spreading on butter, honey, or jelly. Butter, fresh-churned at Mr. J. K. Cunningham's dairy, was on its crystal plate, and each person had his own salt dish. Sterling pickle forks were provided, and stemmed goblets for water and iced tea. China cups and saucers were also on the table, but I didn't drink coffee because I was told that it would turn me black. To this day, I don't drink coffee.

Daddy always sat at the head of the table, a stack of china plates before him. Before any food was served, he always said the grace. During the week, he always quickly said his standard blessing: "Father, make us thankful for this day and for this food we are about to partake. Bless it to our use and us to thy service." But on Sunday he would ask a special blessing covering every sphere of our lives. This was a bit hard to take, far too long with all the fine smells giving rise to pangs of hunger. Once he had thanked God for everything, asked for forgiveness for all wrongs we did last week, and asked for guidance in the following one, he began to carve and serve the meat. With a routine that might have been choreographed by Sister's dance teacher at Alabama College, he would pick up a large silver fork with a yellowed pearl handle and put a piece of meat on each plate. He handed the plate to the left, and it was passed all the way around the table to the person on his right. Then the bowls of vegetables were passed to the left, everyone serving himself.

The food itself was not particularly fancy, just basic home cooking—a pot roast surrounded by carrots, onions, and potatoes, clove-spiked pink hams, or a large platter piled high with golden fried chicken. If forced to make a choice, I would say that the fried chicken was my favorite. It resulted from a ritual that had begun the day before.

The killing and dressing of the Sunday chicken was an event both terrifying and exciting to me. Our maid, Maggie Hale, Momma, or sometimes Dad would wring the chicken's neck, after which the bird would flop around on the ground in its death throes. Once still, it was put into boiling water and plucked of its feathers until the skin was white and clean. Then a sharp knife was stuck in its rear end and a large gash cut, from which the intestines and other organs were pulled. Only then could the chicken be cut up for frying. This process of cleaning the chicken, I was told, was called dressing the chicken, but I thought it was far more like undressing a chicken.

The liver and gizzard were saved to make gravy to serve over rice, mashed potatoes, or dressing. But I was far more interested in the pulley-bone, which everyone knew was my designated piece. At Sunday dinner, after I had cleaned the bone thoroughly, I would hold it up to one of my sisters, and we would make a wish and pull the bone apart. The one getting the small end was supposed to have his wish come true, though I never remember it working out that way.

After the main part of the meal was over, Momma and Mother cleared the table of all used dishes and then brought out dessert and poured coffee for the grownups. Sometimes Dad wanted his coffee with his meal, and the ladies would not object to this breach of proper etiquette.

Dad was addicted to his coffee. Every weekday he had a ritual before leaving for work. After finishing his eggs and bacon and grits, he took his coffee cup and saucer and put it on his plate, pouring some of the coffee into the saucer and raising the saucer to his lips and drinking it with a loud slurping sound. Then he would reach for any remaining biscuit and crumble it into the remaining coffee, picking up his spoon and eating the mixture with great relish. We called this "eating cuddly-muddly." Unfortunately, I was never allowed to make cuddly-muddly, which is one way I think I might have learned to like coffee.

Food was most important to me, I guess, in the afternoon when I came home famished from school. I would immediately rush to the kitchen stove to find the leftovers from dinner. I didn't mind one bit that the food was at room temperature. I would grab a baked sweet potato from the oven, break the top off and cover it in butter, then wolf it down. Candied sweet potatoes would go between two pieces of cornbread or in a cold biscuit, and sometimes I would put black-eyed peas or turnip greens and their pot liquors over cornbread. I never bothered to sit down to eat these feasts, just stood by the stove and ate off the oven top or counter by the sink. But usually I did sit down to cap off this culinary experience with a dessert—"nanner pudding," rice pudding, or, my favorite, tapioca pudding. I think I liked the tapioca best because of the beady little eyes that stared out at you from the bowl. These afternoon feasts were superior even to Sunday dinners.

When Momma left Montevallo in 1942 to live with her youngest daughter Lorene—or "Ween," as I called her, I wondered if the Sunday dinners would continue in the style we had grown accustomed to. After all, she took her sterling silver with her (and when she died she left it to Ween). Buying new sterling when haircuts were fifty cents might have seemed out

*My grandfather, Henry Cary "Doc" Mahan holding his blind daughter Lucille. The photograph probably was taken during one of Lucille's visits home from the Talladega School for the Deaf and Blind.*

*Right: Studio portrait of Lucille Mahan taken during her Philadelphia days.*

*Below: Late summer 1933 family outing. Back row, Ted Hubbard, a son of my aunt, Lois Mahan Hubbard, and my father. The women, left to right, Cornelia Baird, Adelaide Mahan, my mother, and Lucille Mahan.*

of the question, but for Christmas in 1946 Dad presented Mother with her own sterling service for eight, and the formal Sunday dinner routine could continue. Mother maintained a love of silver throughout her lifetime. When asked what she wanted for Christmas or her birthday, she would always answer that a piece of silver would be nice. She achieved her ambition of having service for twelve as well as a full array of serving pieces.

Besides Mother and Momma, there was one other great feminine influence in my household. Although she only visited us in the summer, my Aunt Lucille—Daddy's sister—was a great presence. "Aunt Cille," who had lost her sight when she was two, came over from the Talladega School for the Deaf and Blind, which we called TSDB. When she was nine, a representative from the school came to Calera to meet Aunt Cille and her father, my Grandfather Doc, whom I never knew. To get to Calera they caught the train in Randolph, rode to Wilton, and then to Calera—a trip of about twenty miles. Lucille was interviewed and accepted into TSDB and plans were made for her to attend. A short while later, she was carried to Randolph and put on a train bound for Talladega. I'm sure that the station manager in Randolph telegraphed the station manager in Talladega about her arrival time, but this must have been a pretty stressful time for a nine-year-old blind girl. Luckily she was met at the station by a school representative and taken to the campus.

Aunt Cille flourished in her new surroundings. At TSDB, she completed both grammar school and high school, graduating in 1912 with high awards in piano and voice. She was so proficient in music that she was sent to study piano, voice, organ, harmony, and composition at the Overbrook School for the Blind in Philadelphia. While there, she became a soloist at Patterson Memorial Presbyterian Church and also distinguished herself by being the first blind woman ever to sing with the Philadelphia Philharmonic Orchestra. After graduation in 1916, she went for further study to Hyperion School of Music in Philadelphia, returning after two years to Overbrook, where she was on the faculty from 1917 through 1925. Then she was offered a job at Talladega, and she taught there until her retirement in 1957.

Aunt Cille was a happy soul. She never acted as if she had been cheated by her blindness, and she always said that she would rather be blind than deaf. That made sense to me, as it was clear that music was the center of her life. She was a great admirer of Helen Keller, and she would quote her to me: "The only thing that is worse than being unable to see is to be able to see and to have no vision." She drilled into me the idea that insight was more important than eyesight, and I paid attention.

Aunt Cille demanded attention. Not that we had to wait on her hand and foot, but she expected to be listened to. Every day and especially every night she would play the piano. The kids from the neighborhood—Martha Ann Cox, Gene Baldwin, Bill Hartley, Ed Bridges, and others—would file in and listen to her play Beethoven and Chopin. But most of all we loved it when she played the "William Tell Overture"—which we were familiar with from listening to the *Lone Ranger* on the radio. She could also play "The Sorcerer's Apprentice," which we had learned from Mrs. Farrah while attending Miss Charlotte Peterson's elementary school. Musical appreciation was an important part of progressive education, which was practiced at Miss Peterson's school.

No one appreciated Aunt Cille's playing more than Mother. After all, she too was a pianist and had taught piano while living in Carbon Hill. Dad loved music too, and, though not very advanced in his musicianship, he never seemed uncomfortable playing with such an accomplished musician as Aunt Cille.

Occasionally when Aunt Cille played sing-along music, he would accompany her on his Martin guitar and they would sing songs like "I'll Fly Away" and my favorite, "She'll be Comin' Round the Mountain." Everybody would clap and yell when we finished a number, and Aunt Cille would wheel around on the piano stool, smile broadly, and, for some reason, raise herself up and down on the stool.

After I started playing violin, one of the joys of my life was when Aunt Cille would do duets with me. Mrs. Claire Ordway, my teacher, gave me sheet music, and I would begin to play the melody of a song. Aunt Cille did not need music, but began by ear to accompany me on the piano, smiling at me as she added obligatos that improved the performance considerably. What other kid could be so fortunate, I thought.

But Aunt Cille's interests were not only in music— she was a great storyteller, too. Sitting on the piano stool, she would look in my direction, her eyes floating rather over my head, and begin telling me about Brer Rabbit in the briar patch or the three little pigs or Alice in Wonderland. Sometimes she made up her own stories, which she delivered in a very melodic way, and I thought them just as good as the others.

Often Aunt Cille would read to me—not from printed books like we read, but from huge books with raised dots on coarse brown paper. She would touch her fingers to them and read, and I was fascinated to watch her. She brought lots of books with her, and when the Braille *Reader's Digest* came to the post office, a friend and I would go down and load my red wagon with large packages wrapped in brown paper and tied with white string. Then we'd pull our heavy load back to our house, marveling at how such a small magazine as the *Reader's Digest* took so many books and how each volume of four or more books would fill my wagon.

After supper, Aunt Cille would read to us from what she called the classics, books like *The House of Seven Gables, Little Men, Little Women, Gulliver's Travels*, and *King Solomon's Mines.* And from her Braille Bible Aunt Cille read stories of Samson and Ruth, stories that made a great impression on me because of the expressive way she read. She loved the sound of words as perhaps only a blind person could, and she taught me to value sound, both in music and in language.

When Aunt Cille packed up her books in late summer, I would feel bereft. I knew that the rich evenings of the summer would be gone for many months, and throughout the winter I would long for her return.

*My older half-sisters, Sue "Tootsie" Peters Hargrove, left, and Mary Hilda "Sister" Peters Baker, in their Alabama College senior and junior year portraits, respectively. Tootsie wanted everything in her life to be first-class, organized, and beautiful. Sister, the younger of the two, was a hard worker, creative, talented, considerate, and loved by all. I thought she was the perfect sister, daughter, mother, and wife.*

4

# Tootsie and Sister

In addition to Mother and Momma, my two step-sisters also fulfilled maternal roles—though very different ones. Tootsie, whose real name was Sue Lorraine, was twenty years older than I, and "Sister," named Mary Hilda, was eighteen. In my early years they were in college in Montevallo, and I was still quite young when they married and moved away. So it was never a matter of having playmates in the house. Rather it meant having an extra nurturer and an extra disciplinarian.

Tootsie, perhaps because she was the oldest child, was the disciplinarian. She often took a dim view of my behavior, and for many years would counsel Mother about my need for punishment or chide her for not being more strict with me. Even after I was older, she let me know that she disapproved of the fact that I had not made a career of music, had such a lackluster college career, and kept returning to Shelby Street and Mother and Dad.

Sister took a very different tack. Although I loved Tootsie and always knew she was looking out for my best interests, Sister really had my heart. When I accomplished anything, she noted it. One of the most delightful nights of my life was when Sister and her husband Bobby took me to the Vestavia Country Club to celebrate the awarding of my degree in dentistry. Recently it occurred to me that I never missed getting a birthday or Christmas present for Sister, but I never gave anything to Tootsie.

Dad loved Tootsie and Sister as if they were his own daughters. His will stated that when he died the house on Shelby Street would be shared equally by the two girls and me.

Tootsie married Sidney Hargrove, whom she met while teaching in Mobile. The two were wed in a ceremony at the Methodist Church in

*Tootsie on Dog River. One of the highlights of my Mobile visits was going to Captain Hargrove's Dog River cabin.*

Montevallo, and I remember distinctly the rice showering about them as they came down the high front steps of the church in their going-away clothes, jumped into his car, and sped away.

They lived in Mobile for a while, and I visited at their cabin on the Dog River several times as a boy. Sidney, an accountant, was employed by a firm in Mobile. Tootsie received a degree in secretarial science from Alabama College, and while living in Mobile she taught typing, shorthand, and related subjects at Murphy High School.

While living in Mobile, Sidney met Jack Schatz, whose family ran a ball-bearing business in Poughkeepsie, New York, that provided bearings for tanks and other military vehicles. It was during World War II, and the company was doing a big business. Jack talked Sidney into moving to Poughkeepsie and becoming an accountant for them. Because the company was so vital to the war effort, Sidney would have no worry about being drafted. Later the business became Federal Bearings Company, and Sidney worked for them until he retired. Following their move to Poughkeepsie, Tootsie was employed by a local business college and taught there until her retirement.

Tootsie returned from New York annually for visits, arriving in Birmingham on the *Southerner*, a great streamlined train. Going to get her with my parents and Momma was a real thrill for a young boy. We would borrow a car or go with Sister and her husband to the train station, and I was always thrilled as we drove under the huge terminal building, which I thought beautiful despite its dirty yellowish-tan color. I was especially taken with the large dome on top. When we entered the building, I gazed at the overhead awning, held up by chains that were anchored to the mouths of large dirty steel lions. Inside, I was awed by the ceilings, which seemed as high as the sky, and the huge curved windows all around. I loved looking at the travelers sitting on the wooden benches, their suitcases placed around them on the colorful terrazzo floors.

It was also fun to check the chalkboards to see if the *Southerner* was on time and finally to feel the pulsation of the huge building as the train neared. I would take Daddy's hand as we walked down the stairs to where the trains unloaded the passengers, and we would wait eagerly for Aunt Tootsie to arrive. Soon we could smell the smoke and hear the whooshing of the air brakes and the clack-clack-clacking as the huge train came into the station. A distinguished black gentleman in a black uniform with brass buttons would go up and place a wooden stool next to the door, and as women came off the train he would assist them. Men would not accept his help, I noticed, but Tootsie and almost all the women did. When I saw her strolling toward us, I would run toward this woman wearing a beautiful dress and high heels, with a coat and purse draped over her arm. Although I was first to arrive, she waited until she had kissed Mother and Dad on both cheeks before tousling my hair and saying one of two things: either I had grown or I needed a haircut.

Then Tootsie would call for one of the red caps standing next to their four-wheeled carts to get her luggage. I learned that the position of red cap was highly coveted by black men in this age of segregation. They could make good tips carrying passengers' luggage to their cars. Tootsie would hand Dad her cosmetic case, but the red cap took the rest, and led us through a secret passage out of the building. I was amazed that there was no need to go back up the stairs we had come down by.

Tootsie always arrived alone. Her husband would travel to Mobile to

*Top: Tootsie and her husband, Sidney Hargrove, on the front porch at Shelby Street. Right: Mary Hilda, "Sister," in the back yard, Shelby Street. Mother's kudzu is still flourishing behind her.*

visit his parents, and after her visit to us she would take the train down to join him.

When I was in high school, Tootsie switched from train to plane. Mother did not like that she would be flying— she thought it was needlessly dangerous— but there was no stopping Tootsie once she made up her mind. When Dad, Mother, Sister, and her husband Bobby took me to Birmingham to meet the twin-engine prop plane Tootsie was on, I'd never felt more excited. The idea of Aunt Tootsie dropping down out of the sky amazed me, but I thought if anyone could do it it would certainly be Tootsie. When the plane had landed, we could go outside and watch the disembarkation steps being put in place and the door opening. Finally, Toosie emerged, dressed to the hilt as usual. The sky cap, a bit less regal than the red caps I had seen at the train station, put Tootsie's luggage on his cart and took it to the car. All in all, Tootsie's arrival by air paled in comparison to her arrivals on the *Southerner*.

Tootsie always brought Mother some new article of clothing—a sweater, a coat, or a dress. Often she would bring Mother and Sister clothes that she had bought for herself, but had worn only once or twice or not at all. They both thought this grossly irresponsible and that she was just too reckless with money. But I noticed that they seemed quite happy to wear the fine New York clothes she brought them.

Although Tootsie liked returning to see her parents in Montevallo, she never really had much loyalty to the town. In fact, when she graduated from Alabama College, she didn't even hang around to go through graduation and receive her diploma— when the college was doing some cleaning up for its centennial celebration in 1996, her diploma was discovered and given to me.

Sister chose a different course in life. When she married Bobby Baker, their ceremony, which took place at the house on Shelby Street, was more modest than Tootsie's. Afterwards, they left for their first home, an apartment in Berney Points, near a small Southern Railroad station in the West End section of Birmingham.

I loved going there for a visit. Many times on Saturday mornings, Dad would borrow a car and drive me to the train station in Wilton, where I would catch the train to Berney Points. In the station, we would walk up to the "white" window and buy a day-coach ticket for me. Then Dad would tell

*Sister was bedridden following an automobile accident in the 1930s. Here my father is carrying her outside for the first time in seven months. Doctors told her she would never be able to dance again, but she was still jitterbugging with me in her nineties.*

the conductor—usually one of his old train buddies—to watch out for me.

Once aboard and seated, I would hear the whistle blow and feel the jerk and hear the clank as the train departed. I would look out the dirty smoked windows as we pulled out of the station. In my pocket I always had a quarter Dad had given me for a drink and candy. When a black man in a white coat walked through the car with a big basket of delicacies, I would pick out what I wanted. I noticed that there was a car for white people and one for black people, or, when whites and blacks would share a car, the whites were in the front and blacks in the back. I didn't understand why this was. I was also confused that the seat backs of the train swiveled so that you could pull them completely around, making it hard to know what was front and what was back.

The trip took a little over two hours. When we arrived at the Berney

Points station, the conductor would put out a black metal stool like the one Tootsie stepped onto so that passengers, particularly the ladies, could exit the train easily. But I was so excited about seeing Sister that I would bounce out of the train and rush to her. Together we would then walk the two blocks to her apartment. Also living in the big apartment building was Bob's sister Dot, and I liked her very much. She made me feel as welcome as Sister did.

Sister's apartment was in a large, dark two-story home on the corner of Pearson Avenue and Alabama Street. A concrete wall surrounded the house, with big concrete steps leading up to the yard and higher steps leading up to the front porch. By the front door were four doorbells, and she showed me which one to ring for her apartment. In the other three apartments were wives whose husbands were overseas. I enjoyed hearing their talk about the war and the letters they had received telling about what their husbands were going through. They also talked about how difficult rationing had been for them—little gas, no sugar, no coffee. They all had trouble getting to work.

Sister, luckily, had a job teaching at Phillips High School downtown, and she could walk to the corner a half block from her apartment to Tuscaloosa Avenue, stand and wait, and soon a streetcar would come by and pick her up. The streetcar, which looked like a single car of a train, had a long rod sticking out the top and touching an overhead wire in the middle of the street. I learned that it was not powered by steam but by electricity running in a wire above the rails, which unnerved me a bit, as I could never understand why if you stepped on the rail you might not get shocked by the electricity going from the long rod to the street car.

My trips to Sister's were a highlight of my childhood. I made friends with the children who lived in the apartment building, and I would feel a little blue when I left them and Sister to return to Wilton and then home.

Tootsie and Sister were close, but they were as different as could be. Tootsie was very tall—five-ten or five-eleven—and very thin, but she had a fine shape. She was always very tan, as she baked herself in the sun at every opportunity. Against her tan skin she loved to lay fine jewelry, especially flashy diamonds. She was quite proud of an antique diamond ring

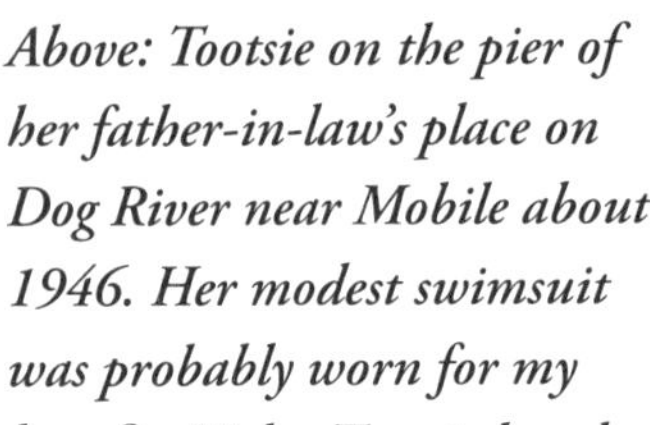

*Above: Tootsie on the pier of her father-in-law's place on Dog River near Mobile about 1946. Her modest swimsuit was probably worn for my benefit. Right: Tootsie loved the good life and adored the pomp and whimsy of Mobile's Mardi Gras.*

presented to her by her mother-in-law, Gracie Hargrove. She always dressed at the height of fashion, favoring black and white spectator pumps with heels so high that Mother was afraid she would kill herself, especially when she walked around the campus at Alabama College, with its uneven brick streets and sidewalks.

If a daring fashion came out, Tootsie was the first to adopt it. When two-piece bathing suits became popular in the forties, she got a turquoise one, wearing it to Sidney's family's cabin on the Dog River and causing much talk among her in-laws. Tootsie did not care one bit about the talk—in fact, she loved it.

Tootsie was really always a rebel at heart. She smoked heavily from an early age, and later she became a very heavy drinker. And she was always quite public about both practices, even smoking and drinking in front of her mother, who greatly disapproved of both habits—particularly in women and in public. Tootsie and her best friends, Todd Jeter and the Weems girls, were much more daring than were most of the other girls, including Sister. It wasn't so much that Sister disapproved of smoking and drinking. Instead she was critical of Tootsie because her behavior upset Mother.

Tootsie craved the good life and gloried in the sense of having made it. High society meant a great deal to her. She always had plenty of money, not just from her husband's ample salary, but also from her work teaching at the secretarial college in Poughkeepsie. Tootsie had married well. Her husband was the son of Captain Hargrove, who piloted on the river at Mobile for many years. When he retired, he was the oldest practicing pilot in America, having piloted sailing vessels, steam vessels, various kinds of crafts in World War I and World War II, and even an atomic-powered vessel. I always found him fascinating when I visited as a boy.

I remember boarding the *Southerner* at Birmingham's Union Station with Mother when I was ten or eleven and riding it to Mobile to visit Captain Hargrove and his wife Gracie, who lived on Ann Street in Mobile. Tootsie, who had come down from Poughkeepsie for a visit, met us at the station, which I noted was not as big as the terminal in Birmingham. But I thought its art deco design was even more beautiful. The Mobile terminal had lots of color inside and out, and the ceiling was high, but not reaching the sky as the one in Birmingham seemed to.

Tootsie drove us down Government Street to the Hargrove home, and I was awed by the immense oaks that arced over the street. It seemed as if we were proceeding through a large tunnel made of trees and green leaves. It was early spring when I visited, and azaleas were in bloom everywhere. When we turned off Government onto Ann, I realized that the Hargroves lived in a neighborhood even finer than Highland Avenue at home. Their house was a gleaming white two-story, with porches across the front on both floors. As we got out of the car, I looked out at the manicured lawn with bright pink azaleas blooming everywhere and was amazed at the funny-looking grass growing in the yard, even up under the shade trees. It turned out to be St. Augustine grass, and I told Mother, who often complained about grass not growing under the trees in our yard, that we needed to get some St. Augustine grass.

Gracie, a thin lady in a bright green dress, met us at the door. Behind her stood Captain Hargrove, wearing white pants and a navy coat with gold buttons. I noticed that he was shorter than she was. He bowed to Mother and came over and shook my hand, and I was amazed at how huge and muscular his hands were. I knew what Dad meant when he said be respectful when somebody had a firm handshake.

The interior of the house was impressive. Everything was just so. Although it might not have been quite as big, I thought it rivaled the Craig house across the street from us in Montevallo. I gazed at the furniture and at the drapes, and I knew somebody had to have some money. Gracie said that she knew we were tired from our trip so she had prepared an early supper, and she took us into the dining room, where an elegant table was set. As I looked at the table service, and as I realized I knew precisely what to do with every fork, spoon, and knife, I was glad that Momma had insisted that we set a full table at home. Home training paid off.

I went to Mobile to visit the Hargroves several times, and when I did Captain Hargrove would take me down to his cabin on the Dog River where he kept his boat anchored. We would go out in the *Suzy Q.*, a small white skiff with three seats and a small inboard motor that was named for Tootsie. After cranking the motor with a small rope wound around a black starting wheel, the engine would begin to run melodically and rhythmically. We would lower the tiller into the water and slowly move down the river toward Mobile Bay and travel under the Dog River Bridge, which seemed mammoth to me at the time. Captain Hargrove would let me sit at the tiller, and I would pretend to be a sea captain as I guided the boat. He taught me nautical terms like *port*, *starboard*, *bow*, and *stern*. When I returned to Montevallo, I told the Shelby Street boys about the red buoy on the right (or starboard) going to the bay and about the green buoy on the left (or port) going up Dog River.

Later, Captain Hargrove and his wife would take us all to the Mobile Yacht Club for fried shrimp and stuffed crab and grilled red snapper. On one trip he presented me with a model of a sailboat made of mahogany and birch. It was painted white with green trim and white sails. It had a single mast about twenty-four inches high with string rigging and a bow jib. Complete in every detail, it had a rudder similar to the one Captain Hargrove let me operate on the *Suzy Q*. As I recall the times I spent on the Dog River, I am grateful for the kindnesses of this wonderful, generous man.

Gracie Hargrove was not much like her husband. Mother said she was a Government Street aristocrat, and it might well have been that Gracie set a model for Tootsie to follow. She, too, I have learned since, treasured beautiful things. At some point she gave Tootsie twelve place settings of fine Havilland bone china, which Tootsie gave to Linda and me as a wedding present when we married.

Sister also liked nice things, like beautiful clothes, jewelry, and furnishings, but she was more moderate in her desires than Tootsie. Bobby finally bought her a mink coat, but Tootsie had several fur coats, some with the heads and tails hanging from them. Sister and Bobby were well-off too. They belonged to the Vestavia Country Club, but somehow it didn't seem so vital to Sister. It was just a good place to enjoy her favorite pastime—dancing. In her teens and early twenties she was well-known as a jitterbugger, and for the four years she was a student at Alabama College she had the reputation of being the best dancer on campus. She did it all: tap, ballet, and ballroom dancing. Each year she was the featured dancer in the Purple Show at College Night, a student competition at Alabama College which pitted the purples against the golds and required students to write the show, to do the acting, singing, and dancing, and to compose the music and play it.

The Vestavia Country Club was a great place to dance. When I was older she would take me and we would dance the jitterbug, the mambo, the rumba, and the samba. We did not care much about waltzing, as we thought that the bands at the Club played inferior waltz tunes like "The Tennessee Waltz," rather than, say, the classier waltzes by Strauss.

There was never a question that Sister loved to have a good time, but, while Tootsie seemed almost driven to have a good time and could be quite self-centered, Sister's having fun always seemed more moderate, wholesome, and healthy. Throughout her life she continued to dance, and up into her eighties she was tap dancing with a group that performed at the grand Alabama Theater in Birmingham. At her surprise ninetieth birthday at my home, Montebrier, she and I jitterbugged to the music of Chuck King and Friends. Until her death in 2011, she kept alive the tradition she established with Red those many years ago.

Sister was always more practical than Tootsie. She worked in Mother's beauty shop while she was in college, but Tootsie never had any interest in it. She was an excellent homemaker, a much better cook than Tootsie. Her dress was much more conservative than Tootsie's, but I always thought she looked beautiful.

Mother and Dad were not so sure that Sister had shown her usual practicality when she married Bobby Baker, a high-spirited man who loved fancy cars and made a lot of money in the scrap iron business and more by gambling. He traveled to Las Vegas quite often, sometimes taking Sister with him. When they married, he was working at Tennessee Coal and Iron (TCI) in Birmingham as part of a railroad crew. At

*After Sister's husband, Bobby Baker, was drafted into the Navy during World War II, she posed for this photograph to remind him what he had waiting for him back home.*

that time the engines at TCI were all steam-powered, and Bobby became very adept at the do's and don'ts and why's and why not's of steam power.

When World War II came, Bobby was drafted from his railroad job into the Navy where his steam power experiences fit right in. After basic training, he was assigned to Okinawa to help engineer a destroyer. Soon his expertise and experience were noted by his superiors, and he was sent back to the states to teach young sailor engineers what he knew about steam power. One week after he returned home the destroyer he had just left was sunk and the young sailor who took his place was killed. Bobby never forgot this tragedy.

After coming back from World War II, Bobby returned to West End and his job with Tennessee Coal and Iron. When he suddenly quit, giving up a good salary, health benefits, and retirement, Mother and Dad were sure he had lost his mind. But Bobby always seemed to make the right moves, taking and quitting jobs, forming business partnerships with Harry Jaffe and others, and always getting the most out of his change. He was a natural trader, and he always made money. For a while, he worked for a company that unloaded boxcars and distributed goods in Birmingham. Finally, he went into the scrap iron business for himself, and he was quite successful, bragging about the time he bought a pile of scrap by telephone from TCI and sold it back to them at a handsome profit without ever even having to move it.

Bobby loved classy, cool cars, and he bought a 1947 two-door Ford with double bullets in the grill. I loved it when they came to Montevallo, as Bobby would give me rides, and later when I could drive would let me take a spin in his latest car. He called me Sport, and Squire was the name he gave to Dad. And though he was a son-in-law, he always called Mother Ethel.

Once in the mid-fifties Bob and Sister appeared in Montevallo in a gleaming new Ford Crown Victoria, and everybody on Shelby Street had to come out and look it over. I was amazed when he threw me the keys and told me to take it for a drive. My friend Stinky Harris and I drove the car up and down Highland Avenue, showing it off. At some point Stinky looked in the glove compartment where he found a package of condoms, and we were impressed. Bobby wasn't a kid anymore, but he still must have felt the attraction of girls and gasoline as much as we did.

Successfully dealing in scrap and pursuing his gambling interests, Bobby was doing very well. Sister was also working, first at Blach's Department Store in sales and buying, then until retirement at Phillips High School. Early in their marriage, she and Bobby had a son named Robert A. Baker Jr., who we also called Bobby. This event resulted in the need for more room, so they bought their first house in Crestline Village. Little Bobby's arrival pleased Mother and Dad immensely, but I was told that it made Tootsie even more aware that she couldn't have any children, no matter how hard she and Sidney tried. It became clear to all of us that she was envious of Sister. But I always figured that Sister was much more suited to motherhood than Tootsie.

Whether her inability to have a child figured into it or not, Tootsie and Sidney drank every day and became severe alcoholics. To some degree, alcohol caused the death of both. In Tootsie's case, she drank herself to death. In 1967 she retired, and shortly thereafter she had a massive stroke that left her unable to care for herself. It became clear that Sidney could not manage, and I was not at all surprised when Sister dropped everything and went to Poughkeepsie to care for her. Eventually, however, it became obvious that she would have to be brought to Alabama and put in a nursing home. Bobby and Sister arranged with a friend to use a private plane to fly to Poughkeepsie and bring Tootsie back to Alabama. They were accompanied by our dear friend and nurse, Bennie Fancher, to make sure she had proper care during the flight.

Dad and I went to Poughkeepsie to help Sidney close the house, and we drove him back to Montevallo, pulling a U-Haul trailer. The plan was for him to stay a short while in the apartment in Mother and Dad's basement, but he stayed there for the rest of his life. He was in easy driving distance of Briarcliff Nursing Home in Alabaster, where Tootsie spent the last eleven years of her life. His own life was disastrous. He would be picked up for driving under the influence, and I would have to get him out of jail. I got him into an alcohol treatment center several times, but it did no good.

After Tootsie died, his life became more and more chaotic. I wasn't really surprised to learn that he had put a pistol into his mouth and blown his brains out. One of the hardest things I ever had to do was clean the bloody apartment on Shelby Street, but there was no one else to do it.

Tootsie's life was tragic in many ways. She did achieve the American dream—or at least one version of it—but in it there was a terrible self-destructiveness. Sister was anything but a self-destructive person. Throughout her long life, she was a survivor, strong and solid. Momma used to say that Tootsie took after her father, but that Sister took after her mother. And based on the little I knew of Mr. Peters, that assessment is pretty much on target. But both sisters gave me opportunities, especially as a child and adolescent, to see a world I would otherwise have missed, and I remain grateful to both.

## 5

# Maggie

In addition to all the other women in my life, there was Maggie Hale, who for some years was a member of our household—or at least I thought of her as that. She was, at least nominally, our maid, but to me she was far more. This black woman came into my life when I was an infant. Perhaps because my mother was rather old for child-bearing, she had problems producing sufficient milk for me. And that is when Maggie was pressed into service. It was at her teat that I suckled the most.

Of course, I do not recall that experience, but in my earliest memories I can see Maggie entering through the back door. A tall, chunky woman, she wore a bandanna of red and white checks, tied tightly in the back. If she was wearing her coat, she would hang it on a hook inside the broom closet on the back porch. Then she would take a white apron hanging on a nail and put it on over her shift and full long skirts. She was ready for her day. "Good morning, Mr. Stanley. Good morning, Miss Ethel," she would call out as she entered the kitchen.

I can see her in the kitchen putting coal in the water heater. Although she always washed the coal dust from her hands, I can still picture her going to wipe her hands on "her" towel. It did not seem particularly strange to me that she was not allowed to use the family towels. I also remember how by the end of the day her white apron had black dusty streaks on it. But she kept the kitchen itself spotless.

Maggie was not pretty, but she had a great smile. One side of her lips rose higher than the other because her first husband had cut her with a switchblade. He caught her just left of her eye, making a deep gash down the left of her nose and on down to the side of her mouth. The definitive scar was pink and shiny, and that side of her mouth was higher than the other when it healed. But the most unusual thing about Maggie was that a quarter of her right ear was gone, bitten off by the same man who cut her. Maggie did not try to hide the mangled ear, wearing a gold earring on it as well as on the complete one.

When I was just a small child, Maggie began referring to me as "Mr. Mike" when she spoke about me to my parents or called my name in their presence. After they left for work, and especially when she needed to be firm with me, she dropped the Mr. When things got real serious, she called me boy. When I heard that, I knew to get ready for some sort of punishment. She would never have laid a hand on me, so she adopted my mother's favorite mode of punishment—sending me to the bathroom. Early on I learned to keep toys hidden under the claw-foot tub, and later I learned the rope escape, so that never was much punishment at all.

Maggie did everything around the house—cleaning, sweeping the porch and sidewalk, tending to me and walking me to school, telling me stories, cooking (when Momma was not there), and ironing our clothes. Maggie did not have to wash, as Mother took the laundry uptown to the shop.

Maggie, I was told, lived with her husband "'cross the creek." To many people, that meant "nigger quarters," but we didn't say that in my house. From a very early age I heard the word constantly and even used it myself, but not in our house. Dad taught me that when I addressed Taft Farrington, Gene Prentice, and Rose Cottingham, I was to say Mr. Taft, Mr. Gene, and Miss Rose. That really applied to the older black people I knew, except for the blacks we were extremely close to, like Maggie. I could call black children my age by their given names, so they were Cary or Peanut or Lightning.

Maggie lived 'cross the creek until during World War II, when her husband was drafted into the army. Maggie didn't have enough money for rent and food, so Mother and Dad began to figure what they could do to help her. Mr. Pete Givhan had built a garage between our house and Bloomer Wilson's, and, since we didn't have a car to put in it, it was unused. "Do we dare to fix that up and move Maggie into it?" Dad asked, and he and Mother decided that if Sam and Rose Klotzman on Highland Avenue could have their maid living in their backyard then we could too.

Dad bought some lumber and got Harry Miller, a shoeshine boy at his shop, to help him put in a floor and to install a door and one window. He nailed up the large garage door and cut a smaller opening in the middle of it, using the planks he had cut out to fashion the door, which he placed on runners so it could slide open and shut. He used the same procedure for the window. He did all this work with a handsaw and a few other simple tools. There was no glass in the window, and I wondered how Maggie could see out. Dad showed me how she could open the window, but I thought that wouldn't work very well in the wintertime.

It was late fall when he fixed up the garage for Maggie, and Dad feared that the room would have wind blowing through it. Maggie said he should fill all the cracks with newspaper, and that is what they did. Then they covered it over with heavy wallpaper with big white magnolias on it, tacking it up rather than gluing it. After Maggie pronounced it quite warm and said it looked wonderful, they set about furnishing the room. Maggie brought a little table and a couple of chairs with her, and Mother and Dad found a bed, a small dresser, and a chifforobe with a round mirror in the top. Maggie ran a wire across one corner of the room and hung clothes on it, covering them over with a white sheet.

Dad had Mr. H. G. Parker run an electric wire from our back porch to the garage so that the room could be lit by a single light bulb hanging in the middle of the room. The place had a tin roof and no insulation, so it could get either very cold or very hot in there. Dad installed a small stove for warmth. The stove looked similar to the four-legged monster in our kitchen, but it was not a water heater and did not need a silver water tank. Maggie's stove burned coal, and of course she used our coal from the coal shed. She was very pleased with her stove because she not only could keep warm, but she could even cook on her stove if need be.

For the hot weather, Dad bought Maggie a brass-plated General Electric oscillating fan, which she would plug in to one side of a two-way plug connected to the light bulb socket. If she wanted to run the fan during the night without the light, she had to reach up and unscrew the light bulb. The fan seemed to me far preferable to the ones we had in our house, and I wondered why Dad didn't take Maggie's fine fan for us and replace it with one of our old black ones.

All in all, Maggie's place was quite cozy, and I recall going in the room at night and being charmed by the glow from the light bulb, casting a rich rose light over the furniture and walls covered with Maggie's magnolia wallpaper. And when the oscillating fan was on, there was a low hum I found mesmerizing.

Although at the outset Mother and Dad had worried a bit about what the neighbors would think, once Maggie moved in she was welcomed by all of them. Even though her friends were 'cross the creek, she seemed happy. Of course she still came in the back door, never in the front—she could leave by the front door to clean the porch or sweep the sidewalk, but she could not enter the front door. Maggie had her own dishes in her place in the kitchen, but on lots of occasions she was invited to eat at the table with Mother and me. I liked those occasions. Often, however, Maggie would wait until we finished eating and then sit alone, eating the leftovers from the stove.

After World War II ended, Maggie's husband came home, and shortly thereafter Maggie told us she was leaving and moving to Detroit, Michigan. To say the least, this was a shock. How could she leave us? Some crude neighbors said, "Just like a nigger, she didn't know how good she had it," that Dad and Mother had always overdone for her, and she was ungrateful. But whatever her reasons for going, there were tears on both sides when Maggie left. We knew very well how lucky we were to have loved and been loved by Maggie, and, though we seldom heard from her over the years, we never relinquished her place in our hearts and minds.

After Maggie left, Mother and Dad were without help for a while. They hired other women, but none stayed long until they hired Leonora, a tall thin lady, thought to be dignified and beautiful by most who knew her. I remember how gracefully she walked down the street. She lived across the little red bridge on Depot Street, which ran parallel to the railroad tracks.

Leonora arrived at our house early enough in the morning to cook breakfast and see Mother and Dad off to work. She did our washing in a new wringer washing machine, which sounded like a snare drum when it was running: *para diddle, para diddle, para diddle, slam slam.* I especially liked watching Leonora feed the wet clothes through the two rubber rollers above the tub, with water and soap bubbles squishing out into the tub. Then Leonora pressed a button and the dirty water was pumped out a black runner hose into a grease trap Mr. Shorty Smitherman had installed in the yard. After that Leonora had to take the clothes in a #2 galvanized tub and hang them in the yard. Washing was not a simple matter in those days.

Leonora stayed with us several years, but a new opportunity came available at Alabama College and she was hired as one of the maids at Flower Hill, the beautiful home of the president. Mother and Dad were happy for her, thinking that her smiling face would fit in perfectly in such elegant surroundings. This was certainly a prized job, and even as a boy I thought Leonora looked right at home as she walked up the brick drive to Flower Hill, under the arch of pecan trees lining the drive.

6

# Ancestors

The Mahan legacy in Brierfield began when the Mahan boys—along with the Fanchers, Smiths, Ragans, Lindseys, and Massingales—came upon the site while returning home after fighting in the battle of New Orleans (or the battle of Chalmette Plantation, as it was often called). According to family history, the men of these five families proceeded north and east toward their homes in Tennessee. Following a trail from the junction of the Cahaba and Alabama rivers at what would become the settlement of Cahawba, they came through what is now Brierfield, where they found a wealth of natural resources—longleaf pine, oak, chestnuts, and iron ore. The Mahan boys, being blacksmiths, said this is the place we need to be. The other men felt the same way.

Family tradition has it that the group left a few men behind in an Indian village on the banks of a beautiful stream, and the rest returned to Tennessee to gather their families, load wagons, hook up teams of oxen, and return to the newly found utopia. When they returned, the men they had left were no more. It was said that they couldn't leave the Indian maidens alone and were killed. But these are just stories. At any rate, the families who returned from Tennessee had little time for mourning, and they split up and went upstream and down, settling on the banks of what is now known as Mahan Creek or on the Cahaba River.

My great-great-grandfather, Edward Mahan, was a hoarder of books, personal items, letters, and even clothes. None of this was junk to him. It was preserved carefully so that it would be in good shape when viewed by future generations. Edward married twice, as did his son Jesse. Two of the eleven children born to Jesse Mahan—Adelaide and Jesse Jr.—were not content to stay in Brierfield, given its limited opportunities for education and prosperity, and they sought their fortunes elsewhere. Luckily for our

*Jesse W. Mahan Sr., 1816–84, the son of Edward, one of the original Mahan boys. Jesse was my great-grandfather and a man of many faces who witnessed significant historical changes. Among his accomplishments, he was the first Republican state senator from Bibb County, Alabama.*

*Anna Cunningham Curtis Mahan, wife of Jesse W. Mahan Sr. and mother of Adelaide, posing in Adelaide's studio on the banks of Mahan Creek, May 27, 1910.*

family, both Jesse Jr. and Adelaide left records that allow us to know a great deal about them. I am descended from Jesse's first wife, and the mother of Adelaide and Jesse Jr. was his second.

ADELAIDE, MY GREAT-AUNT, WAS born in 1872. Her mother, Anna, had a first husband, Joseph R. Curtis, a member of the Fifth Alabama that formed in Montgomery, who was killed early in the Civil War in the battle of Seven Pines. Anna's second husband was also a Confederate soldier. A few days after their marriage, he went off to join a Texas unit and was never heard from again. After the war, about 1870, Anna met and married a Bibb County legislator and widower, Jesse W. Mahan Sr., my great-grandfather.

Aunt Adelaide's early passion was art, particularly painting. But her study was postponed while she served as postmaster of Brierfield from 1897 through 1901. Following her term, she was accepted by the Woman's Art School at the Cooper Union for the Advancement of Science and Art in New York City. From 1901 through 1903, she distinguished herself by winning prizes and earning the praise of her teachers at Cooper Union. In 1902, she traveled to Cape Cod to study with the well-known painting teacher Charles Hawthorne in his first outdoor summer school, the Cape Cod School of Art. He was favorably impressed with her human form pieces, and he encouraged her to submit her work to exhibitions.

Returning to Manhattan for another year at Cooper Union, she passed the year successfully. But the summer brought an unhappy experience—teaching art in the city to a set of recalcitrant boys she referred to as "the demons." At midterm she resigned, dutifully returning not long afterward to Brierfield to take care of her seriously ill mother.

In 1911, Adelaide returned to New York to complete her course of study at Cooper Union, again winning prizes, and then bringing her degree home to Brierfield, where she spent the rest of her life. She became somewhat reclusive, supporting herself with her art, her honey production, and by selling timber and leasing her inherited land to farmers. She was a member of the Brierfield Catholic Church and was a founding member of the Catholic church in Montevallo. She had little to do with people in Brierfield, but she did belong to the Birmingham Art Association and had a one-woman show in Birmingham. As the years passed, she painted seriously less and less, as an interest in crafts replaced her devotion to fine art.

As a boy, I paid little attention when I heard of Adelaide's artistic accomplishments. I mostly thought of her as a witch, stomping around in knee-high boots and wearing shapeless hand-sewn dresses. When it was cold, she would wear a heavy woolen sweater and a toboggan cap she had knitted. When Mother and Dad took me to visit her, we would walk up the herringbone brick path to Adelaide's unpainted house on Mahan Creek (the house had been built, but never finished, by her father for Anna, who refused to live in the old family home where Jesse Sr. was brought up). Often we would find Adelaide busying herself with her bees, doing needlework, painting valentines and notecards she would

*Above: Adelaide Eleanor Mahan, 1872–1958, my beautiful, adventurous, creative, selfish, and self-reliant great-aunt. Right: She is at far right holding a palette in art class at New York's Cooper Union, circa 1903.*

sell to local people, or busily working on some other project.

She never seemed particularly happy to see us. Her bearing was austere, and I was rather scared of her. She hardly acknowledged my presence, and I wasn't much interested in the conversations she had with my parents. But occasionally things were enlivened when she would take issue with Dad on some topic. One source of contention had to do with Dad's handling of the Baird House in Brierfield, built by the husband of Adelaide's sister Christabel, who came from Honduras and abandoned the house in the twenties. All had agreed that it had become such an eyesore that it should be torn down. Dad agreed to handle it, and afterwards Adelaide and others felt that he had kept too much of the money he received from selling the scrap lumber. He was quite defensive about it, and if anything about the Baird House came up he and Adelaide would argue. Afterwards, Dad would say he would never set foot in her house again. But Mother would begin to feel sorry for Adelaide out there by herself, and invariably through the years Dad would go back. In fact, at the end of Adelaide's life, Dad and Mother cared for her in their home.

There were four rooms and a large hall in Adelaide's house. On our visits, we entered the dark and shadowy living room. Like the rest of the house, the room was totally unpainted, with beaded ceilings and walls and broad-board pine floors. Its walls were filled with her paintings, and on tables—covered with doilies Adelaide had crocheted—sat pottery and other things she had made. Later when I saw photographs of Victorian salons in Europe, I immediately associated them with this room. I was always a little amazed that one of the pictures was of a naked woman and another of an almost naked man. Nobody ever mentioned them. I also remember being a little surprised to see that some of the paintings had price tags attached.

We never sat in the living room, but usually she led us through the hall to the kitchen. At one end of the hall stood her prized piano. Hung on the walls of the hall—the bee room, we called it—were an oilcloth hood and apron and high-top gloves she used to handle her bees. I was particularly interested in the extracting machine that took the honey from the combs, and I was impressed with the shelves of quart jars and half-gallon cans arranged neatly along the wall, all bearing the off-white labels she had designed, with the words “HONEY by AE Mahan, Brierfield, Ala.” printed in blue ink. Much of her living came from her sale of this honey, which was thought to be some of the best anywhere.

I think now that the only thing back then that really impressed me positively about Adelaide was how organized and precise she was. She knew how to take care of things, and she didn't want to be distracted from doing so.

From the hall, we would enter the kitchen. Taking our seats in the cane-bottom chairs she used at the kitchen table, we sat around the potbellied stove that glowed red on cold winter days. The one attention she paid me was to get the Civil War sword that Mahan slaves had found after Wilson's Raiders came through Montevallo. I was quite interested in the sword—and am lucky enough to own it now—but a boy was really limited with what he could do with it while sitting in a chair. The adults talked, and I quickly became bored and let my mind wander.

Adelaide's bedroom was off limits to all visitors, and I spent a good bit of time wondering why. What was she hiding back there? Her desk was in her bedroom, and some people thought she didn't want anyone to meddle in her affairs. Some thought there were lurid love letters she wanted to conceal. Others thought she wanted to conceal graphic oil paintings of nudes. Her nephew Edward, who had been sent to live with her in Brierfield because he was thought to have tuberculosis, ran up on those paintings, and when Adelaide found out she was quite furious and burned many of the paintings she had done at Cooper Union. Only after Adelaide died in 1958 did we see that room. Packing up her possessions to send to Texas to her nieces and heirs, Cornelia and Sarah, we never found anything we thought she would have wanted to hide. But she was always a private person, and I guess she felt that she needed one place that was absolutely her own.

I was greatly curious about one family story. In the hall there was one wall that did not reach the ceiling, and it was said that Adelaide threw a number of Honduran gold coins in that space when Edward and his friends kept getting them out and playing with them. It was also said that she skipped some off rocks in Mahan Creek, and when I was a boy I sometimes dived in search of the coins, but never found a single one. Once Adelaide heard me telling someone the story about the coins, and she told me in no uncertain terms to shut up.

I had my most memorable experience with Adelaide while I was in college at Alabama Polytechnic Institute (Auburn). I was taking a sophomore course in Alabama history from the distinguished professor, Dr. Malcolm McMillan, and I decided to do my paper on the Brierfield Furnace. My ancestors had been involved in its establishment, and Adelaide herself had been cited in Ethel Armes's book on Alabama's coal and iron industry. She seemed an obvious source for my paper.

Adelaide did not have a telephone, so on a freezing Saturday morning in the winter of 1953 I knocked unannounced at her door. She rushed me in so she could close the door against the cold. When I told her what I wanted, she didn't seem overjoyed to have to deal with me, but she said, "Take off your coat and I'll try to answer a few questions."

The visit ran on for about three hours, and with every question she became more agitated. Probably she wanted to be doing some of her projects, but that did not occur to me then. At one point, when she ventured some observation, I said that I thought she was wrong, that Dr. McMillan had told us something different.

"Well, if you and that professor already know everything, why are you here bothering me?"

That startled me a bit, and I said I was sorry, that I thought she'd be interested in his opinion.

"Well, I'm not," she said.

I had pretty well gotten all I needed from Adelaide, so I decided the smart thing to do was change the subject. I asked her about her pet wren that had for several years been flying into her kitchen and eating breadcrumbs from her hand.

"You know all there is to know about it," she said sternly, still fuming about her authority being questioned. "There's nothing to say."

I should have taken my leave then, but something made me say, "Don't you think that could be dangerous? A bird like that could bring some kind of disease into the house."

Her face reddened, her eyes bulged, and she took in a menacing breath.

She reached down and took a stick of stove wood from the box and hurled it at me with all her might. Luckily, I ducked and it missed me, but I decided not to wait around for another. I grabbed my notebook and my jacket and fled, hearing only two more words out of Adelaide's mouth: "Smart aleck."

I ran up the hill to a house occupied by Adelaide's nephew, Edward. When I told him what Adelaide had done, he broke out laughing. "Well, you are not the first to have a stick of stove wood thrown at him. I thought you knew that was her weapon of choice." In fact, I expect he preferred she use stove wood than her sharp tongue, because Edward had had plenty of opportunities to be assaulted. He told me that once when she was working outside he and a friend got Adelaide's single-shot .22 rifle and wound up shooting a hole through the friend's toe. Adelaide came running when she heard the gunfire, mad as one of her bees, and she threatened to whip them both, but settled for a severe tongue-lashing after viewing the wounded toe.

Adelaide was quite a character, but it was her older brother Jesse Jr. who most captured my boyhood fancy. From an early age I saw photographs of this massive man standing in the company of men, with a pistol in a leather holster strapped on his right hip and a machete in his hand. He wore a large hat, pants that fit tightly below the knee, and high, laced boots. He was without a doubt the central figure in the photo.

Perhaps inspired by his maternal Uncle Kevin Cunningham, Jesse had a strong case of wanderlust. Kevin was himself a world traveler. He was a collector, and when he died the family found menus he had collected at fine restaurants throughout Europe and in the states, as well as buttons and tokens from various places he had visited. I have his small card the size of a credit card from the late 1800s that lists all the places in New York City where one could make long-distance phone calls.

Kevin became an expert on diatom fossils and traded them with others across the country. I have many of his letters, which he printed in India ink in tiny, precise letters. I also have a map of his travels on horseback collecting diatoms in Mexico. It became clear to me that Kevin had plenty of stories that would have inspired both Adelaide and Jesse.

In the late 1800s Jesse, then in his early twenties, left Brierfield with

*Left: Kevin Cunningham, world traveler, adventurer, scientist, and scholar. He was the brother of Adelaide and Jesse Jr.'s mother, Anna. Below: Scribbled on the reverse of this photograph, "The start to Central America, Oulick, Mahan & Creary." Jesse Jr., center, is equipped leaving Brierfield in the late 1890s for the island of Utila, Honduras.*

a friend for Honduras, where he expected to make his fortune. He had been told that the land there was almost free. I began to piece together his story listening to my aunts Maggie and Adelaide, both of whom lived in Honduras for a while, as well as to the tales Dad and others told me. I also learned that Dad's older brother Cary went to Honduras after World War I and helped build a railroad for the United Fruit Company. In addition, the family had saved some letters from Jesse. So I knew a good bit about this distinctive kinsman.

Jesse first set up on the Isle of Utila, one of the bay islands that was settled by the English in the mid-1800s. A woman was among the first to come there, and she populated the island with offspring from two men. It is likely that Jesse was attracted to Utila because English-speaking people

*Jesse W. Mahan Jr., seated middle row, third from right, with banana plantation workers. Note the surveying instruments, machetes, and guns.*

were there. An excellent carpenter, he quickly became a valuable member of the populace. On the island was a Methodist church that needed to be enlarged, and Jesse took on that job. The church had been perpendicular to the sea, but he decided to turn it to make it parallel, and he cut it in half and enlarged it in length and made other improvements. Jesse further established himself by marrying a sea captain's daughter, but the marriage ended sadly when she died giving birth to a daughter, who also died. Subsequently, he married Rosa St. Martin, from a prominent family in La Ceiba, and they moved to the plantation headquarters near the small community of La Union. He began looking around for a plantation site and found one north of La Union, in the flatlands before the mountains began to rise up. He not only grew bananas, but he also built a railroad to take bananas to the port for shipping and established a commissary at the port site.

Jesse took a business partner, a well-heeled, ambitious man named A. D. Baird. This man thought big. He decided that they needed a boat to transport the bananas to market, as there was too much spoilage getting them to the island of Roatan to be loaded on ships bound for the states and other

***Both Adelaide and Christabel Mahan visited their brother Jesse in Honduras. Step-sisters Lois and Maggie also visited and worked for Jesse. Adelaide took this photograph of an unknown couple at the mouth of the El Porvenir River, the location of Jesse's commissary.***

ports. He had one built in Michigan, traveling there himself to supervise its fabrication. It was a forty-footer with two 100-horsepower gasoline engines.

When the boat was completed, Baird took it back to Honduras. He left Michigan, eventually taking the Mississippi River to New Orleans. Then he sailed east along the coast to Apalachicola, Florida, then across open Gulf waters to Key West. From there he proceeded to Cuba, where he hired a captain to make the journey across the Gulf to Honduras. Following a brief stop at Roatan, they arrived at the dock at the mouth of the El Porvenir River, which was the plantation headquarters. Baird's big boat was finally home. How he had accomplished such an amazing feat is still a wonder to me.

When Baird got to the dock on his return, the first person he spotted was Jesse's sister, Christabel, visiting from Brierfield. He fell in love at once and soon they returned to Brierfield where they had a grand wedding at her mother's home on August 16, 1905. Anna even made Christabel's wedding dress, which I now have.

Eventually, the Honduran government told Jesse that he would have to sell his banana business to the Vacarro Fruit Company or it would be

*Top: Abraham Dubois Baird, Jesse's well-heeled partner, far left, with amigos celebrating something. Note the fellows with musical instruments on the far right. Bottom: Father Alfora, left, a priest and Mexican refugee, posed with Baird in a studio photo. Baird made several trips to Mexico on business ventures and was returning home from there when he died in New Orleans.*

nationalized. So he sold to Vacarro, which later became the United Fruit Company. Jesse's partner, A. D. Baird, wanted new fields to conquer, so he and Christabel moved to Brierfield, where he intended to make a fortune as a dairy and mushroom farmer. He bought four hundred acres from my grandfather, Henry Cary Mahan, then went to Wisconsin to buy a herd of Holstein cows, which he had shipped by rail to Brierfield. He built a long milking barn with two concrete troughs, where the cows could be fed and milked at the same time, and he also constructed round concrete silage bins. He then built a home for himself and Christabel. Baird also rented several caves on the Cahaba River, where his visionary dream of raising mushrooms was to take place.

Baird's dreams did not have happy endings. For a while he had luck with the dairy business. He milked twice daily, sending the morning milking by train to Birmingham while it was cooler. The afternoon milking, when the day was warmer, was shipped to Selma, a shorter trip. Unfortunately, the entire herd contracted hoof and mouth disease and had to be destroyed and burned. In addition, he never marketed a single mushroom. Thus ended his farming days. He and Christabel moved to the west end of Birmingham, where he started several business adventures. One was a business making steel-belted radial tires. According to family lore, he sold the design to Goodyear, but Goodyear never produced them because, presumably, they lasted too long; built-in obsolescence was the hallmark of many products of that day.

By this time, Baird was suffering from kidney failure, and he traveled to New York, where he could get the best medical treatment. There he had a kidney operation that was extremely rare in those days. Afterwards, he went to Mexico and then on to New Orleans, where he died on February 19, 1924. Christabel then moved to Dallas, Texas; her daughter Cornelia had earlier gone to Dallas, where she had a job teaching piano and working for the Catholic Diocese.

Jesse and Rosa stayed in Honduras after the sale of the banana plantation, living in the compound headquarters at the mouth of the river, from which he established cantinas in various locations on the mainland. Aunt Maggie Mahan, who also went to Honduras, told stories of how she

*Jesse and his second wife, Rosa St. Martin, on their wedding day in La Ceiba, Honduras.*

would leave early on Monday morning on horseback to pick up the gold coins taken in at the cantinas, putting the money in her saddlebags and taking them back to Jesse. Jesse and Rosa had three sons—Jesse, Edward, and Gerald. Following Jesse's death, they all came to the states, Edward because of his illness and Jesse to serve in the U.S. Navy. Jesse went on to make a career of the Navy, retiring in Norfolk, Virginia. Edward, because of his health, was not accepted in the military, but went to work in a shipyard near Los Angeles. In 1946 he moved from California to Brierfield, buying forty acres from Adelaide and building a house. The third son, Gerald, was disabled, walking with a limp. He kept getting in trouble, and finally A. D. Baird adopted him and brought him to Birmingham, but he could never control him, and he was returned to his mother.

Jesse Jr. also had a daughter who, like her mother, fell on difficult times when Jesse died. Rosa and the daughter became destitute, finally moving to New Orleans in the 1950s, where family gossip says the two became prostitutes. Rosa, it seemed to me, would have certainly been an old prostitute, but the story was widely accepted by the Alabama Mahans. On occasion, some Brierfield relative of Jesse's would receive a pleading letter from Rosa, asking to borrow money. But during those post-war years, times were tough for the family and money for loans was not available.

I was always fascinated with Jesse's Honduran adventure and dreamed of going there to visit his plantation to see if I could possibly find anyone who knew him, but most of all to find his grave. The first opportunity came in 1976, when my wife Linda and I began our plans. We wanted to start on Utila, and we contacted the Honduran Consulate in New Orleans for advice. They told us of a Mr. Rose on the island of Utila who might be able to help. Shortly afterwards, Linda and I flew to Mexico City and from there to the Honduras capital, Tegucigalpa. Then we went by land to La Ceiba on the northeast coast. From there we caught a primitive C-47 "Gooney Bird" to Utila. The weather was scalding, and the inside of the plane was as hot as a June bride in a feather bed. We sat on uncomfortable little metal seats near the floor. The plane flew only two or three hundred feet above the sea, and every once and a while we could feel the plane bobbing down and turning on its wing. I finally asked about it, and the pilot told me that he was delivering mail to the little bay islands.

Linda and I had never seen a place as primitive as Utila. There were no cars, and the streets were dirt. There was no hotel. But we did see one thing that stopped us in our tracks. When we passed the Methodist Church, our jaws dropped. It had the very same columns we have on our home at Montebrier, a house that Jesse's father helped build in 1866. Jesse would have been quite familiar with the Montebrier columns, and we felt sure that he had designed those columns for the church. There were two other houses nearby in Utila with the same columns, and we supposed that Jesse might have built them as well. The columns—six inches square at the bottom up to four feet, then six-sided from there up to two feet from the top, then square again to the top—were common in our country, but the ones we saw on Utila were the only ones we saw in Honduras.

After we had walked around for a while, I asked someone where we could find Mr. Rose, and he pointed out the way, telling us that Mr. Rose rented rooms in his house. That was good to know, as we had no idea where we would lay our heads that night. We came to the house, which seemed pretty run down, its white and green paint quite faded. Backed up to the water, the house sat up on stilts like those I knew from the Gulf Coast. Linda decided to stand in the street in the hot sun behind the fence as I

*Mr. Rose, seated on his porch at Utila, with his handmade walker—his chariot he called it—under his left hand.*

went on the porch and knocked at the door. Slowly emerging from the house was an ancient man on a homemade wooden walker. He professed to know nothing about a Jesse Mahan, and he also said that he did not rent rooms. I was rather worried that the whole trip was going to be for naught when I thought of a tape I had in my pocket. I had recorded Aunt Maggie telling a story about Old Bob, a celebrated criminal in Utila. I said, "Please, sir, can I play something for you?" and without waiting for an answer I switched it on.

The story went as follows: The year was 1905. Old Bob was a black man, well-known and liked in Utila, who with evil intent hid aboard a shuttle boat headed to the mainland for supplies. On board were ten or so passengers, including women and children. He shot all of the adults but one, who escaped, and threw the children overboard to their deaths. One was a baby that was found washed up on the Utilan shore. The survivor reported that the crime was the work of Old Bob, who was by that time was on the mainland. According to family lore, a posse led by Jesse Mahan went to the mainland to arrest him and bring him back to be tried in Utila. Once Old Bob was back, they made short order of the trial, and Bob was taken out and hanged from the highest ramon tree in the town. After he was buried, people became afraid that he hadn't really died, so townspeople dug up the body to make sure. He was indeed quite dead, and he was quickly reinterred.

As he listened to the story, I could tell by Mr. Rose's eyes that he knew it. When the tale ended, he got a wry look on his face and said, "I be damned if people haven't been coming down here for years to ask me to tell them that story. You are the first son of a bitch to bring the story of Bob to me." He looked out where Linda stood in the street. "That your wife?" he asked. I nodded. "Go get her," he said. "I got somewhere for y'all to stay."

He told us to sit down in the palmetto chairs, and he began to talk about Jesse. He even knew Maggie, and became quite animated telling us about how she once got in a fight with a local woman. That lady was still alive, he told us. Then he took us in to show us our quarters. Our room had shutters that closed, but no window panes or screens. The adjacent toilet was merely a hole in the floor, with the waste falling down into the water below. In the corner of the small room was a cold-water shower, which also drained into the water. Then he took us in to meet his wife, and she said she would cook for us. I had the first fried breadfruit I ever tasted, along with some local vegetables, all very good.

The next morning before we were to leave, Mr. Rose asked me if I had my machine, meaning my tape recorder. I handed it to him and he recorded a short message to Maggie about the settling of Utila by the British. Then he insisted on our meeting the woman Maggie had fought with. A dark-skinned woman, she turned out to be very nice. She said that they made up before Maggie went back to Alabama. She also insisted on cooking a breadfruit lunch for us.

Naturally, we were thrilled to meet these people who had known Jesse and the other Mahans, but we couldn't stay any longer. We took the same hot plane back to the mainland that afternoon. Our next step was to find the Mahan plantation and, if we were lucky, Jesse's grave.

We checked into a hotel in La Ceiba, which seemed luxurious after our night with Mr. Rose. Mr. Rose had given us the name and address of a ninety-year-old black man who had known Jesse Mahan, and I asked at the hotel desk for help in locating him. The desk clerk got us a chauffeur who drove for us the rest of our trip.

Our driver took us out to the site of the head of the railroad that ran twenty-six miles to the mouth of the El Porvenir River, where Jesse had his commissary and where the bananas were loaded onto boats to be taken to the ships. There we found an old man, who spoke no English but made me understand that he would guide us. The trip wouldn't be easy, he said. He took us to a small open railroad car, the kind propelled by pumping a T-handle up and down. Linda and I took our seats in the front with the old man between us, and a younger black man, shirtless and powerfully built, standing at the T-handle. In the hundred-plus degrees he was profusely sweating, and his body odor bothered Linda and me. The old Honduran did not seem to notice at all. It was quite eerie skimming down that track—no sound but the pumping. Suddenly it dawned on me that we knew next to nothing about these two men, one of whom was armed with a machete. I found myself getting a little frightened, but my fright escalated when the car stopped and another sweating black man holding his own machete walked out of the bush. He began speaking in Spanish with the old man, and I wondered what was about to happen next. I realized then that the old man was asking him to help the other man pump the car. The young man put down his machete and stood next to the other. Together they began pumping us down the tracks. We went to the end of the line and back without incident.

We explored the area around La Porvenir for a while. I had brought with me a photograph of Adelaide and Aunt Maggie standing on the shore there, and the old man took me to the exact place the photo had been made. Linda and I had him take our picture there. We also located Jesse's commissary and homesite. This was the headquarters compound of the Jesse Mahan and A. D. Baird banana plantation.

Back in La Ceiba, we hired a driver who located a man who knew the St. Martin family, who were still alive and in the grocery business. From them he found out that Jesse was buried in a cemetery in the downtown area. The man at the desk where we were staying found the old Honduran man who had known Jesse and, in fact, shared a birthday with Jesse. They had gotten drunk together every year to celebrate. This man, a St. Martin, was in his nineties now, and the driver took us out to meet him at the cemetery. As we walked along by graves I noticed that a number of St. Martins were buried there. They, I assumed, were the family of Jesse's wife Rosa.

"The grave is right over there," our driver said, pointing to a place where there was no marker but a concrete slab. Aunt Maggie had always said that

*With a great deal of perseverance and a bit of luck, the gravesite of Jesse W. Mahan Jr. was located.*

Jesse was buried under a concrete slab. The driver told us to wait, and he went off somewhere to get a shovel and began scraping back grass. Slowly the slab emerged. To my great disappointment, there was no name or date on it. But the old man assured me as well as he could that it was Jesse's grave.

Linda and I returned to Brierfield in 1976 feeling that we had achieved more than we could have hoped. We had seen people who knew Jesse, we had walked where he had walked, and we had seen his grave. I had, I felt, gotten in closer touch with my childhood hero, Jesse Mahan, father of my most respected and admired cousin Edward Mahan.

Edward came into my life in 1946. Born in Honduras to Jesse and his wife Rosa St. Martin, in his early teens Edward was diagnosed with tuberculosis. His father had died by that time, but his mother decided that he should be sent to the United States, where he could have a drier climate. He first went to Colorado, but after a while was sent to Brierfield, where he would live with his Aunt Adelaide and attend school in Montevallo. It was during this period that he gained from Adelaide a passion for history. Edward was drafted during World War II, but he did not serve in the military. He was instead assigned work in the shipyards in California. There he married a woman named Rita and had a child, but when he returned to Brierfield she refused to live there with him. He was a talented carpenter, and his plan was to build a house for himself, then work as a carpenter in the area. But what he loved most was history and archaeology, and that would indeed become his profession. From him, I gained my own passion for these subjects.

Edward became aware of the opportunities at Redstone Arsenal in Huntsville, which was on the cutting edge of space study and exploration, and he secured a job there. But while what he found aboveground at the Arsenal excited him, the archaeological wonders that lay below excited him more. It was his archaeology, discovering all he could about the area's prehistory, that was really his life's most important work. He moved to Grant, Alabama, where he could pursue this growing interest in pre-historic Alabama. In several years he had become one of the state's most renowned nonprofessional historians and archaeologists. Academic archaeologists sought him out to be taught what he knew. When he died, he had located and registered more Indian sites than any other archaeologist in the state, professional or amateur, and he was an authority on cave dwellings in Alabama and Georgia. He even spent five years living in one of Alabama's cave dwellings, Cathedral Caverns. During this time he studied the caverns thoroughly, meticulously digging and recording his findings. In the 1970s he was pictured at Cathedral Caverns on the cover of an Alabama history textbook used by students throughout the state. He also served as an adjunct professor at the University of Alabama in Tuscaloosa and Birmingham.

Edward had a profound effect on me. Though still a boy when I first knew him, I found that we had similar interests. Edward took me under his wing, regularly taking me arrowhead hunting—or, as he called it, relic hunting. One hot summer day he took me relic hunting in Buzzard's Hollow, just east of Adelaide and Edward's homes on Mahan Creek. He had a childhood memory of having seen a large geode there, but he and the friend with him were unable to move it and take it home. Now as a man, he was sure he could dislodge it, so off we took.

As we walked into the Hollow, he told me that on March 31, 1865, when Wilson's Raiders marched through Brierfield on their way to Selma,

*Edward Mahan and his wife, Rita, with Adelaide Mahan, right, seated on the front steps of the home built by Jesse W. Mahan Sr. for his second wife, Anna, and passed down to Adelaide. January 11, 1946.*

the Mahan family hid out in Buzzard's Hollow, leaving a Negro servant to take care of the house. That afternoon, more than 11,000 troops arrived and decided to camp in that area for the night. The officers, including General James Wilson, spent the night in the home of my great-great-grandfather, Edward. Finding the house locked, they kicked in the front door, which was blocked from the inside by a plantation desk. They knocked the desk over and walked over it with their hob-nailed boots, forever leaving a mark on a family heirloom.

I loved Edward's stories as much as hunting arrowheads and had little thought of the geode we were supposed to be looking for. Edward was finally forced to give up the hunt for it, and we wandered up to Katie's Spring, which is located in Buzzard's Hollow and flows into Mahan Creek. This had been a favorite spot of Indians, and I loved imagining their having been

*Edward Mahan, nationally respected amateur archaeologist, holding a large Native American artifact, circa 1950s.*

there. This was to be a lucky day for me. I looked down and saw a stone sticking up out of the packed dirt. We pried it out, and we saw that it was an Indian grindstone. I announced to Edward that I was going to take it home, and he said fine, but that I had to map the location of where it was found.

It was a hot day. For a twelve-year-old boy weighing no more than seventy pounds, carrying a stone that weighed more than twenty-five pounds was an arduous task. Especially since we had a two-mile trek back home. Half way, I was really getting winded. I took off my belt and tied it to the stone, slinging the tail over my shoulder. That didn't work, but Edward said that if you choose to take something from the woods, you have made a commitment to see it through. After two hours, I had never been more excited to see home. But I had my treasure, and I only had to map the location where I had discovered it.

Edward also sparked my love for guns, both old and new. One day we were at his home on the hill above Adelaide's house, and he took out a rifle to show me. I had never seen anything like it. This World War II .30-06 Garand rifle had been demilitarized, sporterized, blued, and had a beautiful long stock and scope. I almost fainted when he asked, "Do you want to shoot it?"

I jumped at the chance, watching Edward take a black clip filled with shiny brass bullets from the gun case. With a click, he seated it into the receiver. He said, "Let's go out on the porch and shoot it," and I eagerly followed, having no notion of the learning curve required before becoming proficient at shooting this gun. I took the rifle from him, placed the butt end to my shoulder, looked through the scope, put my finger on the trigger, and pulled. Nothing happened. Edward began to laugh, and I felt stupid.

"You don't know about the safety, do you?" he said. Before I could answer he showed me how to release it. He taught me the proper shooting position and instructed me in sighting. "Now, try again," he said.

I gripped the gun, sighted it at a tree, looked through the scope, placed finger on the trigger, and pulled. At the same time I heard the deafening blast, I felt myself being hurled backwards, my shoulder aching fiercely. In a split second, my butt was on the floor. Luckily, the gun was still in my hand. My ears were ringing, but I could hear the sound of Edward's laughter. From him I had learned a lesson I've tried to follow ever since: "Never fire a gun unless you are sure how to do it."

Edward, more than anyone, taught me to respect nature and made me keenly aware of history and archaeology. From him I first heard a quotation he said came from Ben Franklin, "You will never know where you are going until you know where you have been." Until this day, I have never found any reason to suspect the truth of that statement.

*Top: Major Howison's hotel in Randolph, Alabama. Alan Mahan owed his life to the Major, who built his hotel in 1886 across the railroad tracks from the depot, near where the Mahan-Cox duel occurred. Bottom: Alan Mahan, left, standing with his hands in his pockets, hat nattily cocked, was a sport. Whiskey was his weakness and his ultimate downfall.*

7

# Alan Mahan

All the Mahans were not as illustrious as Adelaide and Jesse. Alan Mahan, a cousin of my father's generation, achieved an unhappy fame. He was involved in not just one, but two shoot-outs, and my father never tired of telling the tale of his pistol-toting kinsman. He was nearby for both events.

According to my dad, Alan was a member of a group of rough young men in the Randolph community (Bibb County) who called themselves the Dirty Dozen. He joined with Scott Cox, Grove Cleveland, Morgan Smitherman, and others, mainly to have a good time being rebellious. Alan, at that time a merchant in town, decided one night to have a crap game for this crowd. At the end of the game when they were counting up, Alan and his good friend Scott Cox got into an argument and had a falling out. In fact, Alan got so mad that he ran Scott out of his place of business.

Scott had been a friend of my grandfather, and, because my grandfather's home was so full at that time, Scott had invited two of my father's older brothers to sleep at his house. They were there when Scott came back to his house after the argument with Alan. They said he picked up his pump shotgun and left. He returned to Alan's store, where he saw Alan coming out on a little platform, getting ready to lock up. Scott opened fire. He hit Alan in his shoulder, leg, and groin. Alan, near death, dragged himself a couple of blocks to the old hotel that was run by a wealthy merchant, Major Allen P. Howison. Immediately, Howison telegraphed the Southern Railway and had them send a special train from Wilton, an engine and a caboose, to take Alan to the hospital in Selma. Miraculously, the doctors in Selma saved him.

As for Scott, he walked directly back to his house after the shooting and told my father's brothers that he had just killed his best friend. Luckily, he was wrong, of course, and no charges were ever filed against him. After all, the families were close. The resolution was an agreement that Scott would leave Randolph and never return.

Alan, who owed his life to Major Howison, went down to Brent, Alabama, to manage a farm for him as a means of paying off the expense incurred in his rescue. With him he took his new bride, Para Splawn, his longtime sweetheart. He stayed in Brent until 1923, when for some unknown reason he moved to Montevallo. He and Para lived in the Hoskin house behind the Methodist Church.

The marshal in Montevallo at that time was Dan Walker, a native of Randolph and supposedly a friend of Alan's. But their friendship came to an end on a tragic day in November 1923.

On Thanksgiving Day, Alan and the barber Roy Tatum went bird hunting. They might have started drinking during the day, but they certainly hit the bottle hard when they returned to Roy's barbershop on Main Street that afternoon. Roy, who lived in his shop, decided to take a bath and change clothes, and Alan said he was going home. But for some reason he returned. Roy let him in and went back behind the partition to change clothes. What followed was inexplicable to those who knew Alan. Although Roy was his friend, Alan began shooting up the place. Apparently in his inebriated condition he just wanted to have a little fun, and he fired the pistol repeatedly. One of the bullet holes went through a plate glass window, and when my father bought the barbershop from Roy in 1927, the patched-over hole was still there.

Somebody noticed what was happening in the shop and called Dan Walker, the marshal. He came right away, and he told Alan he wanted to take him home. In those days the streets were not paved, there were no street lights, and there were gullies between Roy's shop and Alan's house, but Marshal Walker managed to get him home, taking a great deal of abuse off Alan in the process.

The next morning, Para said, "Alan, you ought to go up and apologize to Mr. Walker for the way you treated him last night. He brought you home and you treated him something awful." Alan sent word for Marshal Walker to come see him, but Dan didn't come for Alan to apologize to him. In the meantime, a bootlegger named Dewey Lucas, who was an enemy of Dan Walker's because he wouldn't let him sell his liquor in Montevallo, came to see Alan, bringing some moonshine with him. They started drinking during the day, and late in the afternoon they decided to go to the restaurant run by Dan Walker's wife, the Wiggle-in Hot Dog Cafe. The establishment was located on Main Street, just across the street from Tatum's barbershop.

Mrs. Walker was alarmed when she heard they were coming that way, so she sent word to Mr. C. L. Meroney, a merchant just down the street, to come get Dan and keep him out of Alan's way. Mr. Meroney complied, taking Dan to his store. He told Walker, "Now, Dan, the thing for you to do is to go home and let this thing blow over." Dan seemed to agree. While the two were talking, Alan and Dewey arrived at the cafe, taking seats at a counter in the back.

Just as Marshal Walker was leaving Mr. Meroney's store to go home, a fellow named Ollis Wooley walked up and said to Dan, "I'll be damned if I'd let anyone run me out of my place of business." That was like waving a red flag in front of a bull's face. Dan Walker had a high temper, so instead of going home he marched right back into the cafe, walking behind the counter where Alan and Dewey were seated. "Alan," he said, "I understand you have come up here to kill me," and he hauled off and slapped him very hard. That took some courage because Alan was stout as a bull and could whip just about anybody.

When Alan stood up, ready to fight the marshal, Dan pulled out his gun and started shooting. At the same time, Dewey Lucas started shooting, and in the end both Dan Walker and Alan Mahan lay mortally wounded in the doorway of the cafe, Alan killed by Dan Walker and Dan Walker by Dewey Lucas. Neither died immediately, but were taken to Wilton so that they could be placed on a train due at the time and taken to Selma for medical treatment. It was very strange: at one end of the platform lay the wounded Alan, and at the other end lay the wounded Marshal Walker.

Dad, who lived in Wilton at the time, was present that night at the train station, and he rushed to get Alan's sister Sarah, who also lived in Wilton. When they arrived a few minutes before the train got there, my father took her up to Alan's cot. He was facing the railroad tracks, clearly in a terrible condition. Sarah began crying and asking Alan what did he want her to tell his mother, reminding him how much she had suffered after the first shooting some years before. Alan just waved her away, then turned over and faced the wall. He died at that point, his death witnessed by my father.

Mr. Walker was down at the other end of the platform. Daddy said he was hollering like a goat being slaughtered. He lived long enough to get to Selma, but he didn't make it through the night.

The loss of the two lives seems to have grown out of trivial circumstances. Daddy always said that Alan wasn't a killer, that he just got wild when he drank. Some people thought the animus between Alan and the marshal must have grown out of a more serious cause. The rumor was that Alan had been messing around with Dan Walker's wife. If true, that might explain such a violent response. Dewey, it would seem, had his own resentments. In the end, he was tried for the crime, but was acquitted. Montevallo, in those days, was a place of violence, and justice was not easily come by.

# Part II

# *Neighbors*

*Above: Mother and I in front of our house on Shelby Street with my four-wheel pump vehicle known as an Irish mail, a recent Christmas present. The Craig house is in the background. The home has been completely restored by Janice Seaman and now serves as the Fox and Pheasant Bed and Breakfast Inn. Right: Mother obviously thought that the perfect setting for this Easter photo was across the street in Miss Alice's flower garden.*

# 8

# The Elite of Shelby Street

As a kid, I quickly formed the opinion that there could be no better place on earth to live than on Shelby Street. I thought it more desirable than any other neighborhood in our small town, even Highland Avenue, which was on the other side of Main Street near the campus of Alabama College. The most exclusive area in town, Highland Avenue had fine houses occupied by the elite of Montevallo. At some point the City Council decided that Highland Avenue sounded too snooty and officially demoted it to Highland Street, but it was still an avenue when I was growing up.

Shelby Street, however, had a dwelling far superior to any house on Highland, and I could sit on my front porch and gaze at it to my heart's content. It was an immense two-story brick home on the corner of Shelby and Island streets, occupying half a block in each direction. It was such a landmark that people used it to give directions. A widow named Alice Craig lived there with her ancient stepmother, Mrs. Reynolds, whose husband, a prominent merchant and industrialist, had built the home. Miss Alice herself had married well, her husband amassing a fortune in the coal mining industry, which provided the country with the superior and much-sought-after Montevallo red ash coal. Mr. Craig could easily provide Miss Alice with the finer things in life.

Miss Alice entertained grandly. Every Christmas she invited people from all over town to her house for a much-anticipated party. The large dining table, covered with an ironed white tablecloth, had a huge silver bowl filled with cranberry punch, and guests, dressed in their Sunday best, sipped the punch from small crystal cups. The rest of the table and the sideboard were laden with cheese straws, fruitcake cookies, shiny divinity, peppery toasted pecans, and thick pieces of chocolate pecan fudge. My mother would give me a little glass plate and a napkin, and I would marvel at the fineness of the selections. A huge fire would be blazing in the fireplace in the dining room and also in the living room, which guests overflowed into.

When Miss Alice had a party in the summer, she used her side porch, and guests stood or they sat on white wicker furniture under the large black ceiling fan, which hummed and rotated slowly, gently circulating the air. Sipping iced tea with sprigs of mint or wedges of lemon, everyone complimented Miss Alice on the beauty of the ferns and cut flowers she had decorated the porch with. Miss Alice would smile modestly, thank them, and say that the flowers came out of her yard—nothing special.

I liked the big parties, which we never missed, but I most loved the visits my mother and I made to Miss Alice's. We would be met at the front door by Miss Alice's black butler, improbably named Buster, who wore a coat and tie in all weather. Buster had been well trained. He would bow just a bit, invite us into the entrance hall, and go off to announce our arrival to Miss Alice. Even as a small boy, I knew I was looking at something classy.

The house had a soft smell of roses, unlike anything I had ever detected in our house or the houses of others. There were tall empire mirrors with beveled glass, bronze statues of Greek gods and goddesses sitting on marble-topped tables, and oriental rugs in rich red patterns. There was a magnificent elaborate mahogany staircase, and as I eyed the glistening banisters I wished devoutly to slide down them. But that would have to wait for future owners of the house who did not stand so staunchly on decorum.

Miss Alice would come into the hall, usually wearing black, walking slowly and erectly, holding out a hand first to Mother and then to me. We would be invited into the living room, and she would usually have her maid, wearing a black dress with a full-length starched white apron and white lace-up shoes like nurses wore, bring tea for herself and Mother and lemonade for me. The maid brought everything out on a silver tray, and there was always a little plate of thin teacakes. Mother had instructed me that good manners dictated that I was never to eat more than two. I did what she said, though I could have gladly eaten fifty-two.

As Mother and Miss Alice talked about gardening and neighbors, I looked around at the brocade curtains with gold threads in them, the end tables made of cherry, the fine milk-glass chandeliers. Two small horsehair sofas faced each other near the fireplace, which was far bigger than our fireplace at home. Mother told me that was because we burned coal and Miss Alice burned wood. Sitting in the fireplace were some strange-looking large brass objects. They looked like large eyes staring out at me, but Mother said they were firedogs, put there to hold the logs in place. Going into this room in particular was, I suppose, the beginning of my love of beautiful things. Mother certainly thought Miss Alice was the arbiter of taste in Montevallo.

Sometimes Miss Alice would tell us of her travels to Europe. She was one of the two persons in town who regularly traveled abroad, the other being Mrs. Bess Chamberlain of Highland Avenue. Only once was I invited to go upstairs in the Craig House while Miss Alice lived there, and on the landing halfway between upstairs and downstairs she showed us an amazing space she called her trunk room. I was impressed, as we did not have such a room in our house across the street and my mother did not go abroad. She only went up the street to work. "A whole room just to keep trunks in," I said silently to myself in absolute wonder.

Her radiators were concealed by ornate metal grilles, and I loved to hear their hissing noises and occasional bumps and clanks. On one of our visits in the winter, Miss Alice needed Buster for something, and she sent me to the dark basement to fetch him. To get there I had to go onto the screened back porch, where the servants took their meals in summer, down the dark green stairs outside, then around the house to the cellar door. It was dark inside, but a naked bulb hung from the ceiling had enough light to reveal Buster over in a corner. He had removed his coat and was shoveling coal into the stoker, a dark green contraption with a motor that moved an auger, which at preset intervals pushed coal into the furnace. We did not have a stoker. We put our coal directly into the stove with a shovel or dumped it directly from the big snoot on one of our coal shuttles. One of my jobs was to take the scuttles, one black and the other silver, to the coal bin, fill it, and bring it back—the black one for the kitchen and the silver one for the living room. Miss Alice's stoker was a much better way to get coal in the fire, I thought, and I decided that I should advise my father to get us an auger.

The occasions to see the splendor of the interior of Miss Alice's house were not all that numerous, but my family could constantly enjoy the beauty of the grounds. We could see her yardman George toiling every day to maintain the splendor—manicuring the lawn, planting and fertilizing flowers, weeding the beds. The most arresting part of Miss Alice's yard was her rose garden, in a side lawn between the house and the Presbyterian Church. It was surrounded by hedge bushes that George trimmed weekly, and in the summer Miss Alice and her stepmother often sat in this cool, private space. Sometimes I would stand on a concrete wall by the sidewalk and peer into the rose garden, marveling at the color and size of the flowers.

Miss Alice also had a splendid bed of flowers in the front yard near the screened porch and another between the double walkway that led to her front door. In the summer she filled this bed with pink, white, and dark red petunias, and in the winter she replaced them with pansies, whose happy bright faces gave vivid color when there was little else blooming. There were no plantings next to the house, because, as I later learned, Victorians liked to sit on their porches and look at their flowers and shrubs, and Mrs. Craig was certainly a Victorian lady.

Behind the rose garden were giant crape myrtle trees as high as a house. They bloomed white, pink, and watermelon in the late summer, and they were spectacular. But the trees had a practical purpose too. They screened the rest of the backyard, where the Craig vegetable garden was planted. Compared to the flower gardens on the place, I suppose Miss Alice thought a vegetable garden unsightly.

On the left side of the house was a sunken garden with descending concrete steps. Two very large pots of deutzia bushes stood on each side of the steps, and in the sunken garden itself a large translucent amber-colored ball rested on an iron cradle. Looking out the window of Mrs. Craig's breakfast room, I could see the light shining through the sphere and thought it exceedingly beautiful. Also in the sunken garden was a brass sundial, and I was even more intrigued by it. Finally, when I went to school and learned its function, I would go over and read the dial on occasion.

The grass was green year-round at the Craig House because Miss Alice had her yardman plant winter rye every fall. No other yard in town could boast a green yard in the winter, not even the houses on Highland Avenue.

And there seemed to be something blooming in the yard year-round. Even in the cold of winter, Professor Sargent camellias added color to the place. When the gardenias were blooming in the early summer, we could smell the rich aroma all the way over to our house.

Next to Mrs. Craig's house was an edifice whose quality also rose above that of the other buildings on Shelby Street: the Presbyterian Church. The building itself was not particularly imposing. It was smaller than the Methodist Church on Middle Street, to which my family walked every Sunday. It was smaller than the Baptist Church on Main Street, too. When its bells were rung modestly on Sunday morning, I thought they sounded tinny and greatly inferior to those at the Methodist and Baptist churches. But still I thought the place superior. Perhaps it was distinguished by the people who belonged to it. I would see Dr. Harmon, president of Alabama College, getting out of his long black car and entering the church with great dignity, and I loved watching the Presbyterian college girls, dressed in hats and gloves, strolling down the street for services. The leading citizens from Highland Avenue also entered the Presbyterian portals.

In time, the church seemed to me imbued with mystery, a sacrosanct space I would not think of invading. Churches were never locked in those days, but I could never bring myself to join the older boys from the neighborhood when they would sneak in there. I am not sure what made me scared to go in, but I did imagine that strange, arcane rites were celebrated there, rites that made the Methodist services bland and humdrum. My fear of the church's interior did not extend to the churchyard, however, and I spent many hours with my friends sliding down its terraces in pasteboard boxes.

One of the things that intrigued me about the Presbyterian Church was that it had buttresses on one side—an architectural wonder I had never seen before. I asked my father why they had buttresses, and he said that the 1939 tornado that blew away the Episcopal Church, which was also on Shelby Street, had damaged the Presbyterian Church, too, but that they were able to prop the brick church up with concrete buttresses. The church, when I first knew it, was already painted white, and Dad said that when the buttresses were installed, it was painted for the first time. Shortly after

*Above: Original appearance of the Montevallo Presbyterian Church before the cyclone of 1939 took the belfry tower on the roof and necessitated the installation of buttresses. Right: Ruins of St. Andrew's Episcopal Church on Shelby Street following the cyclone of 1939. Eventually, the church was rebuilt on Plowman Street.*

World War II, my parents bought a set of *Compton's Encyclopedia* for me, and it was a source of great information of all kinds. One of the first things I looked up was buttresses, and when I read that Notre Dame in Paris had flying buttresses I wondered if it too had been hit by a cyclone.

If I were feeling puny on a Sunday morning and stayed home, I was able to listen to the services going on across the street. In the summer, when all the windows were open, I'd position myself at my bedroom window and listen to the sound of the little pump organ wafting across the street and to the joyless, sedate Presbyterian voices singing strange hymns. Even though they had a choir and choir director, I wasn't altogether impressed. Our Methodist hymns were better, I thought, but we only had a piano. The Baptists had us both beat. They had a pipe organ.

I was rather frightened to look at Mrs. Straughn, who directed the Presbyterian choir. Her legs were immense, all the way down to her ankles, and as I would watch her waddle by I would almost shiver. Mother said I was not to stare at Mrs. Ina Straughn's legs, that it wasn't nice. She had been cursed with elephantiasis, she said, and it didn't take me long to figure out where the malady got its name. Everyone said that she had a lovely voice and a pretty face.

The Presbyterian Church and Miss Alice's house were exceptions on Shelby Street. Except for them, Shelby Street seemed solidly middle-class. Houses were decent, but not fine, and they sat on a very busy street, which was one of the major routes into and out of town. Large dusty coal trucks from the mines came by quite often, their engines making a deafening sound. But little did we mind. We liked our street, a place where some of the most intriguing people in the world resided.

# 9

# Other Shelby Street Neighbors

Growing up, I was surrounded by a host of interesting people, both young and old, and I was seldom bored. I knew everybody. Because my sisters were so much older, I had no playmates in the house, so Shelby Street provided a number of cohorts. And the adults along Shelby Street became proxy parents.

## The Wilsons

Next door to us on Shelby Street lived a childless couple named Bloomer and Lucille Wilson. Mr. Bloomer ran the local drugstore with his brother, the pharmacist, whom we called Dr. Wilson. I don't think he was a doctor at all, but in those days it was common to address a pharmacist as doctor. Mr. Bloomer was not a pharmacist, but that didn't keep him from filling prescriptions, though he could usually be found behind the marble counter of the town's most beautiful soda fountain. We kids would take a seat at one of the eight porcelain stools at the counter. These stools swiveled, and Mr. Bloomer didn't mind us turning left or right. But turning all the way around was a no-no—Mr. Bloomer would yell, "Boys, don't be spinning on those stools. If you do it again I'm going to send you over to one of the tables to drink your soda." There were six or eight round white tables with porcelain tops and twisted iron legs. If they were occupied by college girls, as they often were in the afternoons and on weekends, he would tell us that we would have to take our sodas outside if he caught us spinning.

From behind the counter, Mr. Bloomer or his assistant Miss Ione dispensed Coke floats, cherry Cokes, single or double ice cream cones, and sundaes loaded with nuts and chocolate and whipped cream and with a maraschino cherry on the top. I personally preferred the chocolate sodas, because I liked the fizzing sensation they caused in my mouth.

Bloomer's wife, whom we called Miss Lucille, worked downtown at Klotzman's, a department store owned by one of the two Jewish families in town. On weekends she baked oatmeal cookies, and she would often call me into their house and give me a stack. They were the best cookies in the world.

Mr. Bloomer was a big fox hunter. Some Saturdays he would come in from the drugstore and have his supper, and shortly afterwards we could hear him going to his backyard, whistling and calling for the bluetick and redbone hounds penned there. He'd bring them around, and they'd jump into a big box covered with chicken wire in the back seat of his blue four-door Chevy sedan. Then men began to gather in Bloomer's driveway. I would look out the window and watch them. Often, one would have a bottle of whiskey, which they would pass around. When I was very small I didn't know it was whiskey, and I thought it must be some sort of medicine you had to take before you could go fox hunting. The men got louder as time passed, laughing raucously and hollering at the dogs. They talked about which ones treed the best and which could run the best. They all seemed to be experts. Daddy never joined them for the fox hunt itself, but he did

*Bloomer and Lucille Wilson rented the house next door.*

occasionally partake of their medicine before they departed.

I had seen a picture of a fox in my reader at school, and I couldn't really understand why anyone would want to hunt one. It finally dawned on me that I had never seen them bring a fox home, and I came to believe that the fox was more of an excuse for drinking and camaraderie than a real object of their pursuit. On occasion I would be awakened—in fact, everyone in the neighborhood was—when the hunters returned after midnight. The men would be talking even louder than before, and the dogs would be barking loudly. For some reason the dogs did not want to get out of the box, which must have meant for them the end of a spell of freedom they enjoyed after being penned up for days on end, and at that point Mr. Bloomer would take a fan belt from the trunk and begin hitting the dogs. They would moan in pain. Once out of their box, the dogs would often begin fighting, and we would hear Miss Lucille yell at Mr. Bloomer, "Shut those dogs up, Bloomer, or they'll wake up the whole neighborhood." Of course, by then they had already awakened the neighborhood. I would hear Mother telling

*The girl next door, Beverly, and her father, Joe Doyle. After the war, my dad and mother bought the house the Wilsons had rented and then sold it to Joe and Mildred Doyle. Beverly still owns and lives in the house.*

Daddy that Mr. Bloomer should be stopped from such savagery. Daddy didn't seem to agree, so finally she would open up a window and scream, "Bloomer, you better quit beating those dogs."

Mr. Bloomer never acknowledged my mother's complaints nor did he ever change his behavior. The next day in the neighborhood, it was as if nothing had happened.

## The Hartleys

Our other next-door neighbors were the Hartleys. Mr. Bill Hartley drove the gas truck for Mr. J. A. Brown Sr., and Mrs. Hartley worked for Mr. Ellis Hoffman in his dry goods store. Their son Bill was my close friend, and I spent a lot of time at their house.

The Hartley house was nicely painted and had two floors, and we loved to play on the porch off the second floor. Mother was always afraid that we would fall over the banisters down into the yard, but we never did. On very hot summer days and on rainy days we especially loved to play under the Hartley house, which was built on a sloping lot, and the back of the house was high above the ground so there was lots of room down there. The dirt was always cool and powder dry, and there were thousands of doodlebugs. We'd get a straw off the kitchen broom and push it down in the hole, saying, "Doodlebug, Doodlebug, where have you been?" Sometimes we would tickle those little bugs out of the ground all day long.

Mother and Dad told me that the Hartley house used to sit where Mrs. Craig's house now was and that it had been jacked up and skidded across the street on logs. This was the first I had heard that you could move a house, and I thought about it a lot. It dawned on me that this move would have presented a special problem, as it would have to be turned all the way around in order to face the street when it was moved.

The house was moved before there were sidewalks on the street, and when the City installed the walks, the Hartley house was about two feet below the sidewalk. When we skated down the sidewalk, we had to be careful in front of the Hartley house, or we could fall down into their front yard.

The greatest thing about the Hartley household was a visitor who came there periodically. He was Mr. Hartley's oldest son Trab, and we knew that

*Next door to the Mahan house and behind Laura Ann Hicks in this photograph was the two-story Hartley house.*

he was famous. He was a professional baseball player, and, though he played semi-professional ball, we all said he was in the major leagues. Once he injured his shoulder and back, and he had to come home to heal up. He spent part of each day under the house hanging from straps, and I'd always have to go over and peek at him when he did that. The truth was that all the boys on Shelby Street idolized him. Sometimes he would play a game with us that he called pepper. He would stand near the garage between our house and the Bloomer Wilsons', and some of the neighbor boys and I would station ourselves at the end of the driveway near the street. Trab would hit grounders for us to catch, and we loved it. Other times he would pitch with us. Bill had a catcher's mitt, and when Trab's ball hit the mitt it sounded like a beaver tail spanking the water. We'd never seen anything like that.

## The Lathams

On our side of the street, two houses toward town from us, lived Mr. Tommy Latham and his wife in a house that had been moved to the lot it sat on and was jacked up like the Hartley house. We called him Mr. Tommy, but for some reason we always called her Mrs. Latham. Mr. Tommy had run his own grocery store, but when I knew him he ran a store up on Main for Mr. Teamon McCully. You knew that Mr. Tommy was in charge because of the giant silver safety pin he wore on his white apron. Under his apron he wore an impeccable shirt and tie and dress slacks. He knew everybody in town, and everybody knew him. In those days, grocery stores delivered, and if he wasn't too busy Mr. Tommy would deliver your groceries himself. I liked to go to the store, so Momma or Maggie would send me up there two or three times a day to get an item or two.

I was especially fond of Mrs. Latham. I thought she was a grand lady, second on Shelby Street only to Mrs. Craig. She might not have traveled to Europe like Mrs. Craig did, but when she left her house it was a beautiful spectacle. She had a two-toned blue and black 1930 Buick sedan with gorgeous blue velvet upholstery. It had large solid wheels, not spokes like other cars in the neighborhood, and a big chrome gearshift with a shiny black ball on top.

Mrs. Latham was my first employer. Every Saturday I would wash her Buick, whether it had left her garage during the week or not. Both she and Mr. Tommy walked to work, so driving was not an everyday occurrence. She also hired me to pick rocks out between the tire treads because she said that it made the tires last longer and because she didn't like the click they made when she drove down the concrete streets. She kept a meticulous yard, and she also hired me to rake leaves and to transfer flower bulbs.

Running down beside the Latham house was Island Street, which at the time was unpaved. On the right at the bottom of the hill was a rundown house occupied by a colored man. Most black Montevallians lived across the creek, but people said it was okay for the black man to live on our side of the creek, as his house was down under the hill.

## The DeSears

Two houses down, away from Main, one of my best friends, Gene Baldwin, lived in a dirty yellow house with his papaw and mamaw, Mr. and Mrs. Robert DeSear. They, like the Wilsons, lived in a house they rented from Pete Givhan, but their house was far older than either the Wilsons' or ours. It was not well-kept on the outside, and there was a broken cement wall along the street, which had cracked when the roots of a large chinaberry tree worked havoc with it.

Gene had a bad case of asthma, and it seemed to me that while other kids got presents at Christmas, Gene got asthma. Mother said that the DeSears did not keep their house warm enough, and that is why Gene had asthma.

We were impressed with Mr. DeSear, but he was always a sort of mystery to us. We weren't afraid of him at all, but he seemed somewhat unapproachable. He sold burial insurance and would leave home early in the morning in his little black car with a rumble seat, working his debit for a company in Birmingham and returning about dark. Mr. DeSear struck a dandy pose. Tall, stately, and gray-haired, he wore gold-rimmed glasses and a flat-brimmed straw hat with a beautiful turquoise band. His black cap-toe shoes were always polished perfectly, and he wore dark blue three-piece suits with a white pin stripe. A rich gold watch chain went from one side of his vest to the other, and he also wore a gold stick-pin in his tie.

Mr. DeSear was a courtly man. He walked along the city sidewalks a great deal, and whenever he met a woman on the sidewalk he would tip his hat to her. When a man asked him how he was doing, he always had the same answer, "Good as they make 'em, don't give a damn where they come from." Mother thought he had little to do to use the word *damn* so casually.

Mr. DeSear owned guns, and Gene and I were fascinated by them. I was not allowed to have a gun, not even a BB gun, and Dad didn't have a gun because Mother objected to them so strenuously. Mr. DeSear joined the fox hunts, carrying a twelve-gauge shotgun, which was stored in the hall closet. Gene and I would slip in there and handle the gun, both vowing that we would have our own shotguns one day.

Mr. DeSear had a chicken house, and every year he planted a vegetable garden near it. He grew corn twice as tall as I was, and he used brush to prop up his tomatoes and beans to keep them off the ground. When President Roosevelt asked all Americans to plant a Victory garden during the war, Dad complied, thinking it was his patriotic duty to do so. But he never really liked it, and when the war was over there were no more gardens at 159 Shelby Street. In response to the president's call, Bloomer Wilson said he was as patriotic as the next man, but damned if he was going to plant any vegetable garden.

I had many meals with Gene and his grandparents, and I always went there for breakfast on Saturday mornings. Gene had a breakfast ritual he invariably went through. He would spoon Mamaw's grits onto his porcelain plate, and put a large pat of butter in the center, stirring them until the butter melted. Then he would take crispy bacon and crumble it over the buttered grits, after which he would smooth the mixture over the entire plate, pick up his fork, and eat the mixture with a look of extreme contentment on his face. At home, I would try to duplicate his ritual, but I never seemed to achieve his level of perfection.

Gene, who along the way had gained the nickname General, left Montevallo late in high school because his mother, Ladean, who was in education, was not satisfied with the educational program at Montevallo High School. She sent Gene to Fort Gordon Military Academy in Georgia for

*Left: One of my best friends, Gene Baldwin, all dressed up in front of his grandparent's house. Below: Gene's grandparents, Alma and Robert DeSear, in front of their Shelby Street home.*

*Right: Home from Gordon Military Academy, Gene Baldwin had his picture made with his buddy and neighbor, Ed Bridges. Below, left: Gene, stationed in Korea, waiting for a scramble at the alert shack. Below, right: June McQueen, Gene's Alabama College girlfriend and later his wife, the girl he "buzzed" while flying his jet down Montevallo's Main Street in 1952.*

his junior and senior years. Afterwards, he returned to Montevallo with his best friend, Herndon Davis, but they decided they wanted more in life and went to Birmingham to join the Navy. At the recruiting office, Herndon immediately signed up, but Gene got cold feet and didn't sign. Instead, he entered Alabama College in 1950, but he didn't do very well and after one year joined the U.S. Air Force, becoming a jet pilot. He had always been interested in planes, and this was in many ways a dream come true. He made many flights, but his most memorable one came in 1952.

In May 1952, residents of Montevallo could not have imagined an F-94 jet with afterburners roaring over town at 500 feet, but that is exactly what Gene did. He first buzzed Alabama College, barely missing both the top floor of Main Dormitory, which was called the Buzzard, and the concrete water tower. His "buzz" of the campus frightened some and it impressed some, but the main thing it did was to make the heart of his lover, June, race almost as fast as the plane was traveling. Leaving campus, he buzzed down Shelby Street. He apparently enjoyed it so much that he turned around and buzzed straight down Shelby Street again. After that, he flew off to his squadron in Pensacola, Florida, leaving June and his townsmen behind, but definitely with a good story to tell about the antics of a wild man, Gene Baldwin.

I was at home on Shelby Street when Gene made his first pass, and I heard the deafening noise as the General passed over. I rushed out into the yard to see what in the world was happening, but I knew in my heart that this had to be the work of Gene Baldwin. I watched as the plane made a sharp turn onto Main Street and gave the town one last buzz. The whole incident had not lasted over five minutes, but what a five minutes!

Gene went on to have a distinguished career in the military. He flew combat missions for twenty-five months in Korea. But in our minds, none of that was nearly so fine an achievement as buzzing his hometown.

## Hobart Love

Another neighbor who got the attention of the neighborhood kids was Hobart Love. He lived just down the street in an apartment with his wife and two daughters. I occasionally played with one of the daughters on a long upstairs porch on the house. But it was not the house that was really Hobart Love's domain. He was the mysterious man who sat above the balcony in the Strand Theater in a metal fireproof booth (because early film stock was highly flammable) running the projector. When we went to the picture show, we would always check Hobart out. Occasionally when I'd have to have a bathroom break during the movie, I would see Hobart downstairs talking to the owner of the Strand, Mr. Eddie Watson, or eating popcorn, and I would wonder how the movie could be running without him. Later we discovered he could be downstairs because he knew how long a reel would last. He would just have to be back upstairs to see some little spots appear in the upper right-hand side of the screen. That was Hobart's sign to switch to another of the three pre-set projectors. My friends and I would watch for those little spots as if they were some vital secret code that we were privy to. Occasionally Hobart would fail to see the spots, and the movie would stop. We kids would whistle and boo and hiss until the movie came back on. Then we would clap loudly.

We especially envied Hobart because he got to see every movie that came to town. We only got to see the westerns on Saturday.

### The McGaughys

Down the street from us lived two of my bosom buddies, Jack and Joe McGaughy, and their parents, Mr. Luther and Miss Rebecca. When I think of their house, I think of the terraces out front that Mr. Luther covered with white rocks to keep from having to mow on such a steep grade. Until the end of World War II, Mr. Luther drove various routes for the Alabama Coach Company located on Middle Street and owned by Mr. Wyman Brown. Like Dad, Luther was too old to be drafted, but he carried workers, including Dad, back and forth to work in the government's gunpowder plant in Childersburg.

Mr. Luther was stricken with rheumatoid arthritis, which affected his hand and foot coordination, making it impossible for him to continue driving. But he continued working for the company, selling tickets in a little room between the white and colored waiting rooms at the bus station downtown. I loved to go down to the station and watch him selling tickets to Pea Ridge, Dogwood, Marvel, and all the little mining towns near Montevallo. You could also buy a ticket from him that would take you to Birmingham, and I was able to do that on several occasions when I would go visit family there.

Finally Mr. Luther's condition got so bad that he couldn't work at all. First he became confined to home, and later he was completely bedridden. Luckily, some great news drifted down from Dr. Hubbard's office: there was a new miracle drug called cortisone, and maybe injections of this miracle drug would get Mr. Luther well. The shots did help enough that he was able to go out onto the porch and could occasionally ride in the car. But his appearance changed. His face got very fat, and he developed a hump on his back. His hair turned a funny color and then fell out, and it wasn't long after that that he passed away. It was the first death of a friend's parent that I experienced, and I found it very stressful. Luckily, Miss Rebecca was a strong woman. She continued her job teaching home economics at Montevallo High School, and, with the help of Carrie Boo Deviner from Brierfield, she kept an orderly home.

Mr. Luther's garden, which he had kept as long as he could, was not abandoned. The boys and Carrie Boo saw to that. Miss Rebecca continued to cook marvelous meals, to which I was often invited. I can still taste the fresh corn on the cob, the sliced tomatoes, the thick slices of onion, the green beans, the cornbread, and the meat—fried chicken, liver, or crisp streak-of-lean.

I shall never forget one event that took place in the barn behind the McGaughy home. Joe and Jack, Dolan Small, other boys, and I loved to take the corncobs and have wars, shooting them with slingshots. A friend named Grady "Beaut" Houlditch, a quiet and serious boy, was playing war with us one day. We had found a sack of lime in the barn, and we would dip the corncobs in the lime so we would have proof if we had made a kill. Jack hit Grady directly in one eye, blinding him in that eye. Amazingly, Grady and his family accepted it as just one of those things that can happen, and there were no repercussions, except that we were forbidden to ever dip the corncobs in lime again.

Carrie Boo was the one who gave the boys their nicknames. Joe, who

*Grady "Beaut" Houlditch, me, and Harry Klotzman in front of Holcombe's grocery store and Dr. Mitchell's dental office.*

was my age, was called Hon Darlin' and his brother Jack, two years older, was called Sugar Babe. The boys in the neighborhood shortened the names to Hon and Shug, and those names stuck. Joe and I started Auburn in 1952, and since we lived in different dorms I didn't see him for a few days. I hadn't realized, but we were in the same ROTC class. I entered the huge hall, which had raked seating for several hundred students, and went down front to take a seat. I looked back behind me to see if I recognized anyone and was thrilled to see my buddy Joe there on the back row. I jumped up and without thinking yelled out, "Hon Darlin'!" Joe jumped up and waved back. Silence fell over the room. In those days you could not call your best male friend "Hon Darlin'" without arousing suspicion, and our classmates eyed us warily. I realized what was okay on Shelby Street was another matter in the larger world.

Carrie Boo later came to work for us, becoming an integral part of our family, maybe even more so than Maggie had been. After I married and returned to Montevallo, Carrie became a companion to my daughter Miki, as Maggie had been to me. Carrie Boo stayed with us through marriages, births, and deaths, and, when Mother died, her head rested on Carrie's shoulder.

## Mr. Dyer

We had yet another neighbor who fascinated me and the other kids on Shelby Street, but he was almost universally disliked by the adults. His name was Mr. H. I. E. Dyer. This was the first person I ever encountered with three initials, and I had no idea what the *H* and *I* stood for, but the *E* stood for Edward, and everybody called him Ed Dyer. Before the war, he had lived in what we called the house under the hill, but I wasn't much aware of him until his return when the war was over. There had once been a gristmill on Shoal Creek, which ran down behind our house, and Mr. Dyer set out to rebuild it. He was a very hard worker, beginning his labors at sunup, and we neighborhood kids watched the project from a distance, much impressed with Mr. Dyer's energy. Once the mill was finished, he began to raise the dam on the creek to get the water he needed to run the mill. He brought in a lot of workers to drill holes in the dam and install iron bars and then to pour a two-foot layer of concrete across the dam. When he finally opened the floodgates, he drained the creek, exposing the rocks above the dam. For the first time in my memory there were actually shoals in Shoal Creek. He also built a millrace to move the water from above the dam to the gristmill's turbine.

All over town there was talk about Mr. Dyer's project, and most didn't approve. Did he, after all, have the legal right to raise the dam? Would he flood Mulkey's Bottom? Would Mr. Jeter's garden plot be affected? Would we be able to have the carnival down by the creek as usual? Despite their fears, people seemed powerless in the face of a determined Mr. Dyer. Everybody just admitted you couldn't do anything with him. The single exception I know of was the young Catherine Bridges, who lived with her parents in a big white house on Shelby Street just above the dam. I was told that when Mr. Dyer began to bulldoze along the creek toward their property, she placed a chair on their property line and told him that he'd have to run over her to bulldoze her place. For once, Mr. Dyer backed down. He had met his match in young Catherine Bridges.

Mr. Dyer finally got his operation up and running, grinding corn and peanuts to make meal and cow feed. He also had a fantastic corn-shucking machine. He did not have a switch to throw or a button to push to change the speed of the wheel for various operations, but would place an iron bar into the works at the proper location. I loved to hear the growling sound diminish as the water wheel in the pit slowed down and watch the dust-covered belts, each wider than both hands, become visible as the speed slowed down. Then

I'd watch the belts move over to other pulleys, which were designed to do another job, slowing down or increasing the speed when the wide belts were moved in one direction or another. I was astounded at Mr. Dyer's engineering.

*Mr. Dyer's infamous Shoal Creek dam.*

I was also fascinated with Mr. Dyer himself, who worked shirtless in most all weather. He was always covered with corn dust from head to belt, the grinding residue hanging from his nostrils, his ears, and his eyebrows. Somebody in the neighborhood nicknamed him the Monster, but I didn't call him that. As time went on, we were not afraid of him and were often down at his mill site. One day he showed us how to drive a bent nail. Most people straightened bent nails, but Mr. Dyer demonstrated how, if you hit the head of the nail at exactly the right angle and with exactly the right amount of force, the nail would straighten itself. We thought it was pure magic how he could do that.

I caught from Mr. Dyer a lifelong habit—collecting "good stuff." He had more treasures on his place than anyone I knew, and his stuff was an endless source of pleasure to me. There were stacks of wood and lumber, tools of every sort, and pieces of machinery here and there. Among the various piles roamed his four cows. Dad always said that Mr. Dyer's stuff was junk, but I knew better. I knew that Mr. Dyer would find a use for it all. Just give him time.

Mr. Dyer cared little for what his neighbors thought. In many ways, he exemplified a quote from Benjamin Franklin that I came to adopt as my own motto. I first encountered it when, as a fifth or sixth grader, I was taken by Dad to a hot dog stand out in Wilton. On the walls there were blue signs with sayings written in glitter. One read, "To avoid criticism, say nothing, do nothing, and be nothing." I asked Dad what it meant, and when he explained it to me I was quite impressed with the idea. Mr. Dyer and I had more in common than might have been seen at first blush. It gives me great pleasure to own the Dyer property today and to have the opportunity to clean it up and create a park on the site.

## The Carpenters

Old Man Carpenter, as we called him, and his sons Brewer and Bill lived in three side-by-side houses down the street from us. They especially did not care for Mr. Dyer and his projects. They were terribly upset when Mr. Dyer tried to get the city to declare that the driveway between Old Man Carpenter's house and the Bridges' house next door was a public street. Mr. Dyer wanted to use the driveway for easier access to his mill. The Carpenters were not about to let this happen, convincing the City Council, on which Dad was then serving, that the driveway was actually a driveway, not a public street.

I never liked the Carpenters very much. Of all our neighbors, they were the least neighborly. Old Man Carpenter lived with his nice, soft-spoken wife, and an unmarried daughter, Madge, in the house nearest us. On Middle Street behind Wilson Drug Company, his sons had a garage that was made from tin and had a dirt floor, and in part of that building Old Man Carpenter ran his shoe repair shop, a place heavy with the smell of neatsfoot oil and leather. He stood behind an L-shaped counter operating a giant, noisy machine that had multiple wheels running on a long shaft, powered by an electric motor. This machine would grind leather off your shoes, polish the leather, put color on it, stain it, and repolish it. He also worked at a big sewing machine that would sew the soles back on your shoes. And there were metal shoe forms on which he would place shoes and drive nails into the soles and heels. Old Man Carpenter's work fascinated

*Carpenter Brothers Garage between Middle and Valley streets. Through the left door was old Mr. Carpenter's shoe repair shop. The large opening to the right was the entrance to Brewer and Bill Carpenter's auto repair shop.*

me and my friends, but we didn't get to see much of it, as he did not like to be watched. We were scared to get too close to him because he would tell us to get the hell out of there.

Madge was not very nice, either. She worked as a dental hygienist at Dr. Orr's office, which was just above Rogan's Store at the corner of Shelby and Main streets. She didn't have a husband, which could have had something to do with her personality. There was, however, a lot of talk about her and her boyfriends. Even as a child, I would hear gossip, but I understood little of it. What I did understand was that she would almost kill me every time I had to get my teeth cleaned. She stood there grimly doing her work, never offering a word of comfort. But we certainly heard from her when we skated down the hill toward her house. "Cut that racket out," she would yell at us through an open window or from the front porch swing where she often sat. When I played at the Bridges's house, which was next door to Madge's house, we were always admonished by Mrs. Bridges to keep our voices down. But it was impossible to keep quiet while we were skating down Shelby Street toward the little red bridge.

I once had the chance to deal Madge some misery, though it did not turn out as well as I had hoped. It was the summer when I was twelve, and Joe McGaughy and I were playing down next to Mr. Dyer's millrace when suddenly Joe grabbed my arm and motioned over to a large flat rock. I gasped at what I saw: sunning itself was the biggest snake I had ever seen. It was easily as big around as my arm and well over a yard long. "What kind is it?" Joe whispered.

"I haven't got any idea," I said. "It's not a rattlesnake though cause it doesn't have any rattles. Let's look for something to kill it with."

Joe eased up toward the snake just a bit. "It isn't poisonous because its head isn't a triangle. All poisonous snakes have a head shaped like a triangle."

"Except for the coral snake," I said, remembering my science class.

We saw some scrap lumber next to a barn Mr. Dyer kept his cows in, and we each armed ourselves with a length of two by four. We advanced like two warriors and made our attack. The snake, sluggish in the warm sun, never knew what hit him, but, taking no chances, we repeatedly struck him. We dragged his mangled body up to the house to show it off, but nobody was there but Carrie Boo. She hollered and said for us to get that thing away from her.

Later we showed it to Dad and Bloomer Wilson when they came home for lunch, and they told us it was a chicken snake. "Y'all go throw that thing in the creek," Dad said, but Joe and I decided we hadn't yet gotten all the mileage we could out of that snake.

"Let's scare somebody with it," Joe said. "It worked with Carrie Boo."

And then we began our plan. We would tie a rope around the snake and hang it vertically in a long narrow hole in the water oak tree in the front yard. Then we'd train the rope out across a limb that came near our front porch. When we saw someone coming we would pull the rope and let the snake fall down toward the sidewalk, landing at their feet.

Once everything was set, we took our seats in the swing and waited for our first victims. In a short while, we could see a black woman and a child coming up the street headed to town. Just as they neared us, with perfect choreography, we yanked the rope. Neither the woman nor the boy seemed at all alarmed, but just walked around it. The woman cast a disgusted look in our direction and said, "What y'all little white boys think y'all trying to do?" The words *little* and *trying* cut us to the quick, but we decided to try again, despite our disappointment with our first effort. We stuck the snake back in the hole, went back to the swing, and waited.

That was when Madge Carpenter headed our way, going back to work at Dr. Orr's office after her lunch hour. Standing around five foot seven and weighing in at more than two hundred pounds, she was a blaze of white—white uniform, white wedge-heeled shoes, and white stockings. She walked slowly but deliberately—like a man, I thought. On her face was her usual glumness. A better victim could not be found.

At just the right time we yanked the rope, and when the snake brushed her shoulder she let out a scream louder than I had ever heard. "Lord God, Jesus," she hollered, and Joe and I got to laughing. By then she had seen the rope and had spotted the two of us.

"You wait til I tell y'all's daddies," she screamed. "Then you'll be laughing on the other side of your damn faces." With that she stalked off toward Main Street. I knew she would not stop until she got to Dad's barbershop.

In a matter of minutes here came Dad, and I could see by the scowl on his face that he was not happy. "Get in the coalhouse, Mike, and you get on home, Joe. Your mama can take care of you." As I headed to the coalhouse with Dad just behind me, I could tell he was removing his belt. The whipping wasn't so bad. I figured it was probably worth it to scare the hell out of Madge, but it galled me that she might think she was the one who won.

Madge's brother, Brewer Carpenter, lived with his wife and son, Brewer Jr., in a little creosote house between his father and his brother Bill. Both Brewer and Bill had reputations for being excellent mechanics, and they were also known for their automobiles, which they would trade in almost every year. While Brewer chose a practical Dodge or Plymouth, Bill chose a flashy Chrysler. Once he got one with special fender, hood, and roof design to make it aerodynamically superior. He told everybody, "Now that's the way all cars will be shaped in the future." Dad said he hoped not, as he thought it was the ugliest car he had ever seen. But I thought it was cool

*Brewer Carpenter inside the auto shop he shared with his brother Bill.*

having a car of the future on our street. Highland Avenue didn't have one.

The Carpenters didn't like dogs to wander onto their property, and when I got Tag, Mother would always tell me to keep him off their place. They also did not like it at all when the boys in the neighborhood would come onto their property to fish along their bank. There was a gum tree on their property next to the creek, and it was reputed to be next to the best bream bed on the creek. We couldn't resist it, despite the fact that we knew that one of the Carpenters would come and run us off. But we fixed them. Mr. Dyer lent us a little skiff, and we went up and anchored next to the tree and fished and fished. The Carpenters told us to leave, but we didn't budge. The Carpenters did not own the creek, and we knew our rights.

Later we got more revenge. Joe McGaughy's father, Mr. Luther, helped Joe and Jack build a plywood speedboat. I thought it was a beauty, about eight feet long and four feet wide with a beautifully curved bow. It would hold two people, but it was better and faster when you drove it alone, sitting in the middle, where you could operate the five-horsepower engine mounted to the stern. At full throttle it would fly, coming up out of the water on a plane. We'd fly upstream to the viaduct and back down to the dam, making sliding turns at high speed. The Carpenters would come out and shake their fists at us and yell. The sound of that big engine happily drowned them out.

We drove that boat for a couple of summers and we had great plans to improve it by adding a windshield or a steering wheel, or—most importantly—a larger motor. But it didn't happen, as Mr. Luther's health worsened and all our plans had to be scrapped. Besides, one afternoon Dad came to watch this speeding monster, and whoever was at the helm turned sharply only a few feet before the dam. Dad became very disturbed and told Mother, and I was grounded from being a passenger or driving the boat ever again.

There were bigger boats without motors on Shoal Creek, but we dreamed of having faster boats with outboard motors. Joe and Jack's plywood boat, built from a plan in *Popular Mechanics*, remained firmly in our memory. It topped out at only twenty miles per hour, but, above that dam, Mr. Luther's little boat surely still holds the speed record.

10

# Frog Holler

Down at the bottom of Shelby Street next to Shoal Creek was a place we called Frog Hollow, pronounced "Frog Holler" by the older boys in the neighborhood—Charles Cox, Brewer Carpenter, and Bill Hartley. I never knew for sure where the name came from, but in the spring when we were sitting in our backyard we could hear a chorus of bull frogs croaking down by the creek.

Shoal Creek ran right through Frog Holler, and on the town side of the creek, at a place called Big Springs, stood Alabama College's water treatment plant. This site was so interesting that the elementary school did a field trip there every year. But I felt like I was lucky because I could go there any time and climb up the exterior stairs and observe the operation. Mr. O. B. Cooper, whose voice was as loud as a foghorn, was in charge of this operation that pumped water from the spring on the other side of the creek and filtered it through sand. Then the water was stored in an open-air pool, so the sun could also help purify it. After that, it was put in a storage tank, where chlorine was added. When you crossed the viaduct in a car and looked over at the treatment plant, you could see an open square concrete tank, filled with the bluest water that you had ever seen. In the summertime with the sun on it, it sparkled brightly.

When the water was purified, Mr. Cooper or one of his men would enter the pump room and start the big pump that loudly pumped the clear blue water from the clean-water side of the filter plant all the way to the college, where it was stored in a big concrete water tank on the end of the east wing of Main dorm. To this day, that tank, painted a dirty gray, is the symbol of the University of Montevallo. With its narrow vertical windows circling in an upward direction, the tower looked to me like the tower of a European castle. I was able to go into it from time to time,

*Right: Alabama College's concrete water tower. Water was pumped from Big Springs into the famous tower. Below, left: At the Big Springs community watering hole, Montevallo's source of wonder and pride. Below, right: At Big Springs in front of the log WPA Boy Scout Hut with my Easter bunny.*

and I remember well its distinct echo and the sound of cool water dripping all around you.

The City of Montevallo had its own water treatment plant, but it was not thought to be nearly as efficient and interesting as the one operated by the college nor did it produce as good water. One often saw citizens of the town with buckets dipping the clear water out of a concrete springhouse to take home with them. Young boys could often be seen lying on their stomachs and lowering their heads to the water and lapping it like a dog. I myself did that many a time.

On the other side of the water treatment plant stood the Boy Scout Hut, built by the Works Progress Administration. A bridge had crossed the creek to it, but it was so badly damaged in a flood that it couldn't be used any longer. Dad went with some other men to the Alabama Power Company and asked for help in creating a new bridge. Instead, the company installed two cables, the lower for walking on and the upper for holding oneself upright. That worked amazingly well, until someone started horsing around when several boys crossed the cable together. Or when Pep Jeter Jr.—a local sadist—would jump up and down on the cable to try to throw us off. If we managed to get across, we knew he would be waiting for us when we came back across the cable, and sometimes we avoided him by going up to the Cunningham house, walking down Spring Creek Road to Middle Street, and crossing the viaduct to get back home.

Big Springs was a great place to fish and to swim. The part of the creek where the water rippled across the pipe running to the treatment plant was thought to be a choice place to fish, and we would sit on the concrete steps at the plant and cast our bait as near as possible to the pipe. If we were lucky, we could pull out a bass or a bream.

The City Council, which Dad was serving on, decided that the town needed a good swimming hole. Big Springs was the natural choice. The older swimming hole, where Dad had taught me to swim, was called John Dock—because we were told a black man named John Dock had drowned in that spot trying to ford the creek. It was deep and murky, and we would sneak off up there to swim. But John Dock became officially off limits when, in the summer of 1944, Wheeler Foshee and a cousin from Centreville drowned there. Wheeler's sister Ruby ran to town for help, but it was too late when the men got there.

Dad was the first recreational director for the city, overseeing the preparation of the new swimming hole at Big Springs. He built a concrete wall on both banks, with iron ladders going down into the pool. Local boys dammed the creek with rocks just below the pool to make the water deeper. We thought it was a first-class swimming hole. Later, a diving board was even added. Gene Baldwin was the champion diver at Big Springs, and he loved to show off his flips and jackknives to any and all.

The City took great pride in this new swimming hole, and once a year, just before swimming season, numerous townspeople showed up to clean the hole. I never missed being there, and my favorite thing to do was jump in the creek barefooted and walk around and feel any trash and rocks that might interfere with swimming. Then I would go underwater and pull out the offending matter. Rocks were added to the dam to make it higher and the pool deeper. As a reward for our work, we got a free piece of watermelon that had been cooled in the springhouse. Sometimes the dining room at Alabama College provided us with their famous homemade ice cream.

Of course, in this era of Jim Crow segregation, Big Springs was limited to whites, and Dad floated the idea, and the city fathers agreed, to fix up Little Springs at the end of Main Street for the blacks. After all, Little Springs was just behind the AME Zion Church, so it seemed natural to make it the black swimming hole. Dad built cement walls on each side of this hole just as he had at Big Springs. I had no desire to swim with blacks, but I recognized something good and fair in my father when he insisted on remembering that black kids deserved a nice place to swim, too. The colored swimming hole did not have a diving board or a concrete diving platform, but it had a large rope hanging from a big limb sticking out over the water. We Shelby Street boys were quite drawn to this awesome attraction, and occasionally we would slip off and swing on the wonderful rope, sometimes with black boys we knew.

Both Big Springs and Little Springs had a special attraction, which all of us enjoyed immensely. On occasion, it was necessary to drain part of the water from the water storage tanks into the creek, causing a great stream

*The Big Springs "white folks" swimming hole with the diving board built by my dad and Milton Jeter's dad, Mr. Sonny.*

of water to spew out of the pipe at very high pressure. If you got under the downpour, you would be pushed around by the fast-moving water, and we all counted that great fun.

Other activities drew us to the Frog Holler area. The Shelby Street boys loved to play in Jeter's Bottom, which was at the end of Middle Street. It had served in earlier days as the site for horse races, and there had been boxing matches for local boys arranged by Joe Doyle. Also staged there were Battle Royals, in which a number of young black men were put in a ring and would slug it out while white men stood around them throwing money into the ring. The last black boy standing took home the money. In addition, after 1929 Walter McConaghy put on cock fights in Frog Holler. He was said to have been a rounder who had learned the ins and outs of cock fighting from his father. I thought it a shame that these fights had ceased by the time I would have been able to see them.

In my day, we had much tamer activities. Jeter's Bottom was the perfect place to fly kites, and Gene Baldwin, Joel Russell, Charles Cox, and Bobby Crowe could be counted on to take advantage of the strong March winds. Most of our kites were pretty sorry, but Bobby made kites that were wonderfully constructed from light, strong sticks he gathered in the winter. When he could get it, he used Bell Telephone wire to tie the sticks together, constructing his frame. While others used newspaper to cover the frames,

*Kite flying contest on the Alabama College soccer field, now the location of Peck Hall. I'm standing far left next to my buddy, Agee Kelly. Others in the photograph include Murphy and Charles McGehee, Pat Kelly, and James Earl Davis.*

Bobby went to Brown Grocery Store and got heavy brown paper they used for wrapping meat. This made a far more substantial kite. While we usually used flour paste, he would go to Mrs. Hicks's Five and Dime store and buy a bottle of mucilage, with its red rubber angled snoot, to glue the paper to the frame. I loved to watch Bobby at work, and I especially loved the pungent smell of the mucilage, which was almost as penetrating as the airplane glue I sometimes used.

Once Bobby had covered the frame, he would get himself a big spool of strong string and carefully tie one end to the bridle in the center of the cross on the kite. When through, he would attach a colorful tail, and he was then ready to go. We would all cheer as he made his launch, and we were ecstatic as the kite rose on the air currents. Occasionally, one of our kites would go so high that it would drift out of sight. Once we even staked a kite to the ground and found it still aloft when we returned the next day.

Frog Holler was, then, a perfect playground for Montevallo people over the years. It was also the home of some very interesting families.

## The Jeters

Probably the most important family in Frog Holler was named Jeter. They owned half the land down there. Old Mr. Ashley Jeter ran Jeter's Mercantile on Main Street, a diversified business housing a funeral home, a general supply, a grocery store, an ambulance service, and I don't know what else. He had three sons: Ashley (Snooks), Milton (Sonny), and Pressley (Pep).

The City of Montevallo decided that the two funeral parlors on Main Street, Rogan's and Jeter's, had to be moved off Main Street. Mr. Rogan just closed his funeral business, but Old Man Jeter turned one of the front rooms of his home on the corner of Vine and Boundary into the remaining white funeral parlor in Montevallo.

I remember one thing especially about Old Man Jeter's house. In those days houses sat up off the ground on brick or stone pillars, and people stored things under the house. Old Mr. Jeter had some real good stuff up under his house, and I never tired of looking at it. There was all sorts of funeral paraphernalia, and I was especially interested in the wagon wheels, bridles, and dusty horse collars, their leather cracked like dried clay. It all looked very much like the gear I saw in the Westerns at the picture show every Saturday.

A block down the street from Old Mr. Jeter's house was that of his son, who was called Mr. Sonny by my friends and me. I was at this place often, as Sonny's son Milton was my close friend. They had a great yard for playing football, and ten or twelve of us would congregate there regularly to play. Finally Mr. Sonny evicted us. He said that we were stomping on his grass and tearing up his yard. We then moved up to the college campus near King Cemetery, where the Highland Avenue boys joined us in our touch football games. This place was better than the Jeter yard. The grass was neatly mowed, and the stone fence around the King family graves blocked the winter winds. Plus there were no cement sidewalks interrupting the playing field, as there were at the Sonny Jeter house. That was significant because sometimes our touch games went beyond mere touch, and several times I had been slammed down on the sidewalk that bisected the playing field.

Milton was known as Weed. There was just one year separating him and me, and we remained close until he died. Milton got his nickname some time after World War II when his father decided he needed to work in the summer. He bought him a rotary lawn mower powered by a gas engine. In no time, Weed himself was not only mowing, but he contracted out mowing jobs to other boys in town. He began to make more money than any of us boys—I was still shining shoes at the barbershop and Joe worked at the bus station—and we were all envious. Mowing was not what Weed would have chosen to do, though, as he hated getting dirty, complaining regularly that he had grass stains on his clothes. Thus, I nicknamed him Grass Stain, but that was soon replaced by Weed after he found he was allergic to some kind of weed in somebody's yard. He sneezed for hours, and all of us laughed and chose the new name, which stuck.

Weed was the first of our group to get a brand new bicycle after the war. It was a Schwinn with a little generator attached to the front tire that made its headlight burn. Milton was very creative and a sort of dreamer. The bicycle had a little tank that ran from the seat to the handlebars, in imitation of a motorcycle, and Weed told us he would put gas in it when he could find a motor off an old discarded washing machine to convert the bike into a motorcycle. He never succeeded with his plan, but it was certainly a good story to tell all the Frog Holler and Shelby Street friends.

Milton's mother, Miss Elizabeth, put up with a lot when the neighborhood boys descended on her house to play ball, to read Weed's great collection of comic books, or to play with his Lionel train, an impressive system that we would set up in the living room when it was raining or cold outside. Miss Elizabeth graciously gave us Coca-Colas, and on some Saturdays she would give us sweet rolls. If I were there at mealtime, she would invite me to eat with them.

Miss Elizabeth was one of the Frog Holler ladies involved in education. She was principal of Dogwood Elementary School, while her sister-in-law Doris was a teacher at Montevallo Elementary School and later its principal. Mr. Sonny's sister-in-law, Mrs. Phillips, who lived just up the street from Weed, was principal of Marvel Elementary School. Others from Frog Holler who worked in education were Todd Jeter, secretary for the dean at Alabama College, and Prude Fancher's mother, who taught at Montevallo High School.

Snooks Jeter, the oldest of Old Man Jeter's sons, built his house in Frog

*The Mulkey house loomed over Mulkey's Bottom and a cute little Laura Ann Hicks.*

Holler next to what is now known as Orr Park. In this house he and his wife Todd raised three kids, Ashley, Sarah, and Beth. The kids were younger than me, but I knew them well. Sarah and Beth kept a horse in what was called Mulkey's Bottom, down near the creek, and they rode often. I never liked horses myself, as I found them rather uncontrollable. I wanted my transportation to have brakes and a steering wheel.

Mulkey's Bottom was an exciting place for us neighborhood boys for another reason. Every year after Mr. Walker Mulkey plowed the bottomland and after the first rains came and washed the dirt away, we would go down there and find arrowheads and shards of Indian pottery just sitting on top of the turned earth. No digging at all. It occurred to me one day how smart the Indians were to choose the beautiful flat land near Shoal Creek to build their village, and I would try to imagine what their everyday life was in that place I myself thought exceedingly fine.

Mulkey's Bottom flooded almost every year, and the waters came up almost to downtown, often flooding Island Street for several blocks. This phenomenon still occurs every few years at Orr Park, which is where the old Mulkey Bottom was. When the floods came, we didn't have much time to enjoy the resulting lake, as the waters always receded in five or six hours. We would wade in it or occasionally swim in it, and once Joe McGaughy and I took his boat and rode all over Mulkey's Bottom.

*My close Frog Holler friend, Ashley "Hen House" Jeter.*

Ashley Jeter was my close friend, and we spent a lot of time together in Frog Holler. I loved to create nicknames for my friends, and I gave Ashley the name, Hen House. A man named Chicken Brown kept a large number of Dominecker chickens just above Mulkey's Bottom and sold eggs in town. We loved to look at these chickens, which had fine black and white speckled feathers, but Mr. Brown was cantankerous and chased us off any time he saw us near his place or his birds. Of course, his demeanor did nothing but challenge us to test just how sharp-eyed he could be. We discovered he was good. One day Ashley slipped into Chicken Brown's chicken house and was caught stealing eggs. Thus Ashley's nickname.

The other Jeter family member I knew was Pep. He lived with his wife Doris, a rather severe woman who ruled the elementary school like a tyrant. Pep and Miss Doris's house was on Boundary Street just behind Milton's house. Boundary was the conduit that led to Big Springs, and Pep tried his best to control the access. He got particularly upset when people made too much noise down there, and he would holler at them to pipe down.

Pep was a big drinker, which we thought made him even more cantankerous. We kids didn't care much for Pep. In fact, we were scared of him and stayed out of his way. Even his nephew Weed disliked him, often feeling threatened by him.

### The Fanchers

The other family of distinction in Frog Holler was that of Prude Fancher, whom we all regarded as a brain. He was two years older than I was, and I admired him very much. His father had passed (as we always said of someone who had died), and his mother taught at the elementary school. It seemed there was always expendable cash in the Fancher household. Prude had fine things. Like Weed Jeter, he had a Lionel train with elaborate tracks and numerous cars he liked to show off to the neighborhood boys. He also had a fabulous collection of comic books, which he would allow us to read.

The Fancher house had some features that amazed me. They had the only carport in our part of town. I thought it was something that they could pull their car up to the right side of the front door when it was raining, get out, go up the stairs, and never get wet. You could drive right through the carport to the garage out back. The Fanchers were also the first people I knew who had forced-air heat in their home. There was a coal furnace in the basement, but there was a fan to blow the heat up though the floor throughout the house. I wanted heat like that in our house.

### The Clarks

In 1947—early in our high school days—Joe and Mack Clark came to Frog Holler from Dry Valley, which was out in the country. Their dad was in the taxi business and was also the policeman for Alabama College. They built the first new house in Frog Holler since the war, and, as the first house we had seen constructed from concrete blocks with marble facing, it was a wonder. To the side of the house was Mrs. Clark's beauty shop. The Clark boys brought a horse named Bink with them, and he was kept in Jeter's Bottom. Many people thought the Clark horse a nuisance, including some of us kids who used Jeter's Bottom, which was across Middle Street from Milton's house, for football, kite flying, and swimming.

*The Frog Holler cowboy, Joe Clark.*

Joe was younger than me, and Mack was even younger. For that reason he seldom wanted to play with us. And Joe seemed only interested in four-legged animals. He was absolutely crazy about Bink, but we thought he was an over-weight, run-down pony.

Wherever Joe and Bink went, you would find Tony, their dog. While we didn't care for Bink, we all liked Tony. One day Tony was hit by a car and had his front leg broken. All the grown-ups said that he would have to be put down, and we boys were terribly upset by their decision. About that time Doc Phillips showed up. Doc was not a doctor of any kind—not even a vet—but he acted as if he were. He asked Joe if he had a cigar box and some black tape, and Joe rushed off to get it. Then Doc Phillips took out his pocket knife and proceeded to cut the box into small strips, fashioning it into a splint for Tony's leg. He put the splint on and wrapped it with the tape. One month later, Tony was as good as ever.

A few years later Joe's Dad moved the family to Florida, but it was not long before they returned to Montevallo, where they opened an eating establishment named Joe's Place out on Highway 25. There you could get the best barbecue and hamburgers served anywhere.

We Shelby Street residents felt close to our Frog Holler neighbors, and we loved going into their neighborhood. In thinking back, I believe that what Frog Holler represented for all of us boys from Shelby Street was freedom. You could do things there you couldn't do at home, and we greatly enjoyed being free of parental control. Plus the idea that cockfighting and boxing had taken place down there excited us.

But in a small town we never could quite escape parental control. Once when I was a senior in high school, a number of us boys began going down by Shoal Creek and engaging in fierce slingshot battles. We'd use rocks mainly, though sometimes metal objects like steel nuts. It wasn't fun to get hit, as I was a number of times. Usually it stung a bit, and occasionally you'd get a bruise. To lessen the impact of the rocks or the steel nuts or balls, we all wore thick long-sleeved denim jackets and heavy long corduroy pants. But one day Bill Kirby climbed a tree and several of us fired on him, causing him to fall out of the tree with a loud thud. He lay there on the ground like he was dead. Most of the boys fled the scene, though Joe McGaughy and I went over and stood over him until he slowly came to. Bill's breath was labored, and he gasped out that he was all right, just a tad stunned. It was no big deal, he said, but Joe and I remained by his side as he checked out his limbs and found them working properly. Then I looked up and here came Dad barreling down toward the scene of the crime. The word had gotten to him that a boy had broken his neck falling out of the tree. He was relieved to find otherwise, but he was badly pissed off with me. "Come on," he said angrily. "You're not too big to whip." And I found that I wasn't. Back home, he took off his belt and gave me several licks. The truth is that I knew I deserved them. But that didn't stop me getting into slingshot wars. I just refrained from shooting someone sitting in a tree.

*Right: Pete and Sassy Givhan with daughter Gene during her wedding to Bob Lightfoot. Below: Ed Givhan was always a leader and even commanded his own Highland Avenue militia. The troops, left to right, were his sister, Gene, Forrest Brown, and brother, Peter Givhan.*

11

# Highland Avenue

It was generally accepted that Highland Avenue was the elite address in Montevallo. College people lived there; prosperous businessmen lived there. The houses and lawns were well-maintained. As much as I loved Shelby Street, I found myself occasionally envying the people on Highland Avenue.

The house on Highland that I knew best was that of Ed Givhan, the son of our former landlord, Pete Givhan. In our many adventures, Ed tended to be the leader and I the follower. He seemed a natural-born teacher. Although the Givhans were higher economically and educationally than my family was, they never seemed to make any class distinction that I could see. I always felt welcome in their home. This was a house in which the life of the mind was treasured, where culture was valued, and I was tremendously affected by the time I spent there. For the most part, my home was not intellectually stimulating. My parents seemed to lack the keen understanding of political and cultural issues that the Givhans had, and I sometimes felt a void when I returned to Shelby Street, feeling I had made a clear step down. My parents cut and washed people's hair, and at times this seemed faintly low-classed as a profession.

Although I always put up a good front, I have to admit that while I was growing up I always thought of myself as second-string. I had some evidence to prove it. I played second trumpet. I was the water boy for the football team. Even though I organized the Montevallo Brass Band, I never played first trumpet. Ed, however, was definitely first-string, excelling at anything he undertook. He was a great reader, and in music and academics he was top-notch. I can't say he excelled in sports, though he did go out for football two years. The other players used to say that Givhan hid behind the huddle. But at least he participated. I never even went out for football.

*Top: Gorgeous Joy Holcombe topped the homecoming parade float in 1952 on Main Street. Others in the court included Mignon Dailey, Clara Young, Annette McBurnett, Emily Vest, and Evelyn Anderson. The Baptist Church and Plaza Grill are in the background.*

*Above left: Strutting their stuff, Lois Hoffman and Clara Young. Above right: Vicious Tiger's head majorette, Eleanor Mitchell, could certainly twirl a baton and spin the heads of teenage boys.*

Highland Avenue contributed greatly to the female beauty of Montevallo. Shelby Street of course had lots of attractive girls, but Highland Avenue had us beat, I thought. Joy Holcombe, the daughter of the Mr. Holcombe who drove me home from the hospital when I was born, was a real beauty. We first met at Miss Bickham's nursery school at Alabama College, and we have remained friends ever since. Joy played in the Montevallo High School band, directed by Victor Talmadge Young (called Vicious Tiger by the students), and she was also one of our majorettes. The gorgeous Eleanor Mitchell was another majorette. Other beauties on Highland Avenue included Marsha Trumbauer, whose father—affectionately called Trummie—was head of the theater department at Alabama College, and Lois Hoffman, daughter of one of Montevallo's two Jewish families.

Marsha and Joy's mothers would have parties and invite local boys, both from the town and from out in the country. I reckon they wanted to provide a little culture for guys like me, Weed, Joe McGaughy, and the Pea Ridge boys. I was somewhat chagrined that the Highland Street girls seemed to be more attracted to the Pea Ridge boys than to those of us from town. They seemed to regard us as mere friends, but they were attracted in some other way to the country guys. You could see it in the girls' eyes.

Also living on Highland Avenue was our other Jewish family, the Klotzmans. Sam and his brother Joe came here from West Blocton to open a general dry goods store, but the two had a parting of the ways, and Joe pulled out, moving down the street and establishing a competing dry goods store. Eventually he relocated to Selma.

Joe Klotzman had two children, a boy and a girl named Melvin and Betty Ann. Melvin was a little older than me, and, due to his age and maturity as well as his forward thinking, Melvin became a hero to some of us, particularly us guys from Frog Holler and Shelby Street. Tall and thin, he was an excellent athlete and was very attractive to the girls. Melvin liked older women, especially the college girls, and everywhere he went the women drooled over him.

But the thing that we most admired about Melvin was his independence. We were amazed by his willingness to explore the unknown. His wanderlust was established while he was still in high school. He took hitchhiking to a

*Left: Frogging around, Elizabeth Chism and Betty Ann Klotzman.*

*Above: My buddy, Harry Klotzman, and me sitting on his father's decked-out Pontiac on Main Street. My dad's Chevy is behind us and next to it is Harry's Model A Ford. Right: Mama Rose Klotzman on Main Street with McCulley's store behind her.*

high art. He would hit the road in the summer, getting jobs along the way to support his travel expenses. About the time school was to start, he would return to Highland Avenue. But Melvin really outdid himself when he headed off in search of Martha Ruth Waldhein, one of the angels from Alabama College who had returned to her home in Colombia, South America. Martha was the love of Melvin's life, and he could not stand to lose her. Eventually he reached her, but this was not to be one of those "they lived happily ever after" stories. He returned to Montevallo a broken boy. But we were still in awe of his courage and his tenacity, and we were sorry when he and his family moved to Selma, leaving Montevallo with one less fascinating person.

I was much closer to Sam Klotzman and his family than to Melvin's family. I was quite close to Sam's son Harry, who was my age, and to his sister Frances, born three years after Harry. I was often in the Klotzman home. I adored Mr. Sam and his wife Rose, whom I called Mama Rose. Maybe I started calling her that because Harry and I were often taken for brothers or even twins when we were boys. This resemblance remains today.

I was fascinated by the differences in the Klotzman house. They had a thing that looked like a thermometer next to the front door, which Harry said was filled with blood and had something to do with the Passover. They fed me matzo balls and other Jewish foods, and on occasion they took me with them for dinner at the Jewish Country Club in Birmingham. This was quite an adventure for me. We often went on Sunday, and Mr. Sam would play golf. Harry and I, wearing our shirts and ties, enjoyed playing on the country club grounds. In turn, Harry would go to Bible School with me. The Klotzmans were devoted to their religion but intended that their children be integrated into Montevallo life.

I remember well when Mr. Sam went off to World War II. We prayed for him at church along with all the Christians who were fighting the Huns and the Japs, as we called them. During the war Mama Rose's mother, whom we called Mama Magoulis, came from Montgomery to live with her, helping her with the household duties and taking care of Harry and Frances. She also helped at the store. Mama Magoulis was the one who taught me to eat and understand Jewish food. It had to be kosher before the family could eat it. Being from Shelby Street, I didn't worry about the religious restrictions or whether it was kosher or not. I just loved all her food, particularly her matzo balls.

I remember Mama Magoulis coming out on the front porch, hollering with her very distinct Jewish dialect, "Haddy, Haddy, Francie—come home. It's time to eat" or "Haddy, Francie, it's getting very late." I was sad when she left to go back home when Sam returned from the war. Other regular visitors in the Klotzman home were Harry's Uncle Leon and Aunt Jo, who ran a dry goods business in Columbiana. I was especially fond of their daughters, Merle and Esta, and I have kept in touch with them though the years. Merle, in fact, has been our family's doctor for a number of years.

When Mr. Sam returned after World War II, he was warmly received by all. He brought home with him a Japanese sword, a flag, two rifles, a canteen, and other items, all of which he stored in a small room upstairs at his store. He never talked about his experiences in the Pacific, but these objects made me think he had been in some pretty rough battles. I was fascinated with the memorabilia, and when Sam was closing his store in the early eighties he called me in and gave me one of the rifles. Later, not long before he died, he gave me the rest of his memorabilia. I was greatly moved by that, and these treasures are still in my possession.

Mama Rose preceded Mr. Sam in death, and I was asked to attend the Jewish funeral with the family. At the end of the service, family members were asked to come forward and sprinkle dirt on the wooden casket. Mr. Sam motioned for me to take some dirt as well, and I have seldom been more touched by a gesture. When Mr. Sam died, Harry and Frances asked me to join in again in the sprinkling ceremony and again I was extremely moved. Gone was a gentleman whose friendship and generosity I had so often been the beneficiary of, and I knew how terribly I would miss him.

The Klotzmans joined the Givhans and other families on Highland Avenue in enabling a boy from Shelby Street to experience a larger world than he would have otherwise known. I shall remain eternally grateful for that.

Perhaps I should mention that Highland Avenue had not always been *the* elite neighborhood in Montevallo. Before the Civil War and during the late Victorian period, the most prominent families lived across Shoal

*Few girls could fill out a sweater better than Emily Vest.*

Creek on Main Street. Interestingly, in those days this was a biracial community, and it remains so to this day. In my youth, I was aware that the area was primarily black, but I also knew several white families who lived there, including my friend Emily Vest and her grandfather and grandmother, Mr. and Mrs. Payne, as well as Dr. Acker, who lived in the same house as had his father, who practiced medicine in Montevallo in the later nineteenth century.

Emily's grandmother and grandfather, the Paynes, lived in the first house on the left after you crossed the wooden bridge over Shoal Creek on Main Street. Her parents lived in the Chicago area, where her father managed country clubs. Emily lived with them, but when it came time for her to start to school her parents decided they preferred for her to be schooled in the small, quaint town of Montevallo rather than a big city. Emily stayed for high school and college. During all those years, she spent summers with her parents in Chicago. In 1955, Emily married my friend Dudley Pendleton, and Montevallo became their permanent residence, where they raised two daughters. Dudley passed away several years ago, and Emily still resides in their home in Montevallo.

Up the street from the Paynes lived the Willard "Milton" Davis family. I thought the Davises were the most interesting family living across the creek on Main Street. I was actually kin to them. Mrs. Davis, whose name was Una (though we all called her Mama Davis), was a Mahan. She was the great-granddaughter of my great-great-grandfather's brother, Archimedes Mahan, who moved to Chilton County from Brierfield in the mid-1800s. One of his children, also named Archimedes but called Arky, was Mama Davis's father. Early in her life she met and married Willard "Milton" Davis, who worked for Alabama Power Company. Later the couple moved to Montevallo with three children in tow. Milton and Una regularly added to the family until the children numbered seven. From the first grade through high school, their son Wayne was in my class, and I think there was a Davis at almost every grade level.

*Milton Davis cut quite an imposing figure around Montevallo.*

The Davis family claimed several firsts in our town. Of course, they had more children than anyone else, and I can remember my parents and their friends asking, "When do you think the Davises will have more children so they can field a full baseball team?" But Mr. Davis was a trailblazer in his own right. He became Montevallo's first Alabama Power Company executive, and he was also one of Montevallo's first volunteer fire chiefs.

The Davis kids were impressive, and we all envied their abilities. Each had special talents, including art, music, athletics—you name it. This resourceful family always seemed ready to meet and conquer all challenges. For example, when the cyclone of 1938 came through, it blew parts of the Davis house from across the creek all the way to the backyard of our house on Shelby Street. To the Davises, this was no big deal. They moved temporarily to Wilton, and the Chilton County relatives, who were all carpenters, quickly arrived in Montevallo and with no fanfare just built a new house.

Because the family was so large, money was always somewhat tight. But somehow Mama Davis was able to put fine meals on the table for nine people three times a day, 365 days a year. And if visitors or kids like me showed up at mealtime, this was no problem for Mama Davis. "Pull up a chair, sit down, and help yourself," she would always say. To this day I can remember the fragrant aroma of the cinnamon rolls and cobbler pie she often served for dessert.

The Davises knew how to have fun. Peggy, an older sister, was the younger children's leader, and in the summer she often took the family down the street to the swimming hole at Little Springs. The vacant lot next door to the Davis home became the ball field. It didn't matter who showed up; everybody got to play. In the summer the family would sometimes take their meals out in the yard. But the neatest thing they did for fun was when Mama Davis took all her kids down to the Strand Theatre on Saturdays and sat on the

*Mama Davis in the kitchen where she spent a great deal of time. One of her sons, Roy, is behind her.*

steps that led from the theater to the street so they could watch the people going in and coming out when the movies changed. They themselves usually did not actually go to the movie, but Mama Davis purchased five-cent bags of popcorn for all children present and they stood there eating it as they watched the movie patrons and conversed with their friends. At the time, no one seemed to think this was strange.

When the Davis boys—Wayne, Paul, Roy, and Willard—learned that a coat hanger would bring a penny at the Deluxe Cleaners up the hill on Main Street, they would pick up, beg for, or somehow acquire fifteen coat hangers each, and for a penny for each coat hanger they would each get a ticket to the Saturday double feature and a bag of Mr. Eddie Watson's popcorn.

When Wayne and I were in the sixth grade, Mr. Davis got a promotion and took a new job in Tuscaloosa. This worked out fine for them, as Alabama College only accepted girls, but at the University of Alabama the boys could also be educated while living at home and thereby have an opportunity to lead rich lives. But their leaving Montevallo was a tragic loss for me, and I missed them very much, particularly Wayne and Paul.

# 12

# Alabama College

The life of Montevallo was inextricably connected to the life of Alabama College, founded in 1896 for the purpose of training women for useful occupations, but having become a liberal arts college for women by the time of my birth. From my earliest years I remember the beautiful girls walking around downtown—always in groups, never alone. The college was called the Angel Farm by the local boys, but we could not claim possession of this prized group. I remember busloads of horny guys from Craig Air Force Base in Selma rolling into town to attend dances, which were highly chaperoned, and sometimes even to date the girls, though under very tight rules.

The Craig men quickly earned a very bad reputation among some of the townspeople for being adept at circumventing the rules. My mother's beauty shop buzzed with stories of how some fellows climbed the fire escape in Main Hall to get to the girls or came up with stories as to why they were late arriving back at the dorm. On occasion it was rumored that some more brazen girls even left doors open so they could stroll right in after the dean of women was no longer watching.

Mother and Dad liked the Craig Field boys, allowing some to spend the night at our house. The only public lodging in town was the St. George Hotel, which had twenty or so rooms—not enough to accommodate all the guys. Plus Dad had a low regard for the St. George, saying, "I hate to see anybody stay in that joint. It might have been a nice place in its day, but it's nothing but a two-stick hotel now." When I asked him what he meant by two-stick, he said, "One stick to prop the bed up with and another to fight the rats off."

We townspeople were keenly aware of the college schedule. I especially remember the melancholy feeling when the girls departed at the close of the

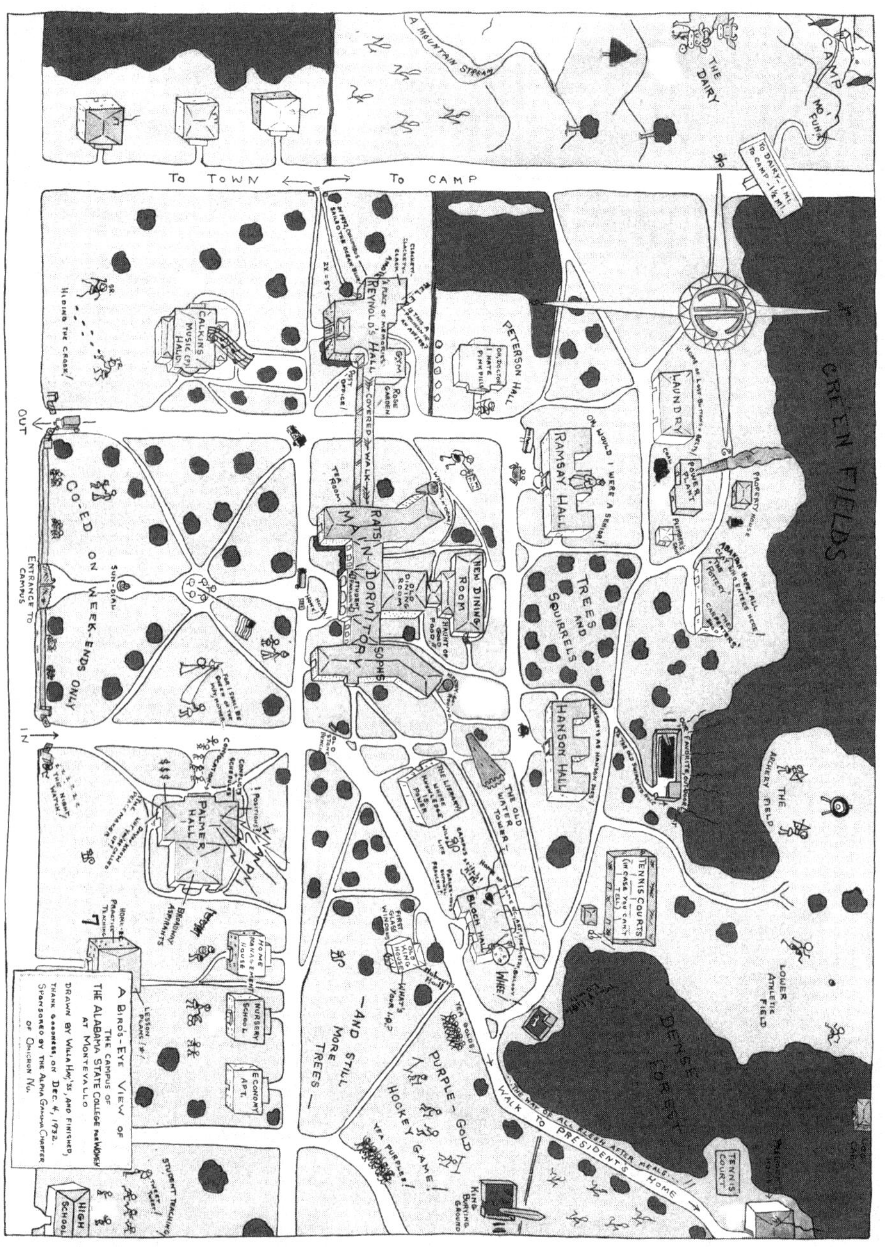


*1932 map of the then Alabama State College for Women campus, drawn by Willa Hay.*

school year. It was an ancient ritual. The college's flatbed truck transported the girls' trunks down to Rogan's Store on Main Street, where a huge line of them was stacked higher than a boy's head out front, waiting to be carried in Mr. F. W. Rogan's truck to the local train stations—Wilton if headed north and Calera if headed south. They were often stacked there for two days, and we local boys could not resist climbing. Mr. Rogan didn't seem to mind at all. After all, if throwing them onto trucks and trains didn't damage them, what could a bunch of playing boys do?

I couldn't help noticing how inferior Mr. Rogan's truck was to the one from the college. Its lights looked like big flashlights attached to the cab of the truck, while those on the college truck were built into the body. While the college truck ran smoothly, Mr. Rogan's could be heard for a mile. Plus it blew so much smoke out its tailpipe that Dad said it killed the grass on the side of the highway. Nevertheless, it did the job, and the freight was delivered every year. After the girls left, the town seemed to shift into a lower gear, and we were always excited to see the girls and their trunks return for the following term.

The college provided the town with some very interesting characters. Perhaps the most imposing figure from my youth was the college physician, Dr. Willena Peck, who presided over the college infirmary. A rather chunky lady wearing a monocle on a retractable cord and a white coat was a sight quite unusual for me, and I was greatly impressed. She came to the beauty shop, and when I was around she was always very nice to me, singling me out to talk to.

I finally got up the courage to enter her domain, the infirmary. Starting when I was about twelve I spied on it fairly often, as it was said that lovely girls were lying half-naked in the infirmary beds, and my friends and I would lie on the lawn behind the building hoping to get a peek. We never had such luck.

But one day I opened the massive maple doors with their mahogany insets and entered the infirmary. The thing that caught my eye in the lobby was a huge plaster medallion—bigger than a washtub it seemed to me. This was Dr. Peck's emblem, I was told. The Queen of England had her emblem and so did Dr. Peck, which seemed appropriate, as Dr. Peck was clearly the queen of the infirmary. I guess I was just plain awed by her. To be responsible for the well-being of more than a thousand girls was amazing. Over the years she dispensed what she called "pink pills for pale people" not only to students, but faculty as well.

Dr. Peck's nephew Billy lived with her in the infirmary. Billy Peck was delicate and thin and wore thick glasses. His head was quite large for his tiny body. People said that a growth had to be cut off the back of his head and that he was never the same after that. Dr. Peck brought him down from Vermont to escape the freezing weather, sending him home to his parents in the summer. Dad cut Billy's hair so I would see him in the shop on occasion, and I would also see him sometimes on campus. He was said to be a genius, but he was not well-adjusted socially. When he came to parties, he always stood on the sidelines. Nevertheless, his classmates seemed to like him. Once when he put a tack in his teacher's chair in an effort to be one of the guys, he was caught and given a whipping by the principal, Mr. Tidwell. Billy's classmates were up in arms about his punishment, thinking it grossly unfair.

Billy's vocabulary outstripped that of most of the rest of us. Once I was on the glassed-in back porch of the infirmary with Billy when he looked down to the pasture where the college's cows grazed. He turned to me and said, "Behold yon quadrupeds." I guessed what he was talking about and retained the word long enough to tell my friends what he said. Soon the story circulated throughout town.

Billy got his big vocabulary from reading. Any spare moment—at school or at home—was spent with a book under his nose. One day Billy failed to return to the infirmary by dark, and Dr. Peck became alarmed. They searched at the school and found him reading in the library, so absorbed he was unaware that the sun had gone down.

When Billy finished high school, he won second prize in a national scholarship competition sponsored by Pepsi-Cola, and he enrolled at the University of North Carolina in Chapel Hill. He had lived in a rather sheltered environment in Montevallo, and he was put in a dorm room with three others. He did not adjust well to that arrangement, but he managed to make it through his freshman year, making all A's. The story was told that in his sophomore year he met a beautiful girl, whose friendliness had led him to profess his love. It was said he became distraught when she rejected him and that pushed him over the edge. During the fall semester of his sophomore year, he went into the chemistry lab and drank sulfuric acid. When the word of his death got back to Montevallo, we were very sorry. Some of us felt guilty for not making a greater effort at being friendly. But the truth was that nobody was terribly surprised. This world was just too hard on one such as Billy. And we especially felt sorry for Dr. Peck, who, for all her stoicism, must have grieved the loss immensely.

Dr. Peck was only one of the Alabama College faculty who fascinated me, though not always for such lofty reasons. I think it is safe to say that there was not a person in Montevallo who didn't observe and comment on Miss Helen Blackiston, who taught biology and was an expert on flowers. Her chosen mode of transportation was a bicycle, and she had a habit of riding her bicycle up hills and pushing it down hills. We all thought it should have been the other way around.

In those days, most bicycles did not have chain guards, and we would put rubber bands around our britches legs to keep them from getting in the chain. Miss Blackiston wore a costume unlike anyone else's. Before anyone dreamed of pedal pushers, Miss Blackiston fashioned herself some knickers so that she would not have to chance getting caught in the chain. Occasionally we would see Miss Blackiston riding her bicycle in a dress, and we watched that carefully, assuming that at some point the skirt would get caught in the chain and be ripped off. Miss Blackiston was not a very attractive woman, which will give you some idea of how hard up my friends and I were for the sight of female flesh.

Another eccentric who appeared in Montevallo when I was in high school was the British writer Pierre Stephen Robert Payne, who was invited to be the chairman of the English department in the late 1940s. We had never seen anybody quite like him, and we immediately gave him the name of Sir Robert. He was the talk of the town for lots of reasons, but for none more than the infamous movie he produced while here. Its story line was the love life of a young woman just going out into the world. For its day, people thought it was scandalously precise. A young student from Calera had the lead, and everybody thought this would launch a great career that would take her to Hollywood. But the most interesting actor in the movie to me was the uncle of my close friend Joe McGaughy. Alvin McGaughy had the male lead, and he cut a fine figure with his good looks, accentuated by a fine moustache. Alvin worked at construction, and instead of heading off to Hollywood, he kept to his old job, bringing the first backhoe to Montevallo.

I could not get in the Strand Theater for the premiere. But I witnessed the huge crowd of well-dressed locals who managed to get an invitation. I also saw them come back out, and I must say that there were lots of baffled looks on their faces. Somebody told me that it was the damnedest thing they ever saw, that a girl even smoked a cigarette she held between her toes. Afterwards, there was an even bigger showing in Birmingham. Among those attending was old Dean Napier, who had tried to maintain standards and decorum on campus for many years. He was not sure that Alabama College would ever recover from such a travesty.

When I was in high school, I encountered another Alabama College person on my walks home from school. This was Mrs. Virginia Barnes, who I was told was Alabama's most noted artist. She first taught at the laboratory school at Montevallo High and later in the Alabama College art department. But that didn't keep her from spending most of her time on her own art. Her specialties were silkscreen, watercolor, woodcut, and portraiture. When I returned to Montevallo after graduating from Auburn University and was working for Alabama College, I learned the silk screening process from her. She showed me how to stretch fine silk tautly on a frame, how to paint those parts with lacquer that you didn't want to print, and to press ink through the silk. Only those parts not blocked out were painted. She became so adept at this method that her silk prints were exhibited in cities of the United States, Europe, Asia, and South America.

Another person on campus whom everybody loved was Dr. W. J. Kennerly, head of the chemistry department for many years. We all called him Dr. Kennerly, though many people said a doctorate was never conferred on him. What made him so special around town, especially to younger people, was that he was an accomplished magician and hypnotist. And he was not reluctant to show off his talents—in class, at Scout meetings, pretty much anywhere. My Cub Scout troop saw him twice. He could make things disappear, could pull handkerchiefs from his sleeve and rabbits from a hat. But the hypnotism was even more impressive. He could put somebody under in a flash and have them telling anything. I decided it would be better to avoid being hypnotized because I didn't want to embarrass myself or anybody else. The hypnosis, however, had a very practical use beyond entertainment. If someone lost some money, for instance, he could put them under and discover where it was. This happened several times, and we were all impressed.

Mr. Kennerly lived on a street off Highland Avenue near the imposing gate to two huge houses in the woods across the road from the President's Mansion. Both were occupied by members of the Alabama College faculty. I was extremely impressed by these houses, and eventually I was able to become familiar with both. I decided that their inhabitants really knew how to live.

Living in one of the houses was a sophisticated couple named Douglass, who had come to Montevallo from England with their two young sons. It was unusual in those days to have two automobiles, but they did. The first, which they called the Little Machine, was an Austin they brought from England, and only two people could ride comfortably in it. Mr. Douglass could be seen quite often tooling around town in it. He often boasted about its gas mileage. The other car was a four-door Dodge sedan, which they called—yes—the Big Machine. It was used for family outings and longer journeys.

Don Douglass was my age, and Mrs. Douglass devoted herself to him and his younger brother. She wanted them to have every advantage, and one thing she instituted toward that end was a Cub Scout den in Montevallo. Joe McGaughy and I made up the Shelby Street contingent in this group, and we were joined by Ed Givhan and Harry Klotzman from Highland Avenue. All told, about ten of us met weekly with Mrs. Douglass, who was the den mother. I was thrilled to have a chance to go through those fine gates and into that handsome two-story house, which rivaled Mrs. Craig's house. Our meetings usually took place in the spacious sunroom, which had large ferns on iron stands year-round.

About once a month there would be a pack meeting at night, attended by our parents. The Cub Scouts were mainly run by women, but each den had an *akela*, a man who could advise us on matters that women folk were thought unable to address. Mr. Douglass was our akela.

Cub Scouts I found extremely fun. I liked to wear a uniform, and I liked the manuals we had to read. We all had projects to earn badges, eventually working our way up through three levels of wolf, bear, and lion. We were also taken on field trips, mainly on campus. In the biology department we were shown the butterfly collection, for example. Outside experts were called in to speak to us. One of my favorites was Martha Allen, a spunky art professor, who would come to our meetings and tell us about art. Mrs. Douglass, whose house was full of original paintings and sculpture, thought art appreciation was vital for persons of quality, which she was determined that all of her Cub Scouts would become.

Sometimes we were allowed to play in the spacious side yard. Next to a small servants' house, the Douglasses had planted a stand of bamboo that grew to an immense size. The stalks were four inches in diameter. It looked like the jungles I saw in the picture show on Saturdays. The scouts were allowed to cut the bamboo and make whistles, and another time we made boats out of some of the largest stalks and sailed them on Shoal Creek.

One big project of the year was a pinewood derby. Mr. Douglass instructed us on making the racers, and then we would have the derby, racing each other. Our cars were about ten inches long. They were made using directions in the Cub Scout manual, and we had to get our wheels from Loveman's Department Store in Birmingham. Mr. Douglas built a track with four lanes and placed it in the sunroom. Four of us would place our cars in the lanes, and upon the signal of Mr. Douglass we released our cars, which traveled down the track that measured about six to eight feet and then down eight or ten more feet on the ramp that went to the floor. We screamed loudly, hoping our car would be the first to cross the finish line. The winner of that race competed then with the winners of the other heats, until finally from the final pair a winner emerged. Although I never won the race, I did very well, as Dad helped me fine-tune my car. He and other fathers came to the race, cheering on their sons.

Near the Douglass home was another imposing house, in which lived Mrs. Chamberlain, the piano professor at Alabama College who regularly traveled to Europe. This lady carried herself so high that people began to refer to her as "The Duchess." Her husband, who was never to my knowledge called "The Duke," was in the coal business, and that enabled them to live at a very high standard. I knew Mrs. Chamberlain because she was a customer at my mother's beauty shop, but I never saw the inside of this house until I was in my teens. The only reason I did then was that my friend, Putnam Porter, who also taught in the music department, rented a room there, often inviting us boys to come by for a visit. I thought the Duchess's house an exceedingly fine place. I remember clearly the grand piano in the living room that was covered with a tapestry. I also remember the giant oil paintings on the walls and the fine oriental rugs. This, I thought, was the way to live.

Later when I began to play in the Alabama College Orchestra I got to know Mrs. Chamberlain, and she was always very nice to me. I was struck with how sophisticated she was as she talked of her travels to Europe and the fine music she heard there. It set me on fire to see the world. In those days nobody flew in airplanes. To get to Europe, one went to Birmingham by car or train, caught the *Southerner* to New York, then crossed the Atlantic by ship. When I saw Mr. Rogan loading the Duchess's trunks onto his old smoking truck to take them to Birmingham, I would be excited thinking about where they might go before returning to Montevallo.

The Duchess's tenant, Putnam Porter, came to Montevallo after World War II. Today he would be called a homosexual or be said to be gay, but in those days we never said any such thing. No one ever called him a queer. In fact, I don't think his homosexuality registered with any of us young men he befriended. But in retrospect it seems strange to think of the keen interest he took in the young men of promise in Montevallo. He took us to dinner in Birmingham. He took us to the beach in his 1949 Chevy sedan. And no one, including Mother and Dad, seemed to think a thing about it. After all, he was a gentleman and nice and a good Presbyterian. And the truth was that I never remember his propositioning anybody. He certainly never did anything untoward with me. We all liked him very much, not just for the attention he paid us, but because he was so interesting to be around. He had seen the world, had served in the Navy during World War II, and wore his sophistication as comfortably as an old coat. There was nothing provincial about him.

We were fascinated that Putnam played the huge E. M. Skinner organ in Palmer Hall on the Voice of America. He recorded two series of programs featuring organ music that went out from Palmer Hall, where he and others

*Above: My friend Putnam Porter at the console of Palmer Hall's great E. M. Skinner pipe organ. Right: Every summer Putt played the organ at the Fourth Presbyterian Church in Chicago. Dudley Pendleton and I took advantage of his free lodgings in the summer of 1953. I wanted the adventure. Dudley wanted to get engaged to his sweetheart, Emily Vest, who spent each summer in Chicago with her parents.*

put on concerts. It thrilled a young boy on Shelby Street to think of people all over the world listening to *Organ Music of the Centuries* and *Music from Montevallo*. It was one of our claims to fame.

While he was teaching at Alabama College, Putnam twice got grants to study organ in Europe. The first time, Dad and I drove him to New York in his Chevy, and there he caught a ship for Europe. I felt connected to the larger world in ways I never had before, and I loved it. The second time, I was in college, and a friend and I drove him to New York. It was on this trip that I gave him a nickname. There were many trailer trucks on the two-lane roads we traveled, and it seemed that most of them were Fruehaufs. Putnam would say, "There goes another Fruehauf," and after a while I started calling him Frue, which I did for his entire life. Putnam did a great deal for me, and I remained a loyal friend until he died a few years ago.

Among the college people, another deserves recognition. Mr. Cooper was in charge of the campus steam plant, a big brick building with a high smokestack. This plant, which roared loudly twenty-four hours a day, generated the college's electricity as well as produced steam heat for the campus. As a teenager I was allowed to go in and look around. Because the workings of the plant were so loud, Mr. Cooper spoke in an extremely loud voice. Even then, you sort of had to read his lips. Down in the basement were mountainous piles of coal, which workers shoveled into the huge furnace. I couldn't help thinking that they needed a stoker like Mrs. Craig had at her house on Shelby Street. Mr. Cooper explained that the steam went underground through asbestos pipes to radiators all over campus.

Mr. Cooper's loud voice sparked stories around town. One day he went to the library to check on something. He approached the desk and bellowed, "What's the problem here?" The librarian, Miss Abi Russell, looked shaken, and she began to answer him in a whisper. "Damn it, lady," he is reported to have roared, "If you're going to talk, TALK."

Probably one of the most colorful arrivals to Alabama College occurred in November 1946. Everyone knew immediately that Ralph and Marcia Sears brought talent, style, and intelligence to our community. Ralph was hired by Dr. Caldwell, the college president, to be a faculty member in radio and speech. He had studied radio broadcasting, and his voice was so

***Marcia and Ralph "Golden Throat" Sears gave so much to so many in their new hometown.***

beautiful that he was immediately dubbed "Golden Throat."

I still have a vivid image of them driving around Montevallo in their maroon 1946 Hudson convertible. It had everybody talking. Staid Dean Napier was not sure how the college personnel would accept a new faculty member who drove a red Hudson convertible.

The Searses first moved up to Nabors Street into a house Dr. Paul Bailey had built, but in 1950 they moved to Frog Holler and rented Hen House Jeter's home, which was vacant because Todd and Snooks had bought a farm, thinking that the country would be beneficial for their family. Marcia immediately took a job on the faculty of Montevallo High School, where she taught English and history. All the Shelby Street and Frog Holler clan were excited to learn that she would be our teacher.

The first major impact Ralph had on the town was establishing Alabama College's radio station, which was heard throughout the town. Earlier there had been a radio station in Comer Hall, an affiliate of WAPI in Birmingham. Ralph's operation was headquartered in Reynolds Hall.

In the summer of 1947, the Searses astounded the town as they loaded up their Hudson convertible and took off for summer studies at the University of Southern California. No one could imagine driving to California just for a summer of studies, and all were relieved to see them return in the fall, not in the maroon '46 Hudson, but in a brand new Hudson convertible. Everyone wondered how they could afford such fine cars and dress as they did in the height of fashion. I think most of these responses resulted from envy. We who lived on Shelby Street liked it that they lived on our side of town and not on Highland Avenue.

The radio station grew, and Ralph became Mr. Alabama College. Marcia continued to teach, but in her second or third year she became pregnant and gave birth to a son, Steve. By then they had caused another stir in the community when they purchased a beautiful green 1950 Packard convertible. It seemed to fit perfectly the image of Ralph Westgate Sears and his glamorous wife. It had a hood ornament unlike any we had ever seen: a big chrome bird sitting right in the middle of the hood. These people were definitely high rollers.

Ralph became director of public relations for Alabama College, and Marcia became a writer and editor. They had two daughters, Sally and Randy. With the birth of Randy in 1956, Ralph and Marcia left Frog Holler and moved to a new home in a subdivision off the Siluria road.

The academic life didn't seem to be all Ralph wanted. He ran for city council and was elected. He spearheaded many new businesses in Montevallo and later became mayor. He established an AM radio station, WBYE, in Calera, in partnership with Ed Ewing, who was from Wilton but had attended school in Montevallo.

Montevallo was always blessed with talent, creativity, and class, but I guess, next to my mother and father, Ralph Westgate Sears, our golden throat, encouraged a little guy from Shelby Street to go up on fool's hill and see what makes the world go round and round.

This does not at all exhaust the long list of colorful and remarkable people at the college during my youth, but it will give you an idea why I always was grateful that Alabama College was in Montevallo.

*Montevallo and environs.*

13

# Country People

When I was growing up, there was a clear distinction between town and country. We in town felt superior to the country kids, who lived in Dogwood, Boothton, Marvel, and other self-contained communities that had sprung up as mining towns in the early twentieth century. They all were largely supported by the coal companies that provided housing, community centers, schools, and commissaries for their workers and their families. Pea Ridge, a small mining community a few miles from Montevallo, was different. Pea Ridge families, for the most part, owned their own homes, and among the community's residents were families like the Picketts and Lawleys—the FFPR's or the First Families of Pea Ridge, as they were called. It sort of seemed to be accepted wisdom that Pea Ridge was as far above the other mining communities as Highland Avenue was above Shelby Street or Frog Holler.

Since the first grade, I had been attending school with country kids from such places as Dry Valley, Spring Creek, and Moore's Crossroads, and we had thought little of it. But they were not mining communities. Until the mining kids began attending Montevallo High School in the seventh grade, we had little chance to know them. I had, of course, seen the mining people when they came to Montevallo on Saturdays to shop at the stores lining Main Street. Some of them even came to the Strand for the Saturday afternoon features. I had seen some of these kids in Dad's barbershop. But I really didn't know them.

We thought these kids were rednecks, even those from Pea Ridge. But we were careful not to offend them, as they were tough as nails. They came in with a swagger, determined not take any crap off these stuck-up Montevallo kids. They upset the equilibrium of the social structure we town kids were comfortable with.

*Bill Allen and Ann Cox on the steps of Montevallo High School. Bill was an athletic giant who all the girls looked at and dreamed about.*

I was always curious about Pea Ridge, a place so near, yet so far away. I was fascinated to learn just how close-knit the community was. There was little difference in social class, and the same values seemed to be generally accepted. There were no colored people in Pea Ridge. People there were hard-working, and early on the parents expected the same thing from their children. Social life centered on the churches and to a more limited extent the two stores, both of which had porches on which people would gather to play Rook or just while the time away. The town was so close-knit that at Christmas the whole community had a Christmas program followed by exchanging of gifts. The churches conducted a name-drawing exercise so that everyone in Pea Ridge got a gift from a neighbor.

While we kids from town thought we could easily outdo the Pea Ridge kids in academic ability and performance, they made up for that with their superior athletic skills. In fact, they dominated the field. Bill Allen, for example, became one of our star baseball players. One year the team actually won a state championship, playing the final game in Birmingham at Lane Park. Everybody was jubilant when Bobby Crowe—a town boy, I happily boasted—emptied the bases with a ball he hit down the middle of the field and into an adjoining lake. The football team was dominated by the guys of Pea Ridge—guys like Chief Lawley, a bruiser I tried to steer clear of.

But participating in sports took a special effort on the part of the Pea

Ridge guys. For the most part, they lacked transportation. A school bus driven by a student named Lacey Herron brought them to school, but it went back out to the Ridge immediately after school. So after practice, the Pea Ridge guys would go down to the corner of Middle Street and either Main or Valley Streets and wait for someone to come by and take them home. If no one came, they were out of luck. But the problem with transportation was a general one. Pea Ridge people—not just students—would congregate at Pinky Lawley's store or at Peters Store to catch rides into Montevallo, and seldom was there too long a wait until they got one.

The Pea Ridge guys not only excelled in sports; they poached some of the fine-looking Montevallo girls we thought were in our own preserve. But they were very protective of the Pea Ridge girls and didn't like it if one of us townies paid too much attention to them. I remember that fistfights occasionally broke out over girls. It was rumored that the girls from Pea Ridge were wilder than the girls from Highland Avenue or Shelby Street, but we had little opportunity to test that theory. You didn't want to get those Pea Ridge guys riled up.

The boys from Pea Ridge told us about a game that was popular out there. It was called candy. The party was typically held in someone's home, and the girls would go into a separate room from the boys. There, they would choose the name of a candy bar—Baby Ruth, Almond Joy, Hershey—and then go back in the room and let the boys choose a candy bar. This was a device for pairing up the sexes, after which the couples would take walks together. The boys tried to fix the game by having an understanding in advance about what candy bar their girl would choose or, on occasion, even go outside to listen at the window outside the room where the girls made their choices. This was Pea Ridge's version of Spin the Bottle.

I got the idea that Pea Ridge, on the whole, was pretty puritanical. One could not buy a drop of whiskey or home brew there. The only alcoholic beverage was the scuppernong wine that Mr. Pickett made every year, though it was rumored that many a pint of moonshine, labeled "For medicinal purposes only," was kept in drawers throughout the community. Teenagers would work up a cough to get a taste of the clear moonshine, flavored with a piece of strong peppermint.

*Top: Montevallo's Joanna Sharp, Alabama's Maid of Cotton, surrounded by adoring fans. Bottom: One of Mrs. Sharp's cultural parties at Joanna's home. Joanna is standing far left. Others in the photograph are Ed Roberts, Joe and Jack McGaughy, Pat Baker, Harry Klotzman, Joy Holcombe, Martha Ann Cox, and Eleanor Mitchell.*

Socially, there was little interaction between town and country, but sometimes friendships were formed between Pea Ridge and Montevallo students. Bill Allen became tight with Bobby Crowe, for example, because of their excelling in sports. The two also spent a lot of time with Agee and Pat Kelly, who lived next door to Bobby. Once when Pat had gotten a motorcycle—the first kid in town to have one—he offered to let Bill ride it. He instructed Bill on the use of the clutch and the accelerator. Unfortunately, he failed to show him where the brake was, a lapse that only occurred to Bill as he was speeding down Shelby Street toward the college. He was able to slow down enough to go safely around the block, and he was moving very slowly when he reentered the Kelly yard. He felt relieved that his friends were not in the yard to observe his running into the brick wall there. Luckily he was going slow enough not to damage the cycle, and his major wound undoubtedly was to his pride.

The Pea Ridge kids were not included in most of the parties we had in Montevallo, but one day Mrs. C. G. Sharp, wife of the chairman of the biology department, decided to change that. The mother of daughters Susan and Joanna, she often tried to bring culture to the town kids, but she liked a challenge and on one occasion decided to see what she could do with Pea Ridge. She ironed her best lace tablecloths and set out her best dishes and crystal. She made congealed strawberry salad, which she put on clear glass plates. She put out a punch bowl with lime punch and an ice ring. She put some Glenn Miller music on low volume on the record player. Everybody was dressed in their Sunday-go-to-meeting clothes.

I was given a first-hand account of the event by Bill Allen, one of the Pea Ridge social climbers there that day. When he and his brother Ted and the Lawley boys entered the house, they felt immediately out of place, he said. Instead of the linoleum that covered the floors in his house, he saw nice oriental rugs. Instead of the coleslaw, which was as close as you saw to a salad in his house, he ate congealed salad for the first time. He awkwardly took a cup of punch, immediately realizing there was no way to hold the plate and the cup and consume anything from either one. So he put the cup of punch on a table and noticed that Mrs. Sharp quickly slipped a napkin under it. After the salad, they were asked to eat little Ritz crackers with cheese on them and spiced pecans. This was a far cry from the cornbread and butter beans that was their usual fare. The longer they stood there, Bill said, the more they began to feel like turds in a punch bowl, and he and the others made a hasty departure. They were never asked back. Apparently Mrs. Sharp just gave up on bringing culture to the denizens of Pea Ridge.

In many ways the most exceptional person who came from Pea Ridge was Donald Dennis. We nicknamed him Stink for obvious reasons. He came to school with a brother who couldn't keep up academically, but Donald was very smart and a high achiever. He always made higher grades than I did. Immediately after graduating, he went into the military. After a year he returned home on furlough, and I saw him crossing Main Street. Without thinking, I thoughtlessly yelled, "Hey, Stink." He turned to me, thrust out his hand, and said, "The name is Donald." I saw then that the nickname had not suited him at all, and I never called him Stink again.

After Donald got out of the military, he returned to Montevallo, where he attended Alabama College and met Elizabeth Stewart, the top student there. She was a biology major, the daughter of the owner and editor of a newspaper in Marion. After she graduated, they married and moved to Atlanta, where she completed master's and doctoral degrees. Donald completed college there, and subsequently received a law degree at Emory and practiced law successfully in the Atlanta area. He certainly shot down our notion that the town boys could outperform the country boys academically.

Among the country communities, we thought Spring Creek superior to Pea Ridge. While the people in Pea Ridge and Dogwood had their own elementary schools, people from Spring Creek did not. Perhaps that made them seem more like us than the others. We could date girls from Spring Creek without there being a problem, as was certainly not true of Pea Ridge, and we guys from Shelby Street and Frog Holler thought there were some real lovelies out in that community.

An exception to most of the country people we knew was the Frank and Sadie Baker family. They were not from Pea Ridge, but owned a dairy farm just north of Montevallo. Tommy Baker, who distinguished himself as an athlete, was about my age, and I loved to go out there to play with him and his brothers. They lived in a comfortable house that impressed many

Montevallians. I remember especially their living room, which Mother always said was as fine a Victorian room as you could find anywhere. In the middle of the room was an exquisitely carved round table—a Sheraton table, according to Mother. On it sat an elaborately decorated oil lamp that had been wired for electricity. Next to the table was a carved mahogany chair covered in wine-colored velvet, and other heavy furniture was nicely placed throughout the room. On the floor was a splendid oriental rug with a red design, and I also remember the cut glass vases on the mantel, which Mother said were extremely fine and expensive. I guess you might say that Miss Sadie was the grand dame of Montevallo's agrarian society. Certainly Mother thought she was.

In late summer, the Bakers hired a lot of boys from town to come out and help get in the silage, and we older boys on Shelby Street were always included in the group. We welcomed the chance to make some money, but we also liked the challenge of the hard work. Early in the morning we would begin cutting silage and loading it into four-wheeled wagons. It had to be taken to the tall steel and stone silos that sat next to the milking barn, where we shoveled the silage into mechanical lifts that dumped into the silos. By the end of the day we were worn out, and we looked forward to bedding down on the sleeping porch on the second floor of the Baker home. It had lots of windows that could be opened to allow evening breezes to cool the hot bodies of us hard-working boys.

The Bakers milked two times a day, at four o'clock in the morning and in mid-afternoon. All year long, the two Baker sons, Bobby and Tommy, were up early to help feed and milk the cows. For the afternoon milking, they were usually at school practicing baseball or football. But on weekends there was no getting out of the mid-afternoon milkings. But the Bakers were hardly slave drivers. They wanted their children to enjoy life on the farm, even constructing a tennis court for them. That really impressed me. No one in town had a private tennis court.

Feeling a part of the Baker family was one of the highlights of my youth. It set for me a model for the good life that I have pursued to the present day.

# Part III

# *Businesses on Shelby and Main Streets*

*From left: Montevallo's dapper and newest professional, Dr. Leslie Hubbard; Montevallo's eligible ladies man, Red Mahan; and Leslie's brother, Lance Hubbard. The men were first cousins and considered "cocks of the walk" around 1930.*

14

# Shelby Street Business and Medical Center

When I was growing up, all of the doctors in town either lived or practiced on Shelby Street. Dr. Charles Acker was an old bachelor who had his office upstairs in an old house just down the street from where we lived. People hardly knew what to think of Dr. Acker. There was a bit of whispering speculation about his sexual orientation, and many people disapproved of his heavy drinking. But he was sought after for his medical skills by a wide number of people around Montevallo well into his eighties. He lived near Little Springs with a woman said to be his niece in a family home that was old enough to have witnessed eleven thousand Yankees passing as Wilson's Raiders were leaving Montevallo for Selma on the morning of March 31, 1865.

Dr. Acker's practice was quite rudimentary. There were two rooms separated by a hall, which served as his waiting room. He employed no receptionist, so people took a seat in the hall on one of the couches and waited for someone to see them. On the right was his examining room, which had a very high ceiling and a bay window in front. Sitting on the examining table, you were able to look at Mrs. Craig's beautiful home. Across from the examining room was a room with a giant X-ray machine that lurked like a black monster. To the side of it were developing tanks for X-rays.

If the door to the examining room was open, you could see patients waiting in the hall. Although Dr. Acker had a white folding screen on rollers that could have been positioned to block the view of the hall, he seldom used it. There was a sink in the room for him to wash his hands, and there were white metal cabinets with glass on all sides where he kept cruel-looking instruments all piled on top of each other and in no observable order. He always had with him a small card on which he recorded information about the patients, but his handwriting was so small and illegible you really could not make anything out. He also recorded the cost of the visit, which I think in those days was $1.50.

There were several other small rooms in the back of the establishment, one of which had a chair I thought looked like a dentist's chair. On the wall were several graded eye charts. Dr. Acker, I learned, was well-regarded as an eye doctor. He also had a small bathroom, and I remember once having to go in there and pee in a bottle.

Dr. Acker had a number of black patients, who entered the side door to the building and took seats in a small, cramped waiting room. Dr. Acker always used the colored entrance himself, parking his car in a designated space next to that door.

No one doubted that Dr. Acker was well versed in the art of medicine. As Mother said many times, "Dr. Acker always kept up." Well after Dr. Acker's death, I went to his estate sale and bought his *Grey's Anatomy*, published in the late 1860s. I discovered that he had first used this book while a student at the Atlanta School of Medicine. I looked at all the other books offered at the sale that day, and there was no later edition of the work in evidence. I suppose it served him well through the years as he lived a life devoted to his profession.

Dr. Acker paid little attention to the affairs of town or gown, and other than taking annual vacations by train to various parts of the country and acquiring Native American jewelry, rugs, and wall hangings, he pretty much kept focused on his work.

I had one memorable visit to Dr. Acker's office. Dad had put up a zip line between our back porch and the garage, and my friends and I would spend hours riding it, hanging by a broom handle attached to a rope that was tied to a pulley. One day when Harry Klotzman and Joe McGaughy were riding it with me, I took a fateful ride on that zip line. When I got about half way to the garage, the line broke and the heavy pulley came crashing on my head. I was stunned for a minute, but then I could see that I was bleeding profusely.

There were no adults at home, and Joe asked excitedly, "What should we do?" He looked a little pale from the sight of all the blood. "Get me to Dr.

Acker's," I said without hesitation, and we set out. We made so much noise climbing the wooden steps leading up to the office that Dr. Acker himself ran out to see about the commotion. When I showed him my wound, he shook his head and laughed a hollow laugh. "Come in here," he said, taking me to the examining room. "This gentleman's going to have to be sewed up," he said. I grimaced in dread.

Dr. Acker pulled back my hair and put something on the wound that seemed to deaden it, as it immediately felt better. After cleaning it thoroughly, he reached up in a cabinet and pulled out a big curved needle. My heart sank. I sucked in air through my teeth as he pulled off some black shiny thread from a spool and threaded the needle. In a rhythmic way, he sewed up the wound, tying each suture in a knot. This procedure of course was done without gloves on him or Novocain in me. Amazingly, it didn't hurt that bad. Maybe I was in shock. When he finished, I had six sutures. "Another crisis past and gone," he said, looking up as my mother entered the room.

Harry had not cared to stay to see the procedure I faced and had run to the shop to tell Mother and Dad what had happened. Mother left a customer under a hair dryer to come to check on me. She thanked Dr. Acker for taking care of me and took me home. But she couldn't stay, as she had to get back to her customer. I lazed around all afternoon unsupervised, and for once I was not looking for more trouble to get into.

In great contrast to Dr. Acker was Dr. Leslie Hubbard. After World War II, following his discharge from the Navy, he appeared in Montevallo to become the partner of another of the town's physicians, Dr. Parnell. I knew Leslie, as he was my cousin, the son of Dad's sister, my Aunt Lois. Very soon he and Dr. Parnell built a new medical building on Shelby Street next to Pete Givhan's Coca-Cola building. This new building was even designed by an architect, and it was the latest thing in medical design. There was plenty of parking space, including a space for each of the doctors near the front door.

Mother and Dad took me to the grand opening, which was attended by many townspeople. As was the case with Dr. Acker, there were two waiting rooms, one for whites and another for colored people, each entered by a separate door. We went into the spacious white waiting room furnished with upholstered leather chairs and nice tables. A receptionist sat behind a big sliding window. We were given punch and cookies, after which we were shown each doctor's suite of examining rooms as well as the lab room. Everything was sparkling, and we were impressed. It was all totally different from Dr. Acker's office. I was especially interested in a demonstration of the centrifuge, which they used when they did blood work, and the sterilizer that sent out great clouds of hot steam when it was opened. Everybody seemed impressed with the new technology.

We didn't see the colored waiting room that day, but I was quite curious about it. Finally, one day I strolled down to the office, opened the door, and peered into it. It had wooden chairs and only one small table with dog-eared magazines scattered on it. I could see that the sliding window into the receptionist's office was very small. I'd like to report that I was bothered by the disparity of the two waiting rooms, but at the time I really wasn't. It just seemed to be the way things were.

Dr. Foots Parnell I remember as being somewhat stiff, but Dr. Hubbard was another matter. He was rather courtly, with a broad smile and a neatly trimmed moustache. He drove a sporty '39 Ford five-window coupe and could be seen scratching off as he headed out to do a house call, maybe to deliver a baby. Females of all ages were quite taken with him. He was married, but had no children at that time. He liked children very much though and was said by everyone to be very sympathetic when they were ill. But when I went to him when I was about twelve, I did not find that to be entirely true. I had a risen—our word for a boil—on the back of my neck that, despite my mother's good efforts, would not come to a head. I had had risens before, and she would take two wooden matches and place them between her finger and thumb on either side of the boil and roll them together until the core of the risen would shoot out like a little sack covered with blood and white pus. But this time the method just wouldn't work, and she sent me to Dr. Hubbard to see what he could do. The nurse took me into the examining room where Dr. Hubbard waited for me wearing a white physician's coat, under which he had on a white shirt and a tie. He seated me on the stool and asked his assistant to get him a sharp silver instrument, one end of which looked like small pliers. He put a white towel around my neck, put on gloves, bent my head forward, stuck this silver thing in the boil, rolled it round and round, and out came the bloody, pus-soaked core. The whole procedure was agonizingly painful. When it was over I expected some sympathetic remark, but he merely chuckled. It certainly didn't strike me as funny at all.

After Dr. Hubbard had taped gauze over the place the risen had been, he went over and wrote out a prescription for some salve he wanted me to use. When he handed it to me, I was amazed to see his chicken scratching, and I wondered how in the world Dr. Wilson at the drugstore would make out these hieroglyphics. When I asked Dr. Wilson how he was able to read it, he said, "His handwriting is no worse than other doctor's. I think they teach them that in medical school."

As I grew older, people often said that I looked like Dr. Hubbard. When I turned fifty, I told Dr. Hubbard, with whom I had shared an office since 1966, "I've been through the last thirty years with everybody saying I look like you. I want for the next thirty for them to say you look like me." Dr. Hubbard, well up in his eighties then, just smiled, his eyes dancing in their usual way. "We'll see," he said.

The other doctor on Shelby Street was Dr. Ted Bridges, who came to Montevallo when they closed the mines at Boothton, where he had been the company doctor. He moved into a large Victorian home three houses down Shelby Street from us toward the little red bridge. He had his office upstairs over the Plaza Grill on Main Street, two doors away from Dad's barbershop. Dr. Bridges always entered the building by way of the fire escape on the back of the building. His office, though not as nice as that of Dr. Parnell and Dr. Hubbard, was nicer than Dr. Acker's. He had a receptionist and an assistant who handled charts, and, unlike Dr. Acker, he was quite organized. You knew once you walked into his office that you were in a doctor's office—everything very clean, green, and sterile.

Like Dr. Hubbard, Dr. Bridges had a wonderful way with patients. Of all the town's doctors, Mother thought he was best with children. He had every reason to be, as he had sired a family of six—Lydia, Eula (also known as Sis), Catherine, Pick, Owen, and Ed. Dr. Bridges was quiet and was very serious about his professional appearance and his medical obligations, seldom clowning or joking the way that Dr. Hubbard did.

With Dr. Bridges, Dr. Acker, Dr. Parnell, and Dr. Hubbard all either living or practicing on Shelby Street, I think it is fair to say that our street was the medical center of Montevallo. But our status was reflected in other ways. Montevallo's only attorney, Owen Bridges, had his office in a building next to the ice plant. So I guess you could say Shelby Street was the legal center of our town as well.

We were the business center of Montevallo, too. Although we had never heard of an industrial corridor or industrial park at that time, I think that is exactly what you had on Shelby Street. There were Pete Givhan's Coca-Cola warehouse, Mr. Dyer's grist mill, the ice plant, Mr. Brown's saw mill, Mr. Brown's molding plant, the Gulf Oil Distributing Center, Acme Oil Company, and the Southern Railway Depot. Mr. Brown installed the first generator for electrical power in Montevallo. He needed steam power to run the refrigerants needed for the ice plant, but, being the entrepreneur he was, he saw the opportunity to use the excess steam to provide electrical power to the town. He ran power lines up Shelby Street to Main Street. Shortly after that, Alabama Power bought and enlarged Mr. Brown's system, the site of today's main substation.

Taken altogether, these businesses provided the lifeblood of Montevallo. All of the incoming and outgoing goods shipped by railroad came down Shelby Street, and if lightning struck the Alabama Power distribution center on the right just across the little red bridge, then Montevallo went dark.

Mr. Dyer's grist mill was also vital to Montevallo's well-being. Without the cornmeal he ground, Montevallo folks would not have had the major staple of their diets. Without his feed mill, there would have been no feed for Mr. J. K. Cunningham's cows and many Montevallians would have been without milk. Nor would they have been able to get Mrs. Russell's goat milk. Without the ice plant and delivery service, there would have been no way to make homemade ice cream in those hand-cranked ice cream makers. Refrigerators in those days did not make enough ice to freeze ice cream.

Also vital to Montevallo's operation was Mr. Eddie's Gulf Service Station, which stood on the corner where Shelby crossed Main Street. Without it, things would have come to a standstill in Montevallo. The Alabama Power Company trucks and the college delivery trucks would have never made

*J. A. Brown, Jr. and Sr. inside Brown's Grocery near Brown's ice plant, saw mill, cotton gin, and Acme Oil.*

their rounds, and the fire trucks and Mr. Rogan or Mr. Jeter's ambulance or funeral home services would have been unable to operate. And then there was the gin. The farmers from Brierfield, Dry Valley, Spring Creek, and all around couldn't get their cotton ginned in the fall except at the gin down Shelby Street. This was especially important, as cotton was so vital to our economy. I well remember that every September school would let out for a week so girls and boys both could help their families pick cotton.

And one last effect of Shelby Street businesses on the community was quite important to me as a boy. Had it not been for Pete Givhan's Coca-Cola warehouse, all of us for miles around Shelby Street would have had no Cokes to enjoy, and the soda fountain at Wilson's Drug Store could not have served Coke floats. And what would a Bulldog football game have been without Coke at the concession stand? The lack of Cokes would surely have affected my Dad and his friends, as they would have lacked their favorite chaser to cut the moonshine they liked to drink.

As I look back, I have to conclude that Montevallo would have been a very dreary place without all that Shelby Street offered.

*Above: Dad opened his barber shop in 1923 on Main Street next door to the Strand Theater. Cashing in on the hair style fad of the time, he called his place Red's Bobber Shop. Later it would be known as the Mahan Barber & Beauty Shop. Top: The notorious dead pecker bench in front of Dad's shop where George Wallace once campaigned for governor. Pete Givhan's Insurance Agency was located next door.*

# 15

# Main Street

Although I thought Shelby Street was the center of the universe, much less of Montevallo, many would have argued that Main Street was the central focus of our town. We lived just a short walk from Main Street, and my friends and I considered it part of our playground. Naturally, the most important establishment on Main Street, as far as I was concerned, was Mother and Dad's shop. It was there that I regularly saw not only people from Montevallo, but also from the nearby communities who thought of Montevallo, then the wealthiest and busiest city in Shelby County, as "town."

Dad always kept his shop, which was constructed of painted brick, clean and neat. He had Harry Miller, his shoeshine boy, sweep the sidewalk every afternoon. Harry or Dad also rolled down the striped fabric awning every morning and rolled it up at closing time. Under the awning sat a bench, sheltered from the sun and rain, and this bench was seldom empty. We called it the Dead Pecker Bench, though for many years I had no idea why. It was usually occupied by various old men in the community who wanted to escape their own households and have the company of each other. They hardly moved and the conversation was minimal, but I was always struck by the look of contentment on their faces.

That bench was occupied once by a man well known in Alabama annals, but he did not sit on it. He stood with a microphone in his hand, addressing people up and down the street. George Wallace came to Montevallo in 1958 the first time he ran for governor, a race he lost. But he became friends with Dad, who became his campaign manager in Shelby County. Much later, while Wallace was governor I had the occasion a number of times to see him in his office when I was trying to get funding for Brierfield Park. Each time I told him who I was, he would say, "Oh, yes, you are Red

Mahan's son." Wallace had a phenomenal memory—especially of those who supported him.

Dad's shop got pretty hot in the summer, but people were used to heat then. We always had the front and back doors propped open to have a cross breeze, and two ceiling fans made a lazy flop, flop sound all day long. Dad proudly pointed out that the Hunter fans had been installed when the shop was built in the early twenties, and all he had to do was oil them three or four times a year.

When you walked through the door of the shop you were immediately struck by the smells of, I thought, age and cleanliness. There was always something a little melancholy about the smell of the shoe wax and leather, of the Vitalis hair oil and talcum powder. Plus there was always the smell of shampoo and permanent wave dressing drifting in from Mother's beauty parlor, and on wash days—Monday and Thursday—there was the smell of Oxydol washing powders and Clorox coming from the washing shed out back.

Before World War II, Mother and Dad did the family wash along with the shop towels in the wringer washing machine that was housed in a corrugated tin shed out back. Monday was the main wash day, but there was always more washing to be done on Thursdays. On Mondays, the first thing Dad did when he arrived at the shop was to take up the ashes in the stove in the washroom, shoveling them into a coal scuttle and taking them out back to add to a huge mound of ashes at the back of the lot. Then he would come in and make a fire to heat the water. It felt great back there during the winter, but in summer the heat was stifling. Then he and Mother would throw the towels and other items in the machine, adding scoops of Oxydol from a 25-pound box that sat in the corner. When the water was sufficiently hot, he would add it to the washing machine through a rubber hose, also adding cold water through a separate hose. Once the clothes were covered, it was safe to pour in some Clorox bleach. Only then could the machine be turned on, and its big paddles began slowly swishing back and forth, back and forth in its quarter turns. Once the wash was through, the machine would have to be emptied of dirty water and rinse water added. When the rinse was over, the dripping clothes and towels were fed through the wringer, which squeezed the water from them. Daddy rigged up a piece of tin to route the squeezed-out water to the floor so that a new load could be begun. Then after the wringing was done, the towels and garments were taken out back and pinned to a line—everything except unmentionables that Mother made quite sure that the populace of Montevallo would not see.

All morning long Mother and Dad were running back and forth between customers to take care of the washing. Although today it appears to be a back-breaking job, they never seemed to think it was onerous. I suppose they might have envied people over on Highland Avenue who had automatic washing machines or Mr. Hartley on Shelby Street, who had a gasoline-powered washing machine. I was especially interested in the gasoline washers, as I knew you could take the motor off one of those and hook it up to your bicycle and have a motorized bicycle. Several boys had done it, but I never was able to find an unused gasoline-powered washing machine lying around. When we finally got a machine at home, it was a shiny new electric wringer, and it simplified things greatly for Mother, who no longer had to lug our clothes, including our unmentionables, to the shop on Main Street.

Harry Miller, the shoeshine boy, started to work for Dad when he was fourteen. He helped Mother and Dad with washing and cleaning, but, of course, his main job was presiding over the shoeshine stand in the barbershop. He was tall and serious, very much aware of his place. He spoke very little, but without a trace of black dialect. I have thought about Harry through the years, and I realize that in doing his job he functioned as an artist, a musician, a physicist, and—perhaps most of all—a psychologist. His very work was high art, and as a small boy I was dazzled by his talents.

When a customer entered he would ask succinctly, "Shoe shine, Mister?" That usually elicited no more than a nod or a shake of the head, and if it was a nod, the man would climb up into the shoeshine stand, a high structure made of twisted wrought iron, much in the fashion of drugstore furniture. The seat, arms, and back were a tawny oak, glistening from the numerous times customers had slid into the chair. In those days, almost everybody smoked, and there were cigarette burns up and down the arms of the chair.

Harry's routine was a wonder to behold, one worthy of praise from the most demanding systems analyst. Normally, the customer pulled up his britches legs, but if he didn't Harry would roll up the legs. If he was lucky, the customer would be wearing dark socks, but many of the rednecks wore white socks, and Harry would have to take great care not to get even a tiny trace of the polish onto those socks.

Harry first dusted off the shoes with a dry brush, then followed with a thorough cleaning, this time with a brush too, but with a cleaning liquid added to it. He cleaned vigorously, as he knew that the shine that would follow could be first-rate only if there was no grit or dust on the shoes. He always paid as much attention to the back of the shoes as the front. That pleased one old man so much that he said, "I like that, boy. A person who don't polish the back of his shoes don't wipe his ass either." Harry smiled in response, but he was always quite restrained, not being sure how his responses would be taken by his customers.

Once the shoes were clean, Harry reached down in his shine box and took out a large tin of Griffin wax polish, turning the wing nut to flip the can open. He then began applying the polish with a soft rag. Dad said that he observed that the number of coats Harry put on corresponded perfectly with the amount of tip the customer gave, but Harry would just grin and deny it.

As he began to polish, Harry, like Prince Hamlet, was faced with his own troublesome question: to spit or not to spit. Some customers expected him to do a spit shine, but others would have been greatly offended by a black man's spit landing on his shoes. Harry had to be sensitive about this. In that era, a shoeshine boy did not offend the white man. He said little, remaining silent as racial epithets and bigoted anecdotes spilled from the mouths of his customers. In fact, for many of those whose shoes he shined, it was as if a machine, not a human being, was doing the job. They did not set out to be offensive; they were just too insensitive to realize the implications of their speech or actions. Such was the nature of pre-civil rights small-town Alabama.

It was when Harry got to the real shining that his artistry shone through the most. He'd take the shining rag in his hands and begin the dittity-dat-dat, dittity-dat-dat rhythms, which ended with a loud pop as he finished the heel of each shoe. No drummer in a big band could have outdone Harry, and when I heard his signature pop at the end I wanted to applaud. Why

*My friend, Earl Cunningham, Dad's hard working shoeshine boy. After enlisting and leaving Montevallo, Earl served very successfully in the Army Medical Corps.*

that would not have been enough to clue the customer that the shine was over I don't know, but invariably Harry would tap the customer lightly on one shoe to indicate that he was through. Usually the customers extracted a nickel or dime from their overall pockets and handed it to Harry without a word and without even looking at him.

Dad thought the world of Harry and was very sad when he left for the service in World War II. He was one of the first colored people from our area to register. Before he left, Earl Cunningham—who, like Harry, lived "'cross the creek" in the quarters—began to come around, watching Harry and learning everything he could from him. Naturally, when Harry left, Earl took over the job. Earl's family was hard up, and Dad developed a rather paternal relationship with Earl, getting even closer to him than to Harry. He made sure that he was well-fed, and he bought clothes for him. I was enough younger than Harry that we never really became friends, but Earl and I became close, spending time out back of the shop when things were slack talking over all sorts of things. Of course we didn't go to school together, and the churches were thoroughly segregated.

When I was young I used to look at a stained-glass window over the entrance to the Methodist Church and wonder what the words Methodist Church South written on it meant. I was told that the Methodist Church split in 1844 over the question of slavery, and that no blacks were allowed to attend. That was only changed after the desegregation battles of the 1950s and '60s. And that change was not easy in the Montevallo Methodist

Church, where a segregationist pastor worked out a deal with the administrative board that the organist, who had an excellent view of the doors, would sound a note on the organ if a black person entered the church. Then the entire congregation would rise and sing the Doxology and be dismissed. But questions concerning segregation and civil rights were not a part of the conversations Earl and I had out behind the barbershop.

When Earl also left to join the military, I was sorry to see him go, but I took great pride in hearing of his achievements, both in the military and in academia. My pride was enhanced by the fact that, in the segregated south, there was still room for my father's humanity to make a difference in the life of a young black man and to know that Earl credited Dad with giving him a sense of self-worth that has served him well throughout his successful life.

The barbershop had many interesting nearby businesses on Main Street. One establishment was Jeter's Mercantile, owned by the Frog Hollow Jeters. They sold everything from baby clothes to caskets. Old Man Jeter was nice to all us kids. He'd give peanuts to Harry, Agee Kelly, Joe, and me. But his son, Pep, who took over the business in the forties, was, I thought, a real bastard. He'd yell at you at the slightest provocation. He had a son named Pep Jr., who took after his dad and was a real badass and a bully.

One part of Jeter's Mercantile was an embalming business in the basement. Caskets were displayed up in the balcony. A hearse was always backed up to the rear entrance to unload the dead bodies. In those days there were no funeral homes, so services were always conducted in the churches.

Jeter's Mercantile always reeked of embalming fluid. My great aim as a boy was to see a corpse. Pep Jr. told us he had seen plenty of them—men and women—naked as jaybirds. I envied him the chance. I was never admitted into the *sanctum sanctorum*, though Pep Jr. did sneak in several girls from Shelby Street. Martha Ann Cox was actually there more than once and, other than Pep Jr., became our chief source of information about the embalming processes.

The Jeters had competition. Across the street was Mr. Rogan's store. He too was diversified. Like Jeter's, he sold hardware, furniture, farm equipment, and operated an embalming business. He also sold clothing (for the

*1940s Montevallo postcard showing Main Street.*

living and the dead). In addition, he ran a delivery service from the train station for other businesses and for individuals.

Although Mr. Rogan's embalming parlor was located on the ground floor and was painted a neat white, the Jeter service was considered to be higher-class. Like the Jeters, Mr. Rogan embalmed only white corpses. Black corpses were taken care of at the black funeral home across the creek, an establishment that also was part of a bigger business, including a honky-tonk.

When word came—often to the barbershop—that someone had died, it was always a matter of great speculation who would embalm them. If we were out of school, we'd watch for the arrival of the bodies. From Pete Givhan's bottling company, we could see them arriving in the alley behind Mr. Rogan's store. From this spot we also liked to watch Mr. Rogan operate a hoist that lifted caskets to the second floor for storage.

Also on Main Street was the Strand, Mr. Eddie Watson's picture show, which he operated from 1935 through 1971. His mother had operated a picture show in Montevallo since 1920, and she continued to sell tickets there and even clean the theater until she was ninety-five.

Mr. Eddie decided to build the Strand in 1935 because he learned that local businessman and entrepreneur Pat Kroell was planning to build a

*Montevallo High School homecoming festivities on Main Street in 1952 with the Strand Theater in the background. The two majorettes with visible faces are Joanna Sharp, left, and Beverly Taft, right.*

new state-of-the-art 500-seat theatre that would be in direct competition with his own theater. By that time Eddie was president of the Southeastern Theater Association, and he traveled to Atlanta to see what could be done to discourage Mr. Kroell. His friends in the association told him that if he constructed a new theater himself, then they could arrange it so that the studios would not honor contracts for films from Mr. Kroell. By then, Kroell had already poured the foundation and footings for the building, but he quickly saw the way the land lay and he suspended construction. Eddie got to work building his own fine new theater.

For many years this theater, with 500 seats downstairs for whites and 100 in the balcony for blacks, was a very successful operation. Eddie, the town's most eligible bachelor, cut quite a figure. No one could out-market him. He printed thousands of handbills advertising his movies, and placed them on the windshields of automobiles all over Shelby County. They were also inserted in the *Birmingham News*, the *Montevallo Times*, and the *Shelby County Reporter*. Probably in violation of all sorts of federal laws, friendly post office employees placed the handbills in the Montevallo post office boxes. Afterwards, it was said, Eddie would go back to the post office and pick up all the discarded handbills to recirculate them.

In addition, Eddie conducted a lottery scheme in which each movie ticket bought during the week was accompanied with a raffle ticket, which was placed in a large round wooden tumbler, built by the excellent carpenter from Wilton, Mr. Jim Splawn. At the end of the Saturday night movie, a number was drawn. If the jackpot was not claimed, the prize money increased, sometimes reaching $300 or $400. The raffle was going so well that Eddie began to sell tickets to those not even attending the movies, and this was seen by the minister of the First Baptist Church and the police chief, Mr. Gardner, as a form of gambling. They brought charges, and he appeared before the grand jury in Montgomery and was indicted. Back in Shelby County, Judge Wallace told him he would be released if he paid a fine of $50 and ceased running the lottery. Eddie agreed, but on the way home to Montevallo he had a change of heart. He went back to Judge Wallace and asked to withdraw his commitment to end the game. The judge said no, but Eddie continued the game for several months before closing it down.

All Eddie's marketing methods paid off. Crowds from Shelby and the surrounding counties swarmed to Montevallo to see the movies. The mining communities of Marvel, Boothton, Aldrich, and Maylene all ran buses two or three times a week to transport their citizens to the Strand, and the girls at Alabama College were a constant pool of patrons. He was able to get new movies as soon as the Birmingham theaters did, sometimes before. He had standing contracts with Paramount, 20th Century Fox, MGM, and all the major film companies. He also had live stage shows there, once booking the country comedienne Minnie Pearl to do a show. He even allowed the president of Alabama College, Dr. Oliver Carmichael, and his brother, an ordained minister, to conduct a men's Sunday School class there. That class was so popular that the ministers of local churches complained that their attendance was being hurt.

In 1948, Eddie married Georgene McCauley, a professor of physical education at Alabama College. She helped him run the Strand until 1971. Through those years, the Strand had seen a lot. Many young couples held hands, and some of them kissed for the first time in the Strand. Romances began and romances ended there.

My memories of the Strand are some of the fondest of my childhood and youth. Every Saturday Dad gave me a quarter, and I followed the same ritual every week. I'd go to Mr. Rogan's store and buy a bag of peanuts and a sweet drink. Mr. Eddie did not permit you to bring in your own refreshments, as that was a major part of his earnings. But we couldn't resist. My friends and I would sneak peanuts and drinks in every week. It was not such a problem in winter, but in summer it was very difficult. Someone had to divert Mr. Eddie's attention so we could rush by undetected. The illicitness of our refreshments made the drinks that much sweeter and the peanuts that much richer. I expect, upon reflection, that Mr. Eddie winked at our breaking his rule. After all, we paid him a nickel admission to see the feature, the cartoons, and the serials, and most of us boys bought a bag of Mr. Eddie's popcorn, too.

Also on Main Street was another landmark, the Kroell House. Occupied by two of the would-be theater owner Pat Kroell's sisters—Miss Kate and Miss Mary, this was an immense Victorian house, featuring many gables and turrets and a great deal of stained glass. Their father had been a very

***By the time this photograph was taken in the late 1950s, the Kroell House had seen better times. The flower beds were gone and the ancient oaks that stood sentinel along the street had been cut.***

successful merchant in town, and they lived on many years after his death. Between the house and the street were flower beds set off by bricks lined up in a rick-rack pattern and divided by walkways, which the Kroell sisters swept daily with brush brooms. On occasion, if some child tried to walk on the bricks in the garden, one or the other sister would come running out the front door and chase them away. Often, a black man could be seen working in the beds and pulling grass from between the cracks on the sidewalk. The Kroell sisters were largely unapproachable. In fact, by the time I came along they had pretty much established themselves as the town recluses. No other place in town was so mysterious.

In the twenties, though, the Kroell House had been the center of local social life. Large parties were held in a dance hall on the third floor. But that all changed. In fact, the only visitor they regularly entertained in the thirties was a Mr. Cassie Fancher, who rode his white horse into town, tying it up on the back side of the house and disappearing inside. He was a most impressive sight for Main Street. I remember that his attire was that of an English gentleman: knee-high shiny black or brown boots and dark riding pants. They looked like the knickers I was made to wear, and I was not sure why Mr. Cassie would have chosen to wear them. I hated mine. He also sported a white shirt that was buttoned high around his neck, with a small bow-tie, and he had a vest with two watch pockets, a gold watch chain coming from one pocket and disappearing into the other. He always wore a flat-billed hat with a pinched crown and a leather band.

Mr. Cassie's appearance on Main Street was always an event, as he never ever acknowledged the cars on Main Street. He just rode straight down the street with no doubt in his mind that he had the right of way. Engine noises, horns, and hostile comments some of the drivers shouted from open windows did not faze him one iota. People speculated recklessly on what was going on inside the Kroell House. Most said he was having an affair with Miss Kate, who entertained him in an upstairs boudoir. But no one ever knew what transpired on those visits, and eventually Mr. Cassie left Montevallo and was said to have emigrated to Australia. So far as I know, he was never heard of again.

Farther on down Main Street was the Ford place, with a repair shop

*Bill Lovelady Ford Motor Company, the corner of Main and Boundary Streets.*

full of cars, their engines roaring as gas pedals were pushed down to check the engines. But the most special thing about the Ford place was the banjo player, Cody Battle, who once played in bands with Dad. He had become a mechanic—the best in town according to Dad, but he still loved to play, and during his lunch break, banjo runs could be heard up and down Main Street. I thought I had never heard a sweeter sound.

You could also hear the ringing from Mr. Hamm's blacksmith shop, behind the Ford place. Sometimes my friends and I would go into the doorway and watch Mr. Hamm, who wore heavy leather boots, a leather apron from neck to his knees, and a long-sleeve denim shirt. He did not wear glasses, but had a cap similar to a railroad cap pulled low over his eyes. He wielded the large steel hammer, pounding on red-hot pieces of iron. He worked with a clear rhythm—one long bang, followed by two short bangs over and over again. Red-hot sparks flew off the iron as he repeatedly hit the hot iron with his hammer—a horse shoe or some other item he held with a large pair of tongs. Ding-ditty-ditty, ding-ditty-ditty. When the fire began to slacken, he would pump the overhead bellows, and, when he deemed the fire sufficiently hot again, he would begin the anvil chorus all over. When our music teacher in elementary school, Mrs. Farrah, introduced us to Verdi's *Anvil Chorus,* I already understood the music.

Another place that intrigued me was the Brown bagging plant, a large two-story building that faced directly to Main Street. As you walked down the street, you could hear the roar of sewing machines, and inside you could see women wearing scarves over their hair leaning over the machines and sewing the croker sack (burlap) material into bags. I could not imagine how so many croker sacks could be used. A colored man would place the sacks on a cart and take them outside, stacking them under a tin awning that ran from the front door out to the curb. In the summer time the sweet smell of the croker-sack material and volumes of dust drifted out the front doors and down the street.

Next door to the Brown bag plant was the two-story Masonic Lodge, with a bowling alley at street level. Mother disapproved of this establishment, thinking it was a den of iniquity. I don't know whether it was or not, but when I passed it I could hear loud male voices and smell a strong odor of cigar smoke. The place never failed to raise my curiosity, and eventually Dad took me in. I was fascinated to see how efficient the black pinsetters were and even more how they avoided getting hit in the small space they had at the end of the lanes. I grew to like this den of iniquity.

In the basement of this same building could be found Times Printing Company, which published the *Montevallo Times*. The Wyatt family owned the company, and I envied Mr. William Wyatt, who became Montevallo's mayor, and his son Pat being able to work in such a wonderful environment. There was a strong smell of ink, kerosene, and cleaning solutions, and I noticed that the fingernails and hands of Mr. Wyatt and Pat and their workers were black or occasionally another color, depending on what the printing job was. The huge press went round and round, producing a clankity, clank as the newspapers were printed. For some reason it reminded me of "Bolero," which Mrs. Farrah played on an old 78 record in our art appreciation class in elementary school.

Travis Killingsworth sat at a huge linotype machine with hundreds of levers moving up and down and back and forth. He printed letters upside down and backwards on wafers of bright silver lead. These wafers, made from molten hot liquid lead, were placed in a pot connected to the machine, and when Travis struck a key, a shiny silver-colored wafer fell out in order in a tray to his right. Travis wore a clear green eyeshade, which I assumed kept the glare off his work, and he always had a cigarette hanging from the corner of his mouth as he worked. I thought he had one of the best jobs in town.

After you crossed the street from Times Printing, you immediately passed by another two-story building with huge oak trees in front. Upstairs there was a porch with rocking chairs and swings, from which the occupants of the building could enjoy a view of Main Street. Below were shops, including the Whaley Furniture Store, which was full of brilliantly colorful sofas and chairs and rolls of linoleum lined up along the walls.

In the next building was Fancher's Radio Shop, opened by Tom Fancher after World War II. I can vividly remember him sitting on a workbench surrounded by all manner of wires, tubes, and electric meters. I was mystified as to how Mr. Tom could find what he needed in such a disorderly place, much less fix a radio that had so many parts that might go bad. Later Mr. Tom went into television sales and repair, and, because the televisions took

*Looking northeast up Main Street about 1959. The large oaks had yet to be cut and the F. W. Rogan house, far right, still faced the street.*

up more space than the radios, the shop became even more cluttered. And there was always a strange smell of burning wire.

When I hung around Fancher's, Mr. Tom and his wife Miss Marie were always willing to answer my dumb questions. I liked the Fanchers very much. Mother particularly admired Miss Marie, saying she could take the worst situation and make it positive. I remained close to Mr. Tom throughout his life, and I still see Miss Marie in church every Sunday. She is in her late nineties, but lovely and lively as ever.

The Kroell house was not the only grand Victorian house in town. Next to the post office on Vine Street were two old multi-story, well-kept Victorians occupied by Alabama College professors and staff. The great Mr. Cooper with the loud voice lived in the one to the left of the post office, and Mr. McConatha lived further down the street.

Just off Main Street was the fine Montevallo Post Office, which opened when I was three years old. Constructed of brick and white marble, it had ornamental iron railings out front and brass-trimmed glass doors that led into the lobby, which was paved with terrazzo tile. Over the door to the postmaster's office was a hand-painted mural entitled *Early Settlers of Shelby County*. I was told that it was painted by a Florida painter named William Sherrod McCall and that it was paid for by the Department of the Treasury. Along the interior walls to the right, there were rows of little brass mailboxes with numbers stenciled on their glass fronts. We had a key for box 448, and Dad made one or two trips to the post office every day. I suppose one of my rites of passage was when I was entrusted with the key to 448 and strolled up the marble steps and pulled the mail from the box. I must have been twelve or thirteen at the time. In those days, most people didn't even include the box number in their addresses. We were small enough that the post office workers had memorized the numbers for everybody.

On Main Street to the right of the St. George Hotel was Dawson's Variety Store, owned and run by Mrs. Dawson, who lived in a small house on Oak Street. The Variety Store was always kept very clean and organized, and she monitored closely those entering and leaving. In fact, she gave everyone who entered the store a once-over that you would think would be reserved for strangers. Mrs. Dawson seemed particularly suspicious of children and

***Looking southwest down Main from Boundary Street about 1959. The St. George Hotel is the two-story building on the right.***

adolescents, and when we went in there we didn't loiter. But people needed the gift items, candies, and school and office supplies she carried, and she never hurt for customers.

Also on Main Street was Mrs. Elliot's grocery store. To enter this drab building covered with dark red brick-patterned tarpaper, you had to leave the sidewalk and go up three wooden steps. It was dark and rather dreary inside, but I learned soon that it held many delicacies. I usually got an RC from a chest near the door and some oatmeal cookies from a canister by the large brass cash register. Sometimes if they had some nice bananas, I'd buy one. But the real treat was a hot dog cooked by Mrs. Elliot, placed on a bun with mustard, catsup, and sauerkraut. This culinary masterpiece sold for a whopping seven cents. When the weather was warm and the front doors to the store were propped open, you could smell those hotdogs all up and down Main Street. I thought no smell was better.

On the left side of the St. George Hotel was the Modern Beauty Shop, which was owned and operated by Mrs. Louise Young. For a while her shop was situated next to Dad and Mother's shop, but Mrs. Young needed more space and built a new concrete block building, utilizing the latest construction technology. In Dad's shop there were many sidewalk superintendents who monitored the construction and predicted this new method of building would not last.

The building actually looked nice inside and out and attracted the ladies from all walks of life. Mrs. Young not only cut and fixed hair, but she had a full stock of up-to-date women's cosmetics. While Mother's customers had to walk through the barbershop to get to her beauty shop, the Modern Beauty Shop was just for ladies, and Mrs. Young especially attracted the college girls. Laurie Orr remembers how the Modern Beauty Shop was the site of the beginning and end of her criminal career. She and Jane Russell and Betty Klotzman coveted an expensive brand of lipstick called Tangee that was on sale there. It came in only one color, but they thought it was the finest they had ever seen. They had enough money to buy either the lipstick or a milkshake at Wilson's Drugstore, and when they thought about it they decided that the milkshake was a necessity, but the lipstick was not. But they wanted this luxury so much that they decided to shoplift it. After all, you couldn't easily shoplift one of Mr. Bloomer's milkshakes. The girls brazenly went through with their crime and were not caught.

Mr. and Mrs. Mitch Young's greatest gift to Montevallo, according to the young male population, was not the Modern Beauty Shop, but was their beautiful daughter Clara. She was the cutest, best looking of the younger generation of Highland Avenue babes, and she had admirers from both sides of town and from the surrounding countryside as well.

Like other fine structures on Main Street, the Modern Beauty Shop was torn down at the same time the St. George Hotel was razed to make room for the new Merchants and Planters Bank.

# Part IV

# *Getting Out of Town*

*Right: My dad's sister, Katherine "Kate" Mahan Lacey, in her World War I nurse's uniform. Below: Some of my Lacey cousins, left to right, Jack, Agnes, and Stanley.*

# 16

# Wanderlust

I always loved traveling, and my parents seemed always willing for me to take advantage of the opportunity to see places, far and near. Sometimes it was weekends with country kin in Maylene or city kin in Birmingham; sometimes it was riding the train to Rome, Georgia, and back; sometimes it was going as far as Mobile and Poughkeepsie, New York, to visit my older sisters. The experiences I had on these travels have had a lot to do with the person I have become.

My Aunt Kate, Dad's sister, lived at Maylene on a 600-acre farm. She was a nurse during World War I, having been trained at St. Vincent's hospital, and after the war had married Bob Lacey. Despite the fact that the farm was quite primitive—no running water or electricity—I loved going there for the weekends. Uncle Bob was a railroad man, and on some Friday afternoons on his way home he would stop his '41 Ford in front of our house on Shelby Street and say, "How about letting Mike go out for the weekend." I was always glad when he came, because I loved my adventures there with my many cousins: Bobby (Bob's son by a previous marriage), Philip, Agnes, Stanley, Jack, and Margaret Ann.

Baths out there were certainly an adventure, especially when the weather was nippy. We'd go out to the creek that beavers had dammed up, making a nice pool, and my cousins would jump right in as if there was nothing to it. I remember jumping into the icy water, jumping back out shivering, and back in again, until I became acclimated to the cold water. I can't say how clean I was when I crawled back out, but I always felt proud that I was tough enough to stay in and wouldn't have to bear the ridicule of my country cousins.

One fall when I was there I looked out at a field with rows of dug sweet potatoes. My cousins told me excitedly that tomorrow George, a black tenant farmer, was taking the potatoes to sell in Siluria. We'd have to get up in the morning real early to load and size the potatoes.

The next morning the two mules stood before the wagon, and George had put the sideboards on the sides of the wagon. "Now y'all kids pick up those taters and bring 'em over to this wagon and dump 'em," he said.

Philip answered, "But we have to size them first."

George looked a little aggravated and said, "Just do what I say. Dump 'em in the wagon."

I jumped up in the wagon, and the others handed me box after box of potatoes, which I emptied all together onto a growing pile. When we were loaded, George got hay and a tarpaulin to put over the yams. Then we all took our seats atop the potatoes, and he climbed up to the seat in front of the wagon.

It was five miles to Siluria on the bumpiest dirt road imaginable, and there were no springs on the wagon. I thought at times my insides might shake out. But eventually we arrived in Siluria. As we prepared to take the potatoes over to a pump to wash them, Philip asked again, "Now, George, when are we gonna size them?"

"Hell, boy," George answered, "we ain't got to size 'em. Didn't you know big taters is always on top? Little taters is always on bottom." We pulled back the tarpaulin, and, sure enough, what George said was true.

Although I was happy at Aunt Kate's house, I was also glad to return to Shelby Street, where we had a good many more of life's amenities. But I was all ready for the next chance to travel, and quite often that would be to Birmingham to visit my Aunt Lorene, who lived in a magical place called Quinlan Castle.

While my Uncle Bill Morrell was in Europe during World War II, Aunt Ween—as we called my mother's sister—took an apartment in the fine old building called Quinlan Castle. She moved Momma in with her, and when I was nine or ten I would catch the bus to Birmingham to see them. Once in the city, I would get on the street car that took me to Five Points South, from which I could easily walk up to the Castle.

Quinlan Castle was a huge stone building, and I thought it looked like something out of a medieval tale. I loved it there. I'd play out in the courtyard with other kids who lived in the complex, and sometimes we would roller skate on the sidewalk out front. At night I slept in a bed next to the steel casement windows, from which I could look down and see all the lights of the city. This was a real excitement for a kid from Shelby Street, where the streetlights were scarce.

There was a tearoom down the hill at Five Points South, and Aunt Ween would take me down for a snack from time to time. The place was shiny and white, and I always placed the same order: cinnamon rolls and iced tea. The rolls had chewy raisins and were covered with the whitest sugar icing I had ever seen. The iced tea was colder than any other I ever had. And I was proud to be sitting there with Aunt Ween, who I knew loved me very much.

When I think of another trip I took twice when I was around ten or eleven, I'm surprised that my parents would have allowed me to make such a trip at such a young age. Mr. Burr Fancher, who worked for the Southern Railway, was the conductor on an old steam train that ran from Montevallo to Rome, Georgia. Perhaps it was because they trusted Mr. Burr, perhaps it was because Dad loved trains so much, but they allowed me to catch the No. 16, which had passenger cars, a mail car, and freight cars. I had been by train to visit Sister in Berney Points, so I was not in the least frightened or anxious. I was allowed to punch tickets for Mr. Burr who gave me pretty much free run of the train. I spent a good bit of time watching the black man who shoveled coal, and at stops, of which there were quite a number, I would follow the brakemen and switchmen around looking for hot boxes. In those days there were no ball bearings, only babbit bearings, so oil had to be put into boxes filled with a mass of string. It was easy for wheels and axles to get damaged and heat up, even catch on fire. I would carry red flags, which the workers would place on hot boxes that needed to be checked at the next stop.

When we got to Rome, I would have dinner with Mr. Burr at a boarding house that catered to railroad men and spend the night in the hotel. Then the next morning after breakfast we'd catch No. 17 back to Montevallo. I'd really feel the big shot for several days. What other boy in my acquaintance had had such an experience?

Other trips took me to Mobile and New York to visit my older sister,

Tootsie. Just as I had done in Mobile, I visited her and Sidney several times in Poughkeepsie, New York, where Sidney took the job with the Federal Bearings Company.

I don't remember much about what we did in Poughkeepsie on my first visit, but I remember the train trip there. After we crossed the Mason-Dixon line, I noticed that the facilities were no longer segregated, and I was surprised to see black families taking seats right in the car where we were. In New York City, we came into Penn Station and had to transfer to Grand Central Station. I was amazed that Mother could negotiate the trip from one station to the other so easily. Later, Tootsie brought Mother and me back down to New York City, and we stayed in the Barclay Hotel. Now that was something for a boy from Shelby Street. I went around with my mouth open for three days. We climbed to the top of the Empire State Building and looked up and down Manhattan. I was especially impressed with the green rectangle that was called Central Park, and I was thrilled when Tootsie helped me pick out where the Barclay was.

I was also amazed at the displays at the Museum of Natural History and the Metropolitan Museum. I could not believe what I saw when they took me to Rockefeller Center to see the Rockettes. When the show was over, the Rockettes disappeared as the entire stage dropped down.

We sat with hundreds of people eating food from the automat. We came well-stocked with coins to pick out our hamburger steaks, Waldorf salads, and pieces of apple pie with cheddar cheese. After lunch as we walked back to the hotel, I looked into the window at Macy's, and there I was stunned by what I saw: a television set. Of all pieces of luck, the Brooklyn Dodgers were playing on the screen. They were my favorite team, and there I was between Mother and Tootsie watching them. I was too shocked for words, and I wished that my friends in Montevallo, especially Joe and Jack, were there to see it with me. There would be no televisions on Shelby Street for a few years yet. Mother and Tootsie had a hard time pulling me away from that window.

When Dad and I drove Putnam Porter to New York City to board a ship, we drove on up to Poughkeepsie after seeing him off. At that time Tootsie had an apartment in an old Victorian home, and you could see the

Hudson River out the window. She and Sidney would take bottles out of a bar, which looked like a radio cabinet to me, and they would shake up martinis or mix Manhattans for Dad and themselves. It seemed to me they drank a lot, and Dad seemed to be enjoying himself mightily. They also drank when we went to restaurants.

In the dimly lit restaurants Tootsie and Sidney took us to, I quickly got a taste of high-class food for the first time. Sidney ordered Roquefort dressing on his salad. I had never heard of it, but I decided to order it too. Then he ordered scallops, which were also a new item for me, but I decided to order them too. I didn't mind trying new things. The Roquefort dressing had a faintly rotten taste to it, but it wasn't bad. When the scallops arrived, I looked at the little medallions closely and said to Uncle Sidney, "What exactly are scallops, Uncle Sidney?"

He thought for a minute, then said very seriously, "Well, Mike, actually they are the muscles out of the eyes of big fishes."

Dad and Tootsie laughed when he said it and I was a little surprised, but Uncle Sidney's answer seemed well within the realm of possibility. I had eaten chitterlings, tongue, tripe, and even mountain oysters, so the idea of fish-eye muscles didn't faze me. Uncle Sidney looked at me closely as I tore into my plate of scallops, and he grinned when I said I liked fish-eye muscles about as well as catfish.

In 1945 Uncle Sidney was diagnosed with tuberculosis and had to be put into a sanitarium that sat up high on a hill on the outskirts of Poughkeepsie. He spent a year confined to a single room that opened onto an uncovered porch. He was supposed to stay on the porch even when the weather was cold, and he complained about the frigid air.

In late May of that year, Mother and I boarded a train and traveled to Poughkeepsie to keep Tootsie company for a while during his confinement. Tootsie's apartment was several miles from the sanitarium, and every day we would take a cab to go over and spend the day with Uncle Sid. For a twelve-year-old, those days became very long, and I quickly became bored. But one Saturday when we went to see Uncle Sid, all that changed.

I had heard on the radio that the Ringling Brothers and Barnum and Bailey Circus was coming to Poughkeepsie, and I asked about going. Tootsie made it clear that the circus was not on the agenda for that visit, but I managed to put it on the agenda for myself.

On that particular Saturday afternoon, as I walked around the grounds of the sanitarium, I heard music coming from down the hill. I rushed excitedly in that direction, and there it was: the circus parade in all its glory and spectacle was passing by. Band members in bright-colored spangled uniforms led the way followed by gaily decorated carts and wagons pulled by trucks, white horses, and even elephants. There were several four-wheeled cages holding tigers and lions, and one cage had a sign that read, "Gargantua: The World's Biggest Gorilla." Gargantua sat in his cage looking as dignified as an archbishop. I had a perfect place to see everything, and when the last wagon came by, without the slightest pause, I fell in with a large crowd of children and adults who followed the parade for over a mile to the fairgrounds.

Now it was time to set up the Big Top, and I was fascinated by all the activity. Amazingly, I thought not once of Mother or Tootsie, or even poor Uncle Sid. I was, I guess, living in the moment. Everything seemed to be going by a preconceived plan. What seemed like hundreds of workers were staking the elephants and tying up the horses. Wagons, carts, and cages were placed in their proper places, and huge rolls of dirty white canvas were spread out in the open space where the tents would be erected. I watched with keen interest as the various pieces of canvas were laced together, creating a single piece of canvas that seemed to me as big as Montevallo High School's football field.

Four-man teams wielding huge sledgehammers stepped forward to drive the tent stakes, which seemed to me as big as automobile axles. One man dropped to his knees and held the stake in place, while another lifted his hammer and began driving the stake into the ground. A loud ringing sound came from the impact. Immediately and in a precise rhythm, the next driver came forward and struck the stake again. This continued until the stake had reached the desired depth. The pattern continued until all the stakes were in the ground. This anvil chorus was one of the most artistic things I had ever witnessed.

The next thing the workers had to do was to put the tent poles into place and lift the canvas on them. But this was too much for the men alone.

Special leather harnesses were placed on the elephants and horses to enable them to do this lifting. The man in charge gave orders, and in a perfectly synchronized way the animals pulled the heavy canvas upwards in the poles and the mighty tents rose magically. I thought it one of the most beautiful things I had ever witnessed. It was like seeing life breathed into a dead body.

With the tent in place, things relaxed a bit and the whole place seemed to become a little town. Smaller cooking tents were put in place, and almost immediately the cooks set to work. Sanitation tents with showers and toilets were put in place. Huge trailers with generators provided the electricity needed for the show.

It was only when the sun began setting that it dawned on me that I should think about heading back to the sanitarium. I have a very good sense of direction, so I had no fear about how to go. As I walked down the street, I noticed a car pulled over to the curb, and Tootsie jumped out. I could tell from the look on her face that she was not happy. Some man I didn't know was driving the car, and I caught a quick glimpse of Mother sitting in the back seat. I learned that Tootsie and Mother had become so alarmed they called Tootsie and Sidney's best friend Jack to come over to the sanitarium to decide what to do. He immediately said, "It's obvious. Like every kid his age wants to do, he followed the circus parade." They just drove in the direction of the fairgrounds until they spotted me.

"Why in the world would you run off without telling us, Mike?" Tootsie yelled. "You could have been kidnapped or anything."

All I could do was bring forth a weak "Sorry," but I wasn't really sorry for having done what I did. I crawled in the back seat next to Mother, who looked relieved and hugged me tightly. All she said was that I should have told them what I was doing, and my wonderful mother never ever mentioned the incident again.

Another memorable trip occurred closer to home when I was in high school. It was spring vacation of my junior year, and Ed Givhan and I were feeling the call of the open road. The weather at home was spring-like, and we thought it was the perfect time for an adventure. Ed's car, Papooshka, had just had some work done on it so it was in top-notch shape, and after thinking it over we decided to go to Gatlinburg, a town in the Great Smoky

Mountains that was a favorite vacation spot for Montevallo people. Since Papooshka could comfortably carry four, we decided that we would ask two others. Our first choice was Harry Klotzman, who lived across the street from Ed, and on a whim we decided that we would also ask a younger member of the Highland Avenue group, James Elbert Mahaffey, who was called Teeny. Teeny was four years younger than Ed and me, but he was very mature for his age. I guess we thought that this excursion would be a learning experience for him.

Harry immediately agreed to go, but Teeny was a bit more reluctant. His mother and father were at work that Friday morning, and he would be unable to get their permission. His older sister, Mary Charles, said he could go, and Teeny apparently decided that would suffice. Ed, Harry, and I had amassed maybe thirty or forty dollars, and Mary Charles advanced Teeny ten or fifteen dollars. With gas being only eighteen to twenty cents

*Milton "Weed" Jeter, a Frog Holler rebel, standing on the running board of Ed Givhan's 1939 Dodge lovingly called Papooshka. The Baptist Church and Plaza Grill are in the background. The magnolia tree to the right of the church was later cut down, for a church addition, over the long and loud objections of many town citizens.*

a gallon at the time, we had enough money to go about anywhere. Ed and I got out some maps and plotted our route. We filled up Papooshka's gas tank at Buddy Allen's Shell Station, picked up some blankets, and gathered up bread, peanut butter, mayonnaise, bologna, chips, Vienna sausage, beans—anything we could find in our parents' kitchens. We each brought along one change of light clothes, but nothing warm because the March temperatures were perfect. We were ready to hit the road for the mountains.

Of course Ed was our number one driver. Harry rode shotgun, and Teeny and I started out in the huge back seat. We drove all day on two-lane roads, beginning to get into the mountains around Gatlinburg late in the afternoon. The higher Papooshka climbed, the lower the temperatures dropped. A few miles outside of Gatlinburg, a heavy snow suddenly began to fall. By this time we were several thousand feet above sea level, and the temperature was in the teens. Papooshka's heater was hard at work, but she could not produce enough BTUs to match the outside temperature. Snow began sticking to the blacktop pavement, making it slick and barely visible.

Our original plan was to camp Friday and Saturday night at a campground in Gatlinburg that we had seen on the map, but we really had no idea where the campgrounds were. Ed, you could see, was getting tense, his hands holding the steering wheel tightly. "Holy shit," he said. "I can't see a blasted thing. What do y'all think we should do?"

For some reason, everybody seemed to be looking at me for an answer. "Well, I don't know about you fellows, but I think we better get our asses off this road. I mean we could get killed in these conditions."

"But where will we stay?" Teeny asked.

I thought a minute and suddenly had an idea that was powerful in its inevitability. "We'll stay in the car," I answered. "We'll find a place to park, and then we'll wrap up in our blankets and let the heater run. We can spend the night in Papooshka. Tomorrow may be better."

The guys agreed there was nothing else to do, and Ed found what looked like an abandoned parking lot and drove to the far side of it. We grabbed our blankets.

"I'm hungry," Teeny said.

"Let me get something out of the trunk," Ed said, opening his door and going out into the whirling snow. He returned with a large sack of food, and we all set to making peanut butter and mayonnaise sandwiches.

"What a hell of a time to have a damn picnic," Harry said.

We all laughed grimly.

Now we were ready to get some rest so we all wrapped up in our blankets. Harry and Ed kept their places in the front, I stretched out on the back seat, and Teeny—who was appropriately nicknamed—lay in the floor space between the front and back seats. But nobody could think of sleeping, as the car seemed to be getting more frigid by the minute. Papooshka's heater was putting out all it could, but it just wasn't up to the job. We tried to keep our spirits up by telling jokes, but by midnight no one had slept a wink.

"All right boys," Ed said decisively, "this is just not going to cut it. I'd rather slide off the side of the mountain than to freeze to death in a parked car. There is nothing for us to do but turn around and head south to a lower altitude."

We had already thought of returning to Montevallo by way of Stone Mountain, Georgia to see the great stone carvings of Stonewall Jackson, Robert E. Lee, and Jefferson Davis, so we all agreed that we should head in that direction and hope we could escape the snow with our lives.

Ed took the wheel and down the mountain we started, curve after curve after curve, the snow still falling, the six-volt battery powering the headlights wavering. But miraculously Papooshka came through for us. We never saw Gatlinburg, despite its being the purpose of our trip, but we were quite relieved to make our escape. We knew, however, that we were definitely not out of the woods. The snow was still coming down hard, and we were low on fuel. Papooshka was getting thirsty. We had no idea where we could purchase gas at this time of night, but like magic we found an all-night filling station and we were able to breathe new life into our endearing lady.

Harry and I offered to spell Ed at the wheel, but he insisted on driving, so the rest of us went soundly asleep. Luckily, Ed managed to stay awake, and we arrived at the Stone Mountain entrance early in the morning. There was no sign of life—no guards or ticket sellers—so we just drove past the entrance booth and parked in the lot next to it. We decided to walk down into the woods and make ourselves a fire. Our teeth were chattering, and

***Probably no one understood my thirst to roam better than my dad, pictured here with my friend Harry Klotzman, who accompanied me on some of these trips.***

Teeny was shaking so bad he looked like he had the Saint Vitus dance. Luckily, we were all Boy Scouts and knew the proper technique for making a fire. As we huddled around the open fire, we opened two cans of Vienna sausages, which we ate with light bread. "This is the best Vienna sausage I ever ate," Teeny said, and none of us disagreed.

Afterwards, we stumbled back to the car and fell asleep. When we woke up around noon, things had warmed up a bit, much to our satisfaction, and we walked over to the viewing area and marveled at the great stone images of the Confederate heroes. After five minutes, we were ready to hit the road.

"Where next," Teeny said, perhaps a little dispirited.

I must say I was thinking of my comfortable bed on Shelby Street, and I think the others were having similar thoughts. "You know," I said, "Teeny's mother is probably worried about him, so I move that we head back to Montevallo."

"I'll second that," said Teeny.

The others agreed, and Ed cranked Papooshka and we headed for Highway 78, which would take us south toward home. There was mainly silence as we drove along, and we arrived late on Saturday evening. Ed dropped me off, and I walked to the kitchen and raided the refrigerator. Mother and Dad seemed glad to see me.

"And how was the trip?" Mother asked, rubbing my back.

"Just wonderful," I said. "Just wonderful."

The trip to Gatlinburg might not have run as smoothly as many of my travels, but it took its place alongside all my other adventures as something I found essential in my life. I was always pleased to return to Shelby Street, but early on I knew that I possessed a wanderlust that would take me far and wide.

17

# Montebrier

My excitement mounted as I waited on the curb, a pair of roller skates and a small box of clothes on the grass next to me. Would the blue 1937 Plymouth ever turn the corner off Main Street onto Shelby Street to pick me up for a weekend at Montebrier, a large home sitting on Mahan Creek, just a few miles down below Montevallo in Brierfield? Mr. and Mrs. Bill Pittman, the owners of Montebrier, had called from Birmingham before starting the two-hour drive to Montevallo so I had a rough idea as to when they would arrive, but well in advance I stationed myself on the curb. Between the ages of eight and eleven I would replay this excited anticipation time and time again, particularly in the summer. Little did I know then that one day I would own the place and live in it.

From Mr. Pittman I learned the history of this interesting house. Montebrier was built in 1866 as a private residence, but in 1929, Dick Yount, who built Palmer, Bloch, Wills, and Ramsay halls on the Montevallo campus, bought it and turned it into a country club. That didn't last long, however, because Yount lost Montebrier in the crash of '29. It fell into the hands of Merchants and Planters Bank, and they leased it for dances and parties from 1929–35. The Bama Skippers Band, made up of Eddie, Charles, and Mary Lee Mahaffey and a couple of surgeons from Birmingham, played there regularly.

Dad loved Montebrier. He often called square dances there, and he also danced with the Frederick girls, who were well known for their dancing skills. When I was a baby, he took my sisters down there to dance.

For a number of years, Montebrier was a gambling haven. When Sam Klotzman was a young man, he won a T-model Ford with one cast of the dice, but little good did it do him. In those days, one had to ford Mahan Creek to get to Montebrier, and while Sam and others were playing, Jaybird

*Right: Ads appeared in the Montevallo and Centreville papers announcing dances and other events at the Montebrier Club. However, open dances were short-lived due to the rowdiness of attendees. Below: The Bama Skippers, a famous local band, seated on the front steps of the Montebrier Club about 1929.*

**ATTENTION!**

No more open dances will be run at Montebrier Club.

All future dances will be run by INVITATION ONLY.

**Montebrier Club**

By V. P. YOUNT, Owner

*John Steelman was a man of many interests and even dabbled in raising wolves for a while at Brierfield.*

Rutledge, a black man who lived on the property and had worked for Yount, came in and said the creek was rising and anybody who wanted to get out better get out right away. Sam decided he better get his new car out, but, when he drove into the creek, water got into the magneto, killing the engine. The creek kept rising and the water got into the engine, ruining the car. Sam sold it for next to nothing.

Along with her husband John, Mrs. Jean Steelman, an English professor at Alabama College, bought Montebrier from the bank in 1936 and lived there, even though it was not ideal for a family. It had a forty-five-foot square ballroom, a little kitchen, a dining room, and two back rooms. The Steelmans closed in a back porch for a kitchen.

The Steelmans did not live in Montebrier for very long. When Frances Perkins of the Department of Labor came to Montevallo to speak, she met Mr. Steelman and was impressed with him. She invited him to Washington as a secretary. He jumped at the chance, but Miss Jean would not go, remaining in Montevallo with an adopted daughter. A divorce followed, and Miss Jean got Montebrier in the settlement. Later she married Mr. Pittman and moved to Birmingham, but they kept Montebrier as a weekend getaway.

Mr. Pittman absolutely fell in love with Montebrier, and he came there as often as he could. He was dean of Massey Business College in Birmingham, and, though gas was rationed during the time he came there, he was able to get extra gas stickers because of his position. Mother and Dad had befriended

Miss Jean during her divorce, so they became friends with Mr. Pittman, and because of that I became a frequent weekend visitor at Montebrier. It was my favorite place in the world. And because the Pittmans had no children, I became like an adopted son. I called Mr. Pittman by the simple name of Mister rather than Mr. Pittman or Mr. Bill.

When the Pittmans' car arrived on Shelby Street, I would grab up my box, open the back door, and jump in, kneeling on the floor behind the front seat. "Hello, Mister," I would say, because it was Mr. Pittman I was so crazy about. This six-foot-two man had gray hair combed straight back on both sides, but he didn't seem old to me. He always wore a blue and white seersucker suit and a bow tie in the summer, and you never saw him without his pipe. He kept a pouch of Old Northern tobacco in his shirt pocket, and he had a fine metal instrument to tamp down the tobacco with or to scrape the pipe out. With Mister, pipe smoking was a high art.

Miss Jean was not so interesting to me, but I was always cordial to her. She talked incessantly, mainly about Birmingham people I did not know, and to tell the truth she bored me to death. But I could stand it. She was a tiny woman, especially looking that way as she sat next to her gigantic husband in the Plymouth. People always said that Miss Jean was attractive, but Mister was the main attraction as far as I was concerned.

"Got to go by the store first," Mister would say, and that meant a trip to Jeter's Mercantile to get groceries and to McCulley's Store, where Mister had his meat specially cut by Joe Doyle. We always ate well at Montebrier.

Then we would hit the road in the big blue Plymouth, complete with fenders and running board. Mister always drove with his left arm out the window, and he always had the wing window opened to blow on him. Miss Jean also had her wing window blowing on her. The smoke from Mister's pipe constantly blew in my face, but I didn't care. I would peer out the front window through the space between the front seats, but what intrigued me most was the radio. In the middle of its circular dial was an orange button with a needle, which you rotated to tune in the radio. I'd ask Mr. to turn on the radio and, even though he knew we were not likely to find anything, he'd humor me. All we ever got was a shrill *whee-oh-eeh-oh-eeh*, but I liked that sound for some reason. I felt like real dude riding down the road in a car with a radio, even if it didn't play. Mother and Dad didn't even have a car at that time.

After we passed through Wilton, we turned onto the dirt road that took us to Montebrier. When we arrived, we all got out and proceeded to the padlocked front door. Once we were inside, Mister opened all the windows and then went out to open the shutters. I got my box of clothes and my skates from the car, and I looked forward to skating in the huge ballroom. I took my things to the small bedroom they put me in, just right next to theirs. It was in this room that I first heard bed springs creaking and moans coming from the couple, and I knew something was up, though I was not altogether sure what.

After getting the house opened up, Mister would get his Winchester Model 61 pump and go out in the front yard. I would watch him lift it to his shoulder and fire it up into the sky. Then we would get real still and listen. In a minute or so, we heard another gunshot from across the Mahan Creek, which ran near the house. We knew then that the nearest neighbor, Great Aunt Adelaide, was aware that we had arrived. Shortly thereafter, we would walk down to the creek, and she would walk down from her house on the other side. Then she and Mister would chat with each other from across the creek—a creek named for my ancestors. Sometimes Mister would bring Adelaide fruit that she couldn't get in Brierfield or Montevallo.

On our weekends at Montebrier, I got a good education from Mister. I was easy with him from the start, even standing by his side as we pissed in the yard. He was infinitely patient in explaining things to me and teaching me how to do things. It was from Mister that I learned to fish. We dug red worms or pulled Catawba (Catalpa) worms from trees, and sometimes we caught hellgrammites in a sifter Mister made from one-half-inch mesh wire. We never lacked for bait, and we pulled many a line of bream out of that muddy creek. And when we caught them, there was no question but that we would scale and gut them and eat them for supper.

Mister also taught me to shoot, which started a lifelong passion for guns. He first taught me to shoot a .22 rifle, and I learned quickly. "You got to respect guns," he told me. And he was forever saying, "There's no such thing as an unloaded gun." If Dad ever owned a gun, I never saw it, and my mother thought using a gun to kill a bird, a squirrel, or a rabbit was totally unnecessary, unless you were starving and needed something to eat. So it was Mister who was my mentor when it came to firearms.

Mister also taught me to work. He was obsessive about keeping Montebrier neat, and he would spend hours in the yard. Wearing a bow tie, he would pick up the swing blade, which he kept very sharp. He'd say, "If the blade is keen and sharp, you hardly break a sweat. Let the sling blade do the work." I think he was generally right about that, but still it took muscle power on the downward swing if the grass or bushes were large and tough. Mister said the same thing was true of an ax, a hammer, or whatever tool you were using. The tools, not one's arms, he said, should do the work.

Mister also taught me to limb up cedar trees with snippers and a pocket knife. To make a tree grow tall, he said, you had to cut off all the lower limbs and leaves, even if the tree is only three feet tall. That way the trees' nourishment would move to the upper leaves and limbs. "I don't want to duck when I walk through my own yard," he'd say with a slight smile. He also planted a number of trees on the property, and he would baby them until they took hold. Plus he got St. Augustine grass runners on campus after Mr. Spot Jones-Williams brought the grass to Montevallo. Then he sprigged them at Montebrier and eventually got a full lawn.

Mister also showed me the old Delco battery system, a large bank of 48-volt direct current batteries located in a small house down under the hill. From the Delco house large copper wires ran from a battery connection plate up a small utility pole and from there was strung overhead into the house. Inside was a switch box with funny looking switches that turned the DC lights on in each room. There were small cords hanging from the center of the ceiling, and a DC light bulb was screwed into the receptacles. In the ballroom, or the big room as it was called, several cords were required. Of course, by the time I bought Montebrier in 1964, the DC bulbs and lighting system had been replaced by Alabama Power Company's 110-volt alternating current light bulbs. But I was fascinated by the old system.

Mister also showed me the one-cylinder gas engine he used to pump water from the spring into a tank that was located on a steel tower sitting next to Montebrier's back porch. Once the tank was filled, the water flowed by gravity to the kitchen and bath. I loved to hear this old pump engine run, as it had a wonderful rhythmic firing pattern, as if it were played by a drummer. It called out repeatedly, "*Paradiddle, paradiddle, paraddidle, pair; paradiddle, paradiddle, paradiddle, pair.*" Of course, the water was cold when it came out of the brass spigot at the kitchen sink, and there were no electric water heaters to get hot water from. Miss Jean would have to heat it on the stove, then pour it into the tub. She had two stoves, but mainly used a four-legged electric one made by General Electric. It had four eyes on top and an oven to the right above the eyes.

Back when Montebrier was hosting parties, dancing, and gambling events, there was only one commode and one lavatory in the house. In 1936, when Miss Jean and her first husband moved to Montebrier, they put a bathtub, a sink, and a commode in the old kitchen pantry. By the time I first saw that bathroom, the brass spigots had become quite dirty-looking, though

*Mr. Jessie "Jaybird" Rutledge, noted citizen of Brierfield, caretaker of the Montebrier Club, and close friend of "Mister" and Jean Pittman. Mr. Jaybird was close to the Mahan family, befriending my Great Aunt Adelaide, my dad, and finally me. He spent his last working years at the newly created Brierfield Ironworks Park in the 1980s.*

I can't say that bothered me at all. Nor was I bothered by the fact that the commode, tub, and sink drained though a pipe directly into Mahan Creek. Mister informed me that this waste water flowing into the creek made for a good fishing hole.

My favorite time at Montebrier was at night, when Mister and I would sit on the front porch and listen to the cicadas and frogs. Miss Jean would be inside reading so it'd just be us two. We didn't talk much, but we were as close as could be. Occasionally, I would see a shadow coming up the drive, and it would be Mr. Jaybird Rutledge, who had spent most of his life on that property. Now he lived in a house up by the gate. Sometimes he and Mister would just talk for a while, but occasionally Mister would remove his shoes and socks, and Mr. Jaybird would trim Mister's bunions. He would put Mister's naked foot on his knee, take out his pocket knife, which was extremely sharp, and with surgical precision trim the hard, white, dead skin off of Mister's bunions. During all this time Mister would suck on his pipe, and I'd look at the stars and think how good a place this was. But since I didn't have any bunions, I never got to experience Mr. Jaybird's surgical skills.

My trips to Montebrier lasted until I was in the seventh or eighth grade. I'm not exactly sure why they ended. Maybe there were more cool things to do with my cool friends—particularly my girlfriends—rather than waiting on the curb in front of 159 Shelby Street for the Pittmans to pick me up. But when Mister died in 1954 while I was a student at Auburn I was flooded with memories of Montebrier.

During my first marriage from 1956 to 1959, there seemed to be no room for Montebrier, but when I brought Linda to Montevallo in 1961, the first thing I did after taking her to meet Mother and Dad on Shelby Street was, according to her, to take her directly to Montebrier. We could not have known at the time that it would be called home by us and Miki and later by Stann. In 1974, Montebrier was placed on the National Register of Historic Places. If I am truly a stepper, then Linda's and my efforts in saving historic Montebrier by bringing it to life as a home and sharing its historic fabric with so many people over the last forty-five years ranks at the top of my accomplishments.

*Top: Montebrier, my home, May 2013. Photograph by Daphney Walker. Above: Before Linda and I purchased Montebrier, we visited the house with our friends John and Marny Owens and their children.*

# Part V

# *Living the Life*

*Left: Milton "Weed" Jeter and me beginning our formal education at Alabama College's nursery school.*

*Below: Miss Ethel Bickham with Joy Holcombe standing in the background. I learned a lot at Miss Bickham's, including what Joy wore underneath her dress.*

*Below: My dad sitting proudly in the fire truck he almost destroyed forty-five years earlier.*

# 18

# Schooldays

Going to school from first grade to high school was pretty much the same. I'd get up between 6:00 and 6:30, reminded by Mother to brush my hair and brush my teeth. Lacking a family car some of the time and too close to ride a school bus, I made the daily trek to school and back by foot or later by bicycle. In my early grades, Mom or Dad or Maggie would walk me the seven or eight blocks to school, and on rainy days a neighbor would carry me by car. But beginning in the third grade, I was on my own. Most days I would strap my wooden violin case to the handlebars and pedal to school. Occasionally, I wondered what people might be saying about that spectacle.

On my way to school, I would exchange greetings with people like Mrs. Latham, Mr. Rogan at the corner of Main, Smiley Frost when you reached Valley Street, Bloomer Wilson at Middle and Main, Mr. Eddie Mahaffey, Mr. Taft Hill, and others. In the big oak trees that lined Main Street, birds would sing happily and the squirrels would chase each other, and this was all a part of my morning's entertainment. I have always been acutely aware of nature's sounds, I think because the elementary school principal, Mrs. Charlotte Peterson, the music teacher, Mrs. Farrah, and the math and history teacher, Mrs. Minnie Dunn, taught me how to be a good listener.

I started my school days in the nursery school run by Alabama College. It was housed in a two-story Victorian white framed building, and I would spend my mornings and early afternoons under the supervision of Miss Ethel Bickham. This place was wonderful for a three-year-old. I thought the playground, with its swings, sandboxes, and sliding boards, could not be more perfect. There was a special swing, which we called Miss Bickham's swing, that was designed like a saddle. You put your feet on a bar in front of you and your hands on a bar above your feet and you could achieve mobility back and forth without any adult help. The swing was held by four ropes instead of two, and that made it easier to achieve greater heights than you could on a regular swing. The girls, like Sarah Pat Baker, Joy Holcombe, and Laura Ann Hicks, could not make Miss Bickham's special swing go as high as we boys could, so they preferred to play in the sandbox doing girl stuff with little china plates and cups. We boys had no interest in the sandbox, but invariably at the end of play period we would go over and destroy the little sand cakes and pies the girls had created. And invariably Miss Bickham or one of the student teachers would take our hands by the fingers and turn our palms up, striking them with a twelve-inch ruler. Usually it did not hurt too bad, but occasionally a tear would slip from my eye. Yet I never did stop messing up the little girls' creations.

Miss Bickham's school day was extremely structured and ran on a schedule about as predictable as the trains that ran through Montevallo. You ate at a certain time. You pulled out your sleeping mat once in the morning and once after lunch and took a nap whether you wanted it or not. You sang when instructed to do so. You colored and fingerpainted on Miss Bickham's orders. She did not brook any protest from us.

My next school was the kindergarten the college ran. Housed in the Alice Boyd building on campus, the kindergarten was even more structured than the nursery school. We had to be there exactly on time and were given assignments by only one teacher. We sat in one room with little desks and round tables with little chairs. We did have playground once in the morning, and here we learned games like kickball. I quickly discovered on the playground—even at that tender age—that I was not a jock. There were no sandboxes or Miss Bickham's special swing. The swings, with just two chains, were much harder to swing in, requiring some help from the teacher to really get going. We didn't have any rest time or sleeping mats to lie on, but following lunch we were sent home, and I spent the afternoons at the shop with my parents.

Two years before I started first grade, the old elementary school, which sat at the corner of Valley and Boundary streets, burned to the ground. Although I was only five at the time, I remember the excitement it caused because Dad drove to the fire in the brand-new Peter Pirsch fire truck the

City had just bought. In the excitement of dealing with the smoke and flames billowing out of the heart-pine structure, he forgot to turn on the cooling system that pumped fresh water into the block and radiator of the six-cylinder Chevrolet engine. Before long the engine burned up. So the new fire truck met its Waterloo on its first trip out. This was a minor scandal, and Dad was, of course, mortified, but luckily the City had insurance and could replace the motor.

When I began regular school, my first teacher was Mrs. Alice Rice. She intended to get us off to a good start, stressing order, discipline, routine, and punishment as the four elements of a sound education. We were all somewhat terrified of her, as she walked between our desks incessantly, dressed in all black with flat lace-up shoes. But worse than her austere appearance, she was constantly armed with a wooden twelve-inch ruler, which she was ready to put into use at any infraction. My failures were mainly not paying attention, talking, and, as she put it, not cooperating, and on a number of occasions my little white palm was made red by Mrs. Rice's whacks. You knew right away how bad your failure was by the number of whacks she gave you. After that you got a tongue-lashing, explaining why she had had to inflict the punishment.

Very different from Mrs. Rice was my third-grade teacher, a shapely young beauty named Mrs. West, who had been a Wave in the U.S. Navy. While Mrs. Rice seemed old enough to have taught Abraham Lincoln, Mrs. West was new and fresh, full of laughter, walking up and down between the rows of students not to keep order but to converse with us in a pleasant way. If you couldn't answer a question, she didn't make you feel bad, the way Mrs. Rice had. She asked us to report on our interests and hobbies, and she encouraged us to make colorful bulletin board displays. She was a disciple of progressive education that Dr. M. L. Orr, head of the education department, was responsible for bringing to Alabama College.

Progressive education, a liberal philosophy of educating the whole child, was just taking off across the nation, and we were made to feel privileged to attend such a school. I think the whole system went against the traditional Three R's—reading, writing, and arithmetic. We were to progress at our own speed, and we received only pass or fail grades, no A, B, C, or D. Report cards would say something like "Mike has passed his math, history, music, but he could do better if he really applied himself." But progressive education did not really make me want to work at my maximum level, so I just piddled around a lot of the time. In dental school years later, I encountered a philosophy that took me back to my progressive education days. We said that anything above seventy was passing, and any effort beyond that was wasted, as our diplomas would all say the same thing. Except for the few students who graduated at the very top of the class, we had all pretty much adopted that philosophy.

Although I was never a top student, I had a lively curiosity and learned a lot from my teachers, but I never applied myself sufficiently to be distinguished as a scholar. I was never elected president of anything. I ran for vice-president of the student council and lost by seven votes. I never made first chair in the band, and neither was I an athlete. But what I did have was enthusiasm, and my teachers liked that about me. I could energize a group and make them excited about a project. Teachers liked to give me jobs to do, and I was proud to be singled out. I actually liked to erase and clean the chalk boards and to run errands down to the principal's office. If a teacher needed something found for a class project, I would quickly volunteer.

One of my favorite teachers was Miss Susie DeMent, who taught commercial subjects. By the time we were in the ninth grade, we all thought we needed typing. For many of my classmates, especially the girls, it would provide them an avenue for employment, and those of us who planned to go to college were told that typing would be invaluable to us as well. So in the tenth grade I signed up to take a typing class from Miss Susie, whom we called the Mother Superior of Typing.

Mother said I was likely to be very good at typing. After all I had taken piano lessons for nine years, and I also was able to play stringed instruments. Certainly, she said, the dexterity required for those activities would transfer to typing. Alas, my mother was wrong. I sat down dutifully before the manual Royal typewriter assigned to me and began to bang out *a, s, d, f, j, k, l, ;*. Over and over I typed this sequence. It seemed like running scales on the piano, and I felt pretty confident. Then we proceeded to "Let us now praise famous men," which was not quite so easy. Then it was time

***Susie DeMent, aka Miss Susie, aka Miss Montevallo High School. She taught many generations of students the art of typing and shorthand. Her dedication and love for teaching made her a Montevallo legend.***

to be speed-tested. I scored a miserable twenty words the first day. Ed, Joe, and Harry all scored higher, as did every girl in the class. I never was able to reach forty the entire semester, and I had to admit that my musical skills were not transferable.

I liked Miss Susie so much that I felt bad that I was not doing better in her class. But Miss Susie was in charge of the school newspaper, the *Spotlight*, which she reigned over with the care that the editors of the *New York Times* must have given to their publication. She demanded absolute perfection. Maybe if I did well on the staff of the *Spotlight*, she would overlook my deficiencies in typing.

I first signed on as a reporter, a job I quickly realized was not for me. I could interview people pretty well, but my writing left something to be desired, and Miss Susie saw that immediately. Little of my work was deemed worthy of the column inches it would require in the newspaper. So it didn't take long for me to find my niche in the more technical side of the publication. Jobs like cleaning the mimeograph machine or straightening up the printing room I eagerly took on. I also distributed the papers around town and mailed copies to other high school newspapers in Alabama. When the *Spotlight* won state awards, I was as proud as the writers were.

Miss Susie continued her work with the *Spotlight* long after I graduated, taking the paper into full color and digital printing. She also remained a fixture at all school events, particularly athletic competitions. She was the official scorekeeper for the three major sports, and she always dressed in the school colors, orange and blue. Students all seemed to love Miss Susie, and she became a mentor to many. In her eighties, she still was an active fan of the Montevallo High School teams, and when alumni returned for home games, she was the first person they wanted to speak to.

My senior English teacher, Mrs. Vinnie Lee Walker, bore very little resemblance to Miss DeMent. Feared by many and respected by all, this woman was the last great hurdle we students faced on our educational journeys. I knew I was in for it, as progressive education had allowed us slackers to get by with murder, and I had not gained all the basic skills required. This thin, graying woman had high standards, and she was not about to compromise them. We read the best literature, and we wrote about what we had read.

*Vinnie Lee Walker seated on the rocks at Davis Falls during the class of 1952's picnic there. Miss Walker was feared, respected, disliked, loved, and dedicated beyond words to the art of teaching English and literature to generations of Montevallo students.*

I did her assignments quite perfunctorily, as I had done most of my high school career. But here there was one difference. My papers came back with *C*'s and *D*'s written in red. Up until then I had embraced the philosophy of "don't sweat the little things; just get the big picture." The utter failure of that philosophy became abundantly clear when six-weeks grades came out. I fearfully opened the card to see a *D* in English. When my parents saw the grade they were none too pleased, either. As for me, I underwent a conversion, accepting Mrs. Walker as Lord and Savior of Senior English, and with the help of my friends Ed, Emily Vest, Jane Triplett, and the student teachers from Alabama College I was able to make *A*'s and *B*'s the rest of the year. Vinnie Lee Walker accomplished more with an academically cavalier guy from Shelby Street than any other teacher I encountered.

At our high school, you were pegged as an athlete, a brain, a musician, or a nobody. But that changed for a number of boys when a short stocky man named Moon Thornton came to town to teach vocational agriculture. He started a Future Farmers of America chapter, offering opportunities for the nobodies to build their confidence up. He took them places and formed a barbershop quartet that competed with quartets from other schools. He had them entering speaking contests. They proudly wore their FFA jackets, decorated with patches won in hog-calling contests and other such events. For many kids who were getting no encouragement at home, Mr. Moon was just what they needed. He also had a great effect on people who had never been classified as nobodies.

People like Donald Dennis from Pea Ridge greatly developed their sense of self-worth due to Mr. Moon's encouragement. One trip to the state fair with Mr. Moon and his fellow future farmers did not end so well for Donald. Things started off okay, as he won a number of dishes by throwing dimes into them. But when Mr. Moon drove up into Donald's yard when he took him home, Donald dropped and broke every last one of his dishes.

Mr. Moon was always pressing us young men into service for the school. Late one afternoon he had a number of us trying to improve the football field, which was more hard-packed clay than sod. He had re-seeded the field, but nothing was growing much as it was so in need of water. The hose we had would not reach far enough, and he asked if anyone from town had a

***Mr. "Moon" Thornton, the legendary teacher of agriculture, loved and respected by generations of Montevallo students, seen here in his beloved shop instructing two aspiring mechanics.***

hose at home he could go get. Ed said yes, and Mr. Moon said, "Can you drive, Ed?"

Ed quickly answered yes, but he failed to tell Mr. Moon that he had only driven his father's Chrysler a few times or that the car had an automatic transmission. "Go on and take my car," Mr. Moon said. I volunteered to go with Ed, and Mr. Moon said okay.

Mr. Moon's car was a four-door 1940 Chevrolet with the gearshift on the floor. But Ed and I were undaunted by the challenge. After all, Mr. Moon had always drilled in to us, "Don't say you can't do something. Before you say that, go and try it." So we went. Ed took his place in the driver's seat. I knew the gear patterns, and I knew when to press the clutch. Ed engaged the clutch, and pushed the starter button. We were in business. I put the car into low, and told him to let off on the clutch and give it some gas. We jerked forward, but the car didn't stall, which pleased us, as we imagined that Mr. Moon was monitoring our takeoff. "Clutch," I said to Ed, shifting up into second as smooth as you please, and by the time I gave the command for third gear we were moving along quite smoothly. We drove up to Ed's house, got the hose, and returned to school without a hitch. "We are one hell of a team," Ed said as we got out of the car, and I couldn't help smiling in agreement. Ed got the Givhan water hose from the trunk and proudly handed it over to Mr. Moon. He and I felt like something that day, having driven the car of our teacher. We didn't even care it had taken two of us to do it. As my dad would say, "There ain't no hill too high for a stepper," and Ed and I were true steppers that day.

We liked Mr. Moon so much that Joe McGaughy, Weed, Ed, our new friend Bill Kirby, and I all signed up for Agriculture the following fall. We were Future Farmers of America, but none of us had any idea of having a career in agriculture. Mr. Moon told us that didn't matter, that what FFA could teach us would be valuable the rest of our lives no matter what path we took. But we did have to have some sort of farm project. Joe and Dudley Pendleton chose to raise a steer, Ed did a work project with his Dad, and I chose to go into the worm farming business. My partner in that enterprise was Bill Kirby, who appeared in Montevallo the same year Mr. Moon did.

After his father died, Bill moved here from Selma with his mother and his younger brother John. Mrs. Mary Elizabeth Kirby, now having to support the family on her own, enrolled in Alabama College to earn teacher certification. The Kirbys lived in a house on Valley Street between Shelby and Middle Streets across from Frost Lumber Company. The two-story house was unpainted with a long concrete walk to the front steps. Neither the house nor the grounds had been taken care of very well, but Bill's mother made it into a comfortable place to live. There were beautiful large oak trees in the front yard, and there was a fine porch from which Bill and John could keep up with all the goings-on on Valley Street.

Bill was my age and in my grade. We quickly became the best of friends, although our life styles greatly differed. I was a musician and a poor athlete. Having been governed pretty much by the female dynasty on Shelby Street, I was non-aggressive and pretty much afraid of physical contact. Bill was completely opposite. In fact, he loved combat. He was not much for academics, keeping his performance just above the failure line.

Bill pushed his behavior to the precipice, barely avoiding the unethical,

*My close friend Bill Kirby, known far and wide for his prowess socially, romantically and athletically. In 1964, he was a bartender and bouncer in a Key West, Florida restaurant.*

the dishonest, or—occasionally—the illegal, but the coaches, Mr. Moon, and all the teachers saw in Bill all the qualities needed to do anything or be anyone he wanted to be. He was as dear, true, and honest a friend as anyone ever had. I always knew that if I had ever needed physical protection or security Bill would be there. Through our FFA activities and our membership at the Methodist church, we became lifelong friends, and when Mr. Moon said that we had to have a project in our Ag class, we naturally decided to work together.

My dad had for years wanted to have a basement under our house, so he made a business deal with Bill and me to dig a basement, and in return we could use it for our worm business. For our labor he would also pay us ten cents per wheelbarrow of dirt we dug, hauled from under the house, and dumped down a bank in the backyard. Bill and I agreed to his terms, and we formed our partnership for this FFA project. Dad bought a new wheelbarrow, two round-pointed shovels, a pick, and a mattock. K & M Worm Business was launched. We would split the income 50/50 from the dirt removal and eventually from the sale of the worms.

In late spring, we began digging each day after band and football practice. We also dug on Saturdays and whenever there was spare time. It was hard work bending over under the floor using the pick without hitting the floor joists, then shoveling the dirt into the wheelbarrow and pushing it up a 2x12 walkboard through a large hole dad had knocked in the brick foundation walls. We soon worked out a system, one of us digging with the pick and mattock and the other filling the wheelbarrow with the dirt. This allowed the picker to rest before the loaded wheelbarrow was pushed from under the house. As you went up the ramp, you had to duck your head to clear the foundation, then roll the wheelbarrow over to the bank and dump the dirt, then back to the basement. We would do this over and over again. Each time the cash register would ring up $.10.

Studying redworm farming in a book from the college library, we found out that we needed to get some old bathtubs and fill them with a mixture of rotten sawdust and dirt, placing a breeding stock of worms in the mixture. Of course, worms had to be fed, and we used uneaten table scraps, some corn meal, and old milk, which we read was good for worm breeding. We hoped to have our worm business started in early fall and begin selling worms after Christmas. Once we had demonstrated that we could complete the project, we would become full-fledged members of the FFA.

By Christmas we had worms and began to sell some out of the first bathtub. We put 50 or 100 worms in a round ice-cream paper carton we got from Wilson Drug Store. I think the price was $1 per 100-worm carton, but the wholesale price was $.25 a box. Our wholesale customers were Western Auto, the Shell service station, and the grocery store across the street next to the colored funeral home. We also made direct sales from my house and some we even sold in Dad's barbershop. K & M was a successful business, and our friendship became more entrenched and mature. The K & M worm business only lasted part of the ninth, all of the tenth, and a little of the eleventh grades. Both Bill and I grew a bit weary of the project, and our interests began to diverge, making our friendship less intense.

While Bill and I raised our worms, Joe McGaughy and Dudley Pendleton raised their steers. Mr. Moon had told them that they would be expected to show and sell at the State Fair in Birmingham late in the fall. Joe and Dudley had no idea how to get the cows to Birmingham, but, in his usual way, Mr. Moon said, "No problem." He soon found a trailer that would hold two cows, but it was in terrible condition. It had maypop tires, and the tailgate had to be wired shut with haywire. Mr. Moon had a trailer hitch on the rear bumper of his 1940 Chevrolet, and he offered to drive us to Birmingham.

Once the steers were loaded, Mr. Moon—along with Dudley, Joe, Ed, Harry, and me—headed up the dirt road to Alabaster and Siluria, where we got on Highway 31, at that time the busiest highway in Alabama. We crossed Shades Mountain in Birmingham and drove past the famous statue of Vulcan atop Red Mountain, then began driving down to Five Points South. It was on that stretch that one of the maypop tires blew out. The two heavy show steers began to move right and left as the trailer zigged and zagged down Highway 31. Mr. Moon's Chevrolet was not made to pull such heavy loads with good tires, and with this flat tire the load began to shift, threatening to tip over. Mr. Moon looked rather grim as he tried to steer the car down the road, and we guys looked just as grim. We could hear the steers bellowing loudly.

Finally, Mr. Moon brought the Chevrolet to a stop. We all piled out of the car to size up the situation. We discovered that we were not out of the traffic, and we motioned the traffic around us as Mr. Moon maneuvered the trailer off the highway. He got out and told Dudley to get his jack out of the trunk. Then he looked a little pale. It was at that point he remembered that he did not have a spare.

"We got to get that tire off and take it to that filling station back up the hill," he said.

We placed the jack under the trailer, but it was incapable of lifting the trailer and its heavy load. There was nothing to do but undo the baling wire and unload the steers. We tied one to the trailer and the other to a utility pole. Traffic was creeping by us. A few cars tooted their horns at us, and one man rolled down his window and howled in laughter. Joe shot him a bird, but Mr. Moon said not to let on no matter what they did. Luckily, with the steers on the ground, the jack was up to the task and we got the maypop off, rolling it up the road past Vulcan to the Pure Oil filling station.

Once the tire was repaired and back on the trailer, we were ready to reload the steers and head for the fairgrounds. But the steers had another idea. They elected to pull their ropes loose from the trailer and the light pole. Off down the hill they tore, with all of us in hot pursuit. They ended up next to Brother Bryan's statue right in the middle of the roundabout at Five Points South. Brother Bryan was kneeling in prayer, and perhaps it was his intercession that stopped the steers, who stood quite still next to his statue. We were able to take control again.

Mr. Moon slowly drove the trailer into Five Points South. All he could do was shake his head as we reloaded the steers. Everything was pretty quiet as we made our way to the fairgrounds. We were happy to get the two beasts out of that trailer and lock them into the wooden stalls, where they would remain until they were shown and ultimately sold. The sooner those steers became hamburgers, the happier we would be. I couldn't help but feel lucky that I had chosen worms for my own FFA project.

*Joe McGaughy and Dudley Pendleton with the famous escapee steers posing at the Birmingham Fairgrounds ready for the next day's scales and sales. Mr. Moon Thornton and his young son Danny are on the far right. Jack McGaughy, Harry Klotzman, and I are bringing up the rear.*

*Joyce Moncrief, the practice teacher who captured my affection, posing here at Big Springs. I thought she was the epitome of grace, beauty, and intellect.*

In addition to our regular teachers, we had a steady stream of practice teachers from Alabama College beginning in elementary school and extending through high school. We guys loved having these beauties from the Angel Farm in our classrooms, and when we were old enough to cruise the campus we used to see them regularly and engage them in conversation, flirting shamelessly. In our classrooms they were primly dressed, but on campus they seemed much more sexy, with their shorts or slacks. We even went to the campus Tea House, where we would dance with them to music from a big jukebox in the corner. Everything was fine until Mr. Adams, the campus security officer, would come by. He was under orders to expel non-college students from the Tea House, and, although he personally did not mind us being there, he was committed to fulfilling his responsibilities. He would escort us out the front door, and we would go sit in our car until we could see him returning to his office under West Main Dormitory, a place we called the cave. Then we would reenter the Tea House through the back door and resume our socializing with the college girls.

It was not unheard of for a college girl to go out with a high school boy. In my junior year, I became infatuated with my student teacher, Miss Joyce Moncrief. When prom time came, I asked her to be my date. She said she would have to think about it, and I felt encouraged by that, expecting that she would have turned me down flat. I went off and bragged to my friends,

***Only by the grace of God, the successful culmination of my high school career. Back row, left to right, Harry Klotzman, Joe McGaughy, and Kenneth "Hanky-Pooh" Rochester. Front row, me and Ed Givhan.***

and the story was soon all over the school. The principal, Mr. Hurt, called me in and told me that under no circumstances could I take a practice teacher to the prom. Plus, Joyce herself, who was nearing graduation from college, had second thoughts. She did continue to take walks with me by the creek, to pose for pictures, to dance with me on occasion at the Tea House, and to go over to Calera to Pearl's for a burger and a shake. Several times on our way back to campus we would turn off Highway 25, proceed up the dirt road to the monument located in what was said to be the center of Alabama. There, in the moonlight, pulse racing, I would imagine smooching with her. That would have to be enough.

19

# Music

I guess I was destined to be a music lover, given how crazy my parents and my Aunt Lucille were about it. And, like my parents and Aunt Lucille, I loved a wide variety of music, playing classical, country, folk, gospel, rhythm and blues, and jazz during my early years. If anybody had been there to teach me bossa nova and rap, I'd probably have played that, too. There was always music in my house, and from the time I was in elementary school Mother made sure that I attended every concert that came to Alabama College. She also made sure that I got music lessons.

Every Saturday morning for a few years, from the time I was in the fifth grade, I would ride my bike, at Mother's insistence, over to Nabors Street to take music lessons from Mrs. Ziolkowski. I remember that their brick ranch-style home looked pretty ordinary, but inside it was a very different matter. It had what I took to be a very distinct European flavor. There was a heavy black grand piano in the living room, with tables covered with sheet music. Mr. Z, whose pipe tobacco could be smelled immediately when you entered the house, was a beloved member of the music department at Alabama College. An acclaimed Chopin expert, he had studied with the famous pianist Jan Paderewski. But it was Mrs. Z I took piano lessons from.

Mrs. Z was a wonderful teacher, always understanding and patient. How she could put up with students like me, I cannot imagine. I practiced very little, and I lacked good brain to eye to hand coordination, but she never showed that she was anxious or disturbed. Before I began my lesson, Mrs. Z would adjust the bench and ask me to practice scales. When I was sufficiently warmed up, I would take my music book from a small newspaper delivery bag Dad had given me. I tried, but I just wasn't very good. The pinnacle of my piano career came at an annual recital when I played "The Marine Hymn" with both hands, using the forte pedal with great aplomb.

Mother and Dad seemed proud that night, but I certainly knew by then that the piano was not for me.

I much preferred the violin, and I began taking lessons at the same time with Claire Ordway, whom everybody I knew called Chicken behind her back. Chicken was an immense woman. She came straight down—no boobs or butt. That was convenient, for as I came into puberty I had no distractions from my lessons.

Chicken was a classic case of someone who couldn't play worth a damn but could teach music extremely well. Although she taught in the music department, she was not of Mr. Z's caliber. When Chicken played, the strings would often go *cluck cluck*, and that is where she got her nickname. She always played flat, and her vibrato was a howling, yelping sound. But when she taught, everything changed. I was rapt. And on occasion she would open a case and show me a rare violin she kept wrapped in red velvet. She even let me hold it on occasion. Later when I married Linda, a violinist

*"Chicken" Claire Ordway conducting on the stage of Palmer Hall. I am one of the two male musicians in the photograph. In the rear center is Ed Roberts.*

who herself valued fine violins, I appreciated Claire Ordway even more, realizing better what a superb teacher she had been.

Chicken encouraged me to play second violin in the college orchestra from the time I was twelve, and when I was a junior in high school she got me to enter a statewide violin contest playing "The Blue Danube Waltz." I practiced like everything, and I reckon you could say I was almost cocky when I played for the judges. That self-confidence paid off, as I took first prize. When I returned to school the next day, we had an assembly and I played the piece for the entire school, getting a standing ovation. As I surveyed the student body clapping enthusiastically, I couldn't help thinking, "It doesn't get any better than this."

The truth was, however, that for the most part I was a little self conscious about playing violin. None of my friends did. I carried my violin in my bike basket, and when I had American Legion baseball practice I'd hide the violin in the juniper hedge next to the Presbyterian house on Valley Street, two blocks from the ball field. It always seemed to be wiser to head off ribbing than to suffer it.

At church I did play the violin along with Kate McConagee on the flute and her brother Walter on the clarinet. I was also able to play duets with the minister's knockout daughter, Jane Triplett, who was a good pianist. In addition to directing the school bands, Victor Talmadge Young (Vicious Tiger), was music director at our church, and he much favored moving beyond the piano and organ in planning church music. This I enjoyed very much, and it was then that I realized that whatever communication with the Almighty I was to have—in church or out—was to be had through music. I could not keep my mind on the sermons, and scripture reading might as well have been in Greek or Aramaic, as it meant nothing to me. But the music was another matter. Even as a boy of nine or ten, I somehow knew that I was participating in something sacred.

From the seventh to the ninth grades, I added the trumpet to my instruments. I continued to play violin in the college orchestra at the suggestion of Chicken Ordway, and I played trumpet in the school bands under Mr. Young. I began in the junior high band, but Mr. Young told me that if I worked hard I could march with the senior band starting in the eighth grade.

*Mr. Victor Talmadge Young, band director. His occasional stuttering did not keep "Vicious Tiger" from producing excellent concert, marching, and swing bands.*

I did what he said, and the next year I was marching with the Montevallo High School Bulldogs band.

It was commonly said that Vicious Tiger was a grouch, which accounted for the name we students gave him. But the more we were around him, the more we liked him. He had been trained at one of the leading music schools, Oberlin Conservatory in Ohio, and he had a master's in music from the University of Ohio. He encouraged those with talent by forming swing bands, and I was quite impressed that a song he had composed, called "Golden Earrings," was played by the swing band I was in. How many high school band directors were composers, I wondered, a bit in awe of him.

While I was in high school, with Mr. Young's encouragement, I and a number of other boys in town formed a band called the Dixie Cats. Johnny Ziolkowski played cornet, Ed Givhan valve trombone, Teeny Mahaffey trumpet, and Eddie Mahaffey clarinet. Mr. Young allowed us to practice in the bandroom. Ralph Sears let us do tape recordings at his radio station.

Pretty soon, music became more than a mere avocation to me.

I was about fifteen or sixteen when I began to play for money—and in the least likely of places, given this was still in the forties. Sam Brown, a black man who worked at Rat Scott's Chevrolet dealership, had a band called Sam Brown's Band of Renown, a name he had borrowed from the nationally prominent bandleader Les Brown. Sam played dances for blacks at the VFW in Centreville, the Cucumber Club out on Highway 25 near Centreville, and other venues in the area, and he played for white dances at the old cotton mill in Siluria. Sam was always needing players, and he asked Johnny and Teddy Ziolkowski to join the band as the first white members. A bit later he came to Dad and asked, "How about letting Mike play trumpet with my band, Mr. Red?" Amazingly, my parents agreed, and I began earning three or four dollars a gig working with Sam, becoming very close to the man.

I would go down to Rat Scott's place, and I'd seek out Sam. I'd find him in his dirty overalls, usually in the grease pit or at the wash rack. He was probably earning minimum wage, but he was a hard worker and he never slowed down when we talked. We'd talk about the coming gig, or we'd go over song titles. Nobody had more of a positive attitude than Sam. He'd say, "Mike, we gonna knock those cats dead." And he meant it. And we did.

When Sam would come by the house to pick me up to head out for a job, he looked nothing like he did in the grease pit. He'd drive up in his old Chevy sedan, with the trunk tied with baling wire because the drums made it impossible to close it. He would be wearing a natty black suit, with tight pants and a loud tie. His pointed-toed black shoes were always spit-shined, and his hair would be slicked back with grease. The band members did not wear suits—just the leader did—but we did wear matching black pants with either white or black shirts. As I entered the car, I would be sort of stunned by the odor—a combination of cigarette smoke and body odor—a smell my friends and I called the Negro smell.

Sam was a mighty presence. He played both drums and sax expertly, and the other players were also very good. It was a big band. There were two trumpets, an alto sax, a tenor sax, sometimes a baritone sax, one or two trombones, a piano, a bass, and drums. We had sheet music, but we were highly improvisational. In fact, I learned to fake under Sam—which is what we called improvising when you couldn't follow the written music—a skill that has served me well in my musical life. When the dance was over and the managers gave Sam his cut of the door, he paid us off immediately, with his usual quip he had picked up off a preacher somewhere, "Boys, we had a hundred-dollar sermon and a ten-dollar crowd." But I was proud to get the four greasy George Washingtons he pressed into my hand. None of us players were bothered that Sam's cut was bigger. He held us all together. And he was generous. I was still also playing with the Dixie Cats, and he would lend us his drums for our practice and performances.

While I was playing with Sam, I was asked to play with another band that was just about as opposite as you could get. It was the Cofer Brothers Band from Siluria, a country band presided over by Duck Cofer, a friend of my father's. When Duck found out I was playing with Sam, he asked me if I could play bass.

I had fooled around with the bass a few times, which I thought qualified me, so I quickly said, "Yes, sir."

"Can you fake?" Duck asked.

I could improvise on the trumpet, so I saw no reason I couldn't improvise on the bass. "Yes, sir," I said confidently.

My first gig with the Cofer Brothers was to be the next Saturday night at the Buck Creek Cotton Mill. I had a week to learn to fake on the bass. I borrowed country records from Ralph Sears at the college radio station and went over to the college and borrowed a bass fiddle. I practiced every day, and by the weekend I was faking all over the place. This as much as anything qualified me for the compliment I sometimes was given: "That Mike is really a quick study."

The Cofer band played some fast songs, but most often we did slow numbers that couples could clinch dance to. I'd be up there flailing away on the bass, and I would watch those dancers, bellies together and the guy's leg between the girl's legs. I knew they were enjoying it, as I was getting a thrill out of it vicariously. I also noticed those same couples would go out and stay out for a while before they started back dancing. I had a pretty good idea where they had gone. In the Buck Creek Cotton Mill parking lot, everyone knew you could see the parked cars swaying rhythmically, and in cold weather the windows would be steamed up.

I played lots of dances, both square and round, and it was a steady source of income through high school and into college. Like Sam Brown, Duck played for a cut of the door, and he paid us off after every gig.

My favorite song I learned to play while I was with Sam was "Caldonia." It was so popular with the crowd that we'd usually play it twice. Later, when I was a student at Auburn University, a fellow named Cunningham formed a rock and roll band called the Auburn Knights of Rhythm, and when we weren't playing we would often go to a black establishment called the Dynaflow Club, which was near Tuskegee on the road between Auburn and Montgomery. Anybody could come to the Dynaflow Club, but its owner, Batman Poole, had decreed that to *belong* you had to drive a Buick Roadmaster with a dynaflow transmission and four holes on the front fender. Three holes wouldn't cut it. At the Dynaflow Club, I really learned to play rock and roll. He'd invite the white boys to join them on stage.

The Dynaflow Club was pretty basic. It was a cement block building painted a dark brown, and it had a gravel parking lot. There was very little light other than on the sign over the door. There was usually a $1 cover charge, but when they saw the instruments we were carrying they never asked us to pay. Inside, it was smoky and dark, with colored lights hanging down. Tables and booths were arranged around the room, at which black couples were sitting with drinks before them. We were told to go to the back of the room, which was a real reversal for us. We were in for many new experiences there. For the first time in my life I shared bathroom facilities with black men.

A long bar ran all along one side of the room, and there was a stage at the far end, standing about two or three feet above the floor. It had its own colored and white lights. It was here that I saw my first electric piano, electric bass, and electric guitar. The musicians were all black.

When Batman saw us, he would go to the microphone and say, "Hey, here's my musician friends from Auburn." He'd motion at us, saying, "Come on up here, boys. Make yourself at home." I would be carrying my bass and the others had their instruments, and we would join the colored musicians already on the stage. We were thrilled to be there because we were able to see the beginnings of rock and roll. R and R pretty much used the same four chords I used when I played country with the Cofer Brothers and blues with Sam Brown, so it seemed quite natural to me.

Batman was an impressive looking man. He dressed impeccably in dark suits and handsome ties. His kinky hair was cut short, and a part had been made in it with a razor. The Dynaflow Club had no air conditioning, and in no time he and everybody else was sweating. The sweat would be falling from his face, but he always waited to the end of an eight bar to pull out his handkerchief and mop his face. He reminded me of the great Louis Armstrong.

One night while we were sitting in with the band, he said, "We gonna play 'Caldonia' now." Then, with a somewhat mischievous look on his face, he looked directly at me and asked, "Boy, can you play 'Caldonia'?"

"You bet," I said.

He looked surprised. "Where'd you learn that, boy?"

I proudly said, "I learned it from Sam Brown when I was playing with Sam Brown's Band of Renown, from Montevallo, Alabama."

Batman looked impressed and he counted off the beat for "Caldonia." In unison, the horns blew rhythmically and the singers began: "Caldonia, what makes your big head so hard." When the phrase ended, I let out a loud grunt, as Sam Brown had taught me. The audience laughed loudly in approval. By the end of the evening, everyone in the house was doing it. I was thrilled to death.

As I survey the happiest moments of my youth, it is amazing how many of them have to do with music. And that has continued throughout my life.

*Ain't no hill (or tree) too high for a stepper. Climbing the wonderful chinaberry tree on top of the wall at Gene Baldwin's house.*

*The annual wading party at Little Springs behind and down the bluff from Agee and Pat Kelly's house. Teachers furiously yelled, "You be careful, and don't get your clothes wet." That command always led to a "who pushed who" discussion.*

20

# Having Fun

Having fun has always been a very high priority in my life, and my life on Shelby Street was filled with fun. I spent hours skating down our sidewalk or riding scooters. Just after World War II, Dad bought me a used bicycle and painted it bright red. Then my adventures spread out beyond Shelby Street. The neighborhood guys played marbles—or deebees, as we called them—and slid off the terraces at the Presbyterian Church on sleds made from pasteboard boxes we got at the stores downtown. We played cowboys and Indians all the way down to Frog Hollow.

Another activity on Shelby Street was rubber gun battles. E. G. Smitherman and Charles Cox were master builders of these weapons. They cut a strip of inner tube and attached a clothespin to the end. When it was released with skill, the rubber would fly off and hit its mark. I was hit by many of them, and it hurt like everything. In addition to the guys who played with the rubber guns, there was one girl—Catherine Bridges, the neighbor girl who stared down Mr. Dyer. Catherine was fearless, we thought, and we admired her for joining in.

One thing we all loved occurred not on Shelby Street, but not far from Highland Avenue. If you went through the college campus and up behind the president's home, there you would find what we dubbed "big ditches." A barren red clay hill with hardly any vegetation had been eroded over the years, the rain having washed large deep ditches and gullies on the surface of the hill. The grade of the ditches varied from straight down to angles as steep as those of the terraces at the Presbyterian Church or Ed Bridges's house on Shelby Street. We boys were overtaken by a desire to live dangerously, and we would take cardboard boxes up there to slide down the ditches. The dust would be as thick as the dust coming from behind the stagecoach in a Saturday afternoon Wild Bill Hickok or Johnny Mac Brown movie.

After about a half day of big ditches—up the slopes on foot and down on cardboard box tops, we would be "red clay dirty." Returning home with our clothes caked with the red dust, we always knew that our mothers would not be happy. But sliding the ditches was worth it.

Living as I did on Shelby Street, with Shoal Creek right in my backyard, I could not avoid being interested in swimming and fishing. Before Big Springs swimming hole was completed, I usually swam at Little Springs, which served as the water source for the town of Montevallo. Later, Little Springs became the swimming hole for blacks. It was located just behind Mrs. Maggie Lou Kelly's house, and there was a park there. I envied Agee Kelly because he could see Little Springs Park from his back steps, and many times he and I and other friends would walk down the stone path and cross the little wooden bridge that took you to the park. The bridge was close to the water, and we would lie down on our stomachs on the bridge, put our heads down and lap up the cool water. Next to the park, the creek was wide and shallow, and I remember at school picnics when I was a small boy spending hours wading in the creek. My lifelong fascination with the Civil War had its beginnings in this very place when I learned that this was where the Yankee soldiers forded Shoal Creek after camping in Mulkey's Bottom for three days.

Later I was occasionally invited to swim at the college, and after summer term was over we townspeople could swim there for a small fee. Located behind Hanson and Tutwiler Hall, the large concrete pool was filled with clean, blue water that was always cold, even on hot summer days. It was surrounded by a tall green wood fence with only one gate to go in and out.

The pool had a regulation I disliked. Before you could swim, you had to put on a shower cap and take a shower. Even the boys had to. I hated those rubber caps, which always hurt my ears.

Since Alabama College was a girl's school, the boy's dressing room was quite small. As young inquisitive boys, we learned quickly that you could go outside and sneak a look through the knotholes into the girl's dressing room, and you could sometimes see girls with almost no clothes on, or occasionally no clothes on at all. How we managed not to get caught, I could never figure out.

Later the city started a recreation program, with Dad as the first director. Under his leadership, Big Springs was improved greatly. The City Council hired lifeguards to be on duty during certain hours to ensure the safety of the swimmers. The beauty of going to Big Springs was you didn't have to take a shower or wear a shower cap like you did at the college pool. The Alabama College bathing beauties we all admired had to wear a one-piece black bathing suit with a white cap, but at Big Springs the girls wore whatever they wished, including revealing two-piece suits.

We guys especially liked it when Martha Ann Cox, Laura Ann Hicks, and the other girls would swing on the rope tied to a sycamore tree and drop into the water. We always hoped that the impact of hitting the water would cause their tops to fall down. We watched and watched them and hoped and hoped, but every suit stayed in place. But that didn't keep us from wishing and watching.

Fishing always appealed strongly to me. The fishing was especially good below Mr. Dyer's dam, and many a time I grabbed a pole, dug some worms or night crawlers, or found crickets under the water meter coverings, and went to the creek bank. Getting the crickets proved difficult. The heavy steel water meter covers had to be pried up with a screw driver enough to

*Dolan Small, left, and Joe McGaughy waiting for a top to fall at Big Springs.*

get your fingers under the lid. I had many a mashed finger trying to get that cover off. Also you never knew what one might find in the meter hole. Occasionally you could find large black lizards, long-legged spiders, roly polies, hard-shelled thousand legs, black roaches, and other critters. We never found a snake, but we always feared we might.

The best place to fish, by far, was the Sewer Hole. It was called the Sewer Hole because it was at the point that Alabama College dumped its raw sewage into a small creek flowing into Shoal Creek. Only blacks fished there.

It was at the Sewer Hole that I met Montevallo's champion fisherman, a huge jet-black muscular fellow named O. C. That's all I ever knew him by—O. C. He rolled his own cigarettes and usually had one stuck in his lips. The thing that impressed me first was how beautiful his fishing poles were. They had a golden glow, as if they had been varnished. He kept all his gear in perfect order, and he was an excellent teacher. It seemed to me that everyone who encountered him respected him because of his knowledge and his ability to teach what he knew. He taught Montevallo boys, black and white, to find hellgrammites—or thousand legs, as we called them—by seining with screen wire in the shoals of the creek, though I had already been introduced to hellgrammites by Mister Pittman out at Montebrier. It took two people to catch hellgrammites. One person held the seine, which was two sticks to which the screen wire was attached. He stood downstream from the other fellow, who turned over rocks and kicked the bottom of the creek. The many-legged hellgrammites would wash downstream into the screen wire. Hellgrammites were not the only critters that would wash into the seine. Sometimes you would catch a small turtle, minnows of different colors, and all kinds of black water bugs. But it was the hellgrammites we were after. O. C. instructed us on how to put a hook in just the right place on the hellgrammite's back and set him a-wiggling. We'd make our cast, hoping he'd entice a prize big-mouth bass. Truth was, we never caught a prize fish, but we did catch our share of more modest fish.

O. C. also introduced me to the use of the quill, and he was the one who taught me to catch suckers. Suckers are very tricky to catch because, unlike the bream or bass who grab the bait and run with it, they bite the bait very gently. The cork or quill, I discovered, would not bob up and down very much, but just ease away and slightly go under water. O. C. said that just as the bobber went under I was to set the hook. I came to love to watch the quill slowly moving down as it tacked along the water, and I got very good at picking out just the moment to make my catch.

Ordinarily the fish we caught wound up on the supper table, crisply fried, and we would eat the fish tails and all, even crunching the little bones. But Dad and Mother would not hear of our eating the fish from the Sewer Hole. In fact, no white people I knew would eat fish caught in the sewer hole. They said they were nasty. But O. C. straightened me out on that. He said, "The fish always likes the Sewer Hole cause there is plenty of food, but lots of time fish gonna leave and swim upstream to the dam after they eat down here. So them dam fish the same as the Sewer Hole fish. It's funny how some people will eat fish caught up by the dam but won't eat these down here. They the same fish."

Any fish I caught in the Sewer Hole I gave to O. C., who had no reluctance in eating them. He said that, after all that stuff passed through the fish's body, it was clean as a whistle. I wasn't so sure about that and could never bring myself to eat a Sewer Hole fish.

O. C. didn't limit himself to the Sewer Hole. He also loved to fish on the discharge side of the gristmill. "Those fish got plenty to eat here so they lots of fish in here," he would say. Then he would add with a wink, "Course they ain't as hungry as they are in some other places." O. C. would sit and fish for hours, sometimes accompanied by Miss Lilly, an old black woman who was almost as crazy about fishing as O. C. Both had infinite patience.

At some point, my friends and I heard about redhorse fishing, and we were eager to try it. To get a redhorse fish you had to go to the Cahaba River, which was over near the coal mining towns of Marvel or Boothton. You didn't catch redhorse with a hook. You snared him with a lasso made of copper wire on a bamboo pole. You had to get to swift water where the bottom was covered with small rounded pebbles. Redhorse only came upstream in the river a few days each year to spawn, usually in the middle of May.

The male, which was called the horse, was the first to come upstream. He would find a place where the water was swift and the bottom was covered with pebbles. With his horny head he would dig out a "bed" maybe a foot and half or two feet in diameter, waiting for his mare to come upstream and lay her eggs in the bed. She would go just above the bed and thrash about, muddying the water. The clear Cahaba would become reddish or brown for two to three seconds as her eggs came out of her, washed downstream and settled into the bed. Immediately the horses would fight to see who would have the opportunity to deposit their sperm over the eggs. Typically, the horse who built the bed dominated the others. He was a mean dude who did everything to keep the young horses away from his home life.

Redhorse had been coming up the river hundreds of years. It is said that in the nineteenth century there would be thousands of redhorse beds covering as much as an acre. There were so many fish congregated there that people could wade out in the water, take their snares and lasso all the redhorses they wanted. People used to come in their wagons loaded with salt, take big treble hooks tied to a heavy piece of string, throw the big treble hook out over into the river, and just snag the redhorse. They were thrown onto the bank, where they were cleaned, salted down, and taken home to cook. Redhorse, which are somewhat like a mullet, have a lot of bones and are somewhat tricky to prepare. But once a person learned to prepare them properly, they were mighty good eating.

As a boy I always wanted to go redhorse fishing, but I never got to. When I was about forty-five, I went for the first time with a third-generation redhorse fisherman, Charles Griffin. Now I go every year for a day or two when they are running and Charles will take me. But things have changed. No longer is the redhorse plentiful. So I always free them after they are lassoed. I can't stand to see them bleed.

After World War II, fishing took on a new meaning for the boys on Shelby Street. Mr. DeSear's daughter Roberta married a veteran named Tony Elliott. When he visited, he would go down to the creek bearing great big casting rods and reels, and we were astounded at how far he could throw his lures, their triple hooks glistening in the sun. I saw him catch two fish at one time more than once. He taught us boys to bottom fish. We didn't have rods, but he taught us to tie two or three Golden Eagle claw hooks (which he introduced us to) on the line above the lead and drag the baited hooks on the bottom. We were very successful with this way of fishing, but none of us would rest before we had our own rods and reels. I was shining shoes at Dad's shop, and I would hardly part with a nickel I made before I got my own rig. We would announce proudly that we were bottom fishermen.

Tony Elliott became our hero, not only because he taught us to bottom fish, but because he would show us the M1 carbine he had brought back from the war. He was an excellent shot, and we would watch as he slipped in the clip and began firing at fish and snakes down at the creek. He killed quite a number. All of us boys now wanted us an M1 carbine, but he said we'd have to join the military to get one, and that was off in the future somewhere.

For now we had to get our excitement some other way, and we were presented with lots of excitement when the "viadock" (as we called the viaduct) was begun in the late 1930s. Jeter's Bottom had been at the end of Middle Street, but this viaduct was built through it to give those coming from Calera better access to Montevallo. Until then, Calera people had to ford Shoal Creek and bounce along the railroad tracks until they reached town. Or they could drive farther to Shelby Street, crossing the little red bridge into town. Dad called the viadock the Eighth Wonder of the World because it was said to be the first bridge in the United States to cross a creek, a road, a railroad track, and a footpath. Besides, it was an engineering wonder. It was curved in the middle and was banked, and it was the first bridge Dad knew of that was designed with rollers in the expansion joints, making it expand and contract with the changes in weather.

Ramps had to be built up to the bridge. The dirt came from Hooker Hill on the Calera side of the viadock, and it had to be hauled over the little red bridge and down Shelby Street when the Montevallo ramp was built. Finally, there was a thirty-foot sheer cliff of red clay where the dirt was mined for the ramps.

That cliff was irresistible to the Shelby Street boys. Several years after the viadock was completed, I began a mining project with my white friends Dudley Pendleton and Alonzo Clay Galloway (whom we called Buddy) and a black friend named Peanut. It is telling that I never inquired about Peanut's last name. The project was top-secret, and we covered over our entrance to the mine with brush every day after we finished our work.

There was a ledge about ten feet down the cliff, and that is where we began our excavation, eventually digging ten feet in. Dudley was our engineer. When dirt began to fall, he said we had to put up timbers, the way they did in the coal mines. Peanut was the smallest of the four, and we usually made him do the work in close places, which was most of the work. When we had finished our work for the day, we took great delight in seeing who could piss the farthest off the ledge. Eventually, we abandoned the project, as it became clear that the mine served no useful purpose.

The viadock opened up an industrial corridor between Montevallo and Calera. In the forties, Westinghouse was located along Highway 25 between the two towns, and other smaller industries were opened. The biggest effect it had on Shelby Street, however, was that now the coal trucks from Boothton, Marvel, Aldrich, and Dogwood traveled Middle Street instead.

After the viadock was built, what was left of Jeter's Bottom became the site of an annual carnival. The first ones were run by Lee's Carnival Company, and they were family oriented. There was no gambling or striptease. But there were fine rides—the tilt-a-whirl and Ferris wheel were my favorites. I loved the bright lights, the motion, and the calliope music resounding from the merry-go-round. People came in from all the outlying communities, and it was the most festive event of the year in Montevallo.

After a few years, Mr. Lee sold his carnival, and things got better, or worse, depending on your point of view. The new carnival had strippers and gambling games, and we boys thought it was wonderful. Joe McGaughy and Beaut Houlditch, so-named because he was so very ugly, would sneak off with me late at night and crawl up to look in the tents where the strippers were. It was there that I copped my first look at a non-maternal boob.

I can also remember grown men standing around outside the tent hoping to see the strippers. Ever so often a barker with a cheerleader's megaphone would come out and tell you all about what you could see inside. He would always be accompanied by a lady in a night robe, slightly opened, who on the barker's commands would quickly open and close the robe. Cheers, hoots, vigorous clapping, and whistling erupted from the crowd. The men would slap each other on the back and urge the barker to have the woman flash them again. Unfortunately, we never saw much of all this because the men would block our vision, but we eagerly waited for even a few seconds of visualizing bare skin. We never looked at the men because we neither wanted to see who they were nor let them see us.

My buddies and I pretty much kept on the move. As a kid, I was always an outside person. It took a lot to keep me still. But in the afternoons I would stay inside to listen to my favorite radio shows—*The Lone Ranger*, *The Shadow*, and *Superman*. We were very late getting television. Not only were televisions in almost every house on Highland Avenue—Ed Givhan even had a big outfit with TV, radio, and stereo all in one—but Frog Holler was even ablaze with TV when Dad got Tom Fancher to come and put us up an antenna and install the set. Lots of people didn't want to miss televised sporting events, but I was never much interested. I preferred *The Sixty-Four Thousand Dollar Question* and followed the Van Doren scandal with keen interest.

The first people in Montevallo who had a television were the Klotzmans. They got their console set with a round screen in the late 1940s. Harry became even more popular as his friends would come over and crowd around the small black and white screen. One day we were told that Joy Holcombe had the first color set in Montevallo, and my friends and I tore up to her house to see it. It was not worth the time because we discovered that all she had was a plastic covering to place over a black and white set. All you could see was bands of colors that did not go with what was on the screen. People had blue faces; trees were red. We laughed and laughed. "Gotcha," Joy said, laughing louder than we did.

When we got old enough to drive, we broadened our opportunities to have fun and to get in trouble. Of course, Ed Givhan had Papooshka, and we spent many hours cruising in it. Our favorite thing to do was to get a girl to ride around with us and have her sitting between us on the front seat. It quickly became clear to me that when you shifted the car from second to third, the gear shift lever would rest right down between her legs. I'd beg Ed to let me do the shifting even when he was driving, and sometimes he'd let me. But he once complained that I was doing way more shifting than necessary and that it was going to burn out his clutch trying to keep up with me.

One Halloween Ed and I were riding around in Papooshka. In the back seat were Harry Klotzman, Joe McGaughy, and Milton Jeter. We were all more interested in tricking than in treating, and the idea emerged, why I don't know, to pull down the mailbox of Dr. Mitchell, a dentist who lived out on the Siluria Road. We got us a rope and pulled that box right out of the ground, yipping and laughing and very proud of ourselves.

The next day at school we bragged to our friends about what we had done, and everybody thought it was real cool. But about mid-morning, as I was sitting in math class, a student worker brought the math teacher a note saying that Ed, Harry, Joe, Milton, and I were to report to the principal's office. "Oh, shit," I thought, as our gang of five headed down to Mr. Seymour Hurt's office. When we got there I was more alarmed because sitting next to Mr. Hurt was a strange gentleman wearing a black suit and a very stern look on his face. "Oh, Lord," I thought.

Mr. Hurt sat at his desk, and directly behind him on the wall was his famous paddle, a clear symbol of where the power lay in any meeting between him and the students in his school. He began speaking slowly, in a voice more serious than I had ever heard him use. "Gentlemen, I want to introduce you to Mr. Montclair. Mr. Montclair is an inspector for the U.S. Postal Service." The inspector flashed a badge at us, and five grim boys were impressed.

"Now gentlemen," Mr. Hurt continued, "don't start lying to me. I know what you did. It was witnessed and reported to me. You all five are guilty of vandalizing government property. You may not know it, but once a mailbox is put in the ground it becomes the property of the federal government. Did you know that?"

We all shook our heads, looked over at the investigator, who was eyeing us gravely, and waited for Mr. Hurt to lower the boom. "Gentlemen," he said, "Dr. Mitchell has agreed not to press charges if he has a new mailbox in the ground in thirty minutes. Is that understood?"

"Yes, sir," we shouted in chorus, all sweating like brass plated monkeys.

"Well, consider yourselves lucky. The investigator here tells me there are boys all across America who are incarcerated for lesser infractions. Just get on out of here and get that mailbox up as quick as you can."

We scrambled out of his office and out into the parking lot. We piled into Papooshka, pooled our money, and went down to Frost's Hardware and bought a new mailbox. We never learned who witnessed our crime, but we did learn that whoever it was went to Dad and told him. He, in turn, told Mr. Hurt. "Give them hell," he said. As it happened a salesman was coming through Montevallo High School that day, and Mr. Hurt thought of letting him pose as a postal inspector. We never learned where the badge came from.

One thing we learned through this episode was how fast word travels in a small town. By noon of the day after we pulled the prank it seemed that everyone in town knew about it.

Another caper that got us in trouble occurred when Joe and I found out how to make firecracker cannons out of one-inch galvanized pipe. We asked the electrician Mr. Parker to cut the lengths of pipe for us, which he did for some reason without asking any questions. We borrowed an electric drill from Western Auto, where I was working, put a hole in a one-inch galvanized pipe cap, and screwed it on to the threaded end of the pipe. We then placed a big red firecracker in the pipe, threading the fuse through the hole. Then we placed scraps of metals, nuts, bolts, rocks, acorns, or anything solid in the pipe. Finally, we packed a little bit of newspaper on top of that and placed the pipe on the ground aimed at a target. One of us would then hold the pipe in position with his foot, bend over and light the fuse and bam what a sound. Our projectiles would go half a city block.

At high school there was a teacher, Mrs. Ruth Frederick, who was generally regarded as a real bitch. She had a tin garage, which we thought made an excellent target to fire on. After making our attack, we all scattered, but unfortunately our stunt was witnessed. Mrs. Frederick called the police, and Harry Kendrick was the officer who called all our fathers. At the time, Ed's dad, Pete, was mayor, and Dad and Joe's father were on the City Council. Kendrick said that he believed he could calm Mrs. Frederick down if he convinced her that the boys were being disciplined by their fathers. Dad told Kendrick, "You can tell her that Mike, for one, will be punished."

Dad was rather pissed when he called me in. "Boy," he said, "sometimes you act like you haven't got the brains God gave a billy goat. You and those others are lucky you weren't put under the jail. And I'll tell you one thing, I wouldn't have gotten you out." I acted chastened for Dad's sake, though I felt rather confident that Dad would not have let me spend a night in the Montevallo jail. I felt lucky that Dad seemed to think a good talking to was sufficient punishment.

Our group got away with another Halloween prank, in many ways the worst we ever did. Dr. Sharp—he didn't have a doctorate, but was accorded the title in the same way that druggists were—was in the chemistry department. We didn't think much of him, though we were fond of Mrs. Sharp, who hosted those classy parties for her daughters and their friends. But that did not stop us from the revolting thing we did.

On Halloween night, about midnight, we got a sack of ashes from the pile behind the barbershop, and each of us, in ceremonial solemnity, pissed into the ashes. We drove over to campus and parked the car, then sauntered over to the Sharp house. They had one of those mail slots next to their front door that allows the mail to be sent directly into the house. We crept up on the porch and delivered our package, emptying the foul smelling ashes through the slot. We hoped very much that we would hear around town about the prank—especially how upset Dr. Sharp was. But Dr. Sharp demonstrated that he was properly named: silence was the best policy. We would have gloated to know that he had been greatly upset by our caper.

With the arrival of puberty, our games became more daring and sensuous. During my senior year I began to play what turned out to be my favorite, a game we called "pass it." If we were lucky, we got to play it with college girls. These girls were hungry for male companionship, and it didn't take a lot to lure them out. They were quite susceptible when music, an automobile, and alcohol were a part of the planned activities, and these elements could produce quite a sensuous night. If the weather was warm, we'd go out to Bulldog Bend on the Little Cahaba River, which was about ten miles south of Montevallo. We'd often have two or maybe three carloads of people, and we'd pull off the dirt road at some point, walk down to the river, and build a fire on the sandy shore. We'd take out our blankets and put them down, sometimes sitting and sometimes lying on them. Someone would get out our stash of liquor, which was usually vodka, as we thought no one could smell it on our breaths. At first we mixed the vodka with Seven-Up and felt quite sophisticated drinking our cocktails, but we quickly moved to straight vodka.

Often we would bring along a black guy named Goochie, who could play the blues on a guitar better than anyone we knew. We would give him a dollar or two and some vodka, and he would play while we began the game of "pass it." The first boy would pass the bottle to the girl next to him. She had to drink from it or do one of two things: kiss the boy next to her or pass him an article of her clothing. This pattern was followed, and some threw clothing into a pile, while others smooched with the boys next to them. This routine was followed until a body of semi-clothed bodies were writhing in passionate kisses on the blankets. Goochie's music supplied the exact right touch.

This bacchanalian evening would continue until someone realized we had to be back at the college before lock-up, which was ten during the week, eleven on the weekend. There was a great scramble to get the discarded clothes back on and the couples piled back into the cars for their return to the college. "Pass it" had given us an excuse for making out, and when mixed with a measure of vodka we thought life couldn't offer much more.

*Stinky Harris, Joe and Jack McGaughy, and dates enjoying "pass it." The sandy beach and seclusion of Bulldog Bend was the perfect place for this coming of age game.*

*Stinky Harris, left, Joe McGaughy, and friends.*
*The group's motto, "Whenever, if available."*

21

# Alcohol

Alcohol was a no-no in my house. I never saw even a sip of wine poured in the house. Because of Mother and Momma's hatred of the demon rum, all of Dad's drinking had to be done on the sly outside the house. He kept a bottle of moonshine whiskey in the coalhouse, and I felt sorry for him when he would head out there and take a pull off the bottle. Sassy and Pete Givhan on Highland Street had mixed drinks and served them to their friends. The Jeters had liquor in their house. So did Mrs. Rogan. And Dr. Acker kept a bottle of bonded whiskey in his office at all times. When I had visited Aunt Tootsie in New York, they always served Dad drinks, which he seemed to enjoy mightily. I was embarrassed that my parents ran a dry household on Shelby Street. Social drinking, I thought, was cool. But, because of my upbringing, I greatly disapproved of overdrinking.

All of us boys wanted to imbibe, but drinking had to be a clandestine affair. Occasionally Ed Givhan, another classmate named Kenneth (Hanky-Pooh) Rochester, and I would slip a drink of whiskey from the Givhans' stock, but usually we bought our alcohol from a black man named Moses, who lived out at New Camp, which was the colored camp at Aldrich. He sold pints of bonded whiskey and cans of beer, but we thought those cost too much, so we usually bought his home brew. It packed a lot of wallop for the money. Stinky Harris would drive us out there, usually at night, and one of us would go up on the porch of Moses's unpainted cabin and knock on the door. I was a little scared, but I'd go up pretty often. Moses would crack the door no more that eight inches and look you over. His face was backlit and eerie.

"What you want, boy?" he'd ask in a gruff voice.

"Three bottles of brew," I'd say.

"Boy, I'm of a good mind to tell Mr. Stanley what you doin'," he would say, but I knew that was an idle threat. He certainly did not want to miss a sale. He would then come out the door, and I'd follow him across the road to the spring. He'd lift the door to the spring box and pull out the Clorox bottles of cool home brew. "These are four bits a bottle," he'd say, as if we didn't know, and I'd hand him the crumpled dollar bill and the quarters.

The next step was open to debate. Where would we go to drink it? Usually we decided on the Montevallo Cemetery, though sometimes we'd go out to Ed Givhan's cabin on the creek. But we couldn't wait. We'd unscrew the lids off the bottles, and the yeasty home brew would foam out over the neck. The malty smell hung heavy in the car, and we would take gulps of the brew, relishing its strong, slightly rotten taste. And wonder of wonders, I was never made sick by the stuff nor did I ever have a hangover. That was not true for some of the others, and I quickly got a reputation for being a cool drinker.

Everyone knew that Moses sold whiskey and home brew, but there were no policemen in Aldrich to interfere with his business. Shelby County was dry, of course, but no one enforced the law. I heard the matter discussed in the barbershop, and someone said, "Oh, he's out there in nigger quarters. They ain't gonna pay no attention to him." I knew for a fact that he was selling liquor to prominent people in town.

Another opportunity to drink came because Pete Givhan's Coca-Cola bottling company served the Shelby County Gold Coast, a series of honkytonks on Highway 31 South and on Highway 280. Sammy Fiorella had a joint on the Shelby County side of the Cahaba River, and on the other side of the river was the First Stop. We'd send the oldest boy in to buy beer at these establishments, and often times they would return with a six pack. This area was known as lawless territory, and we were the beneficiaries of that status.

My drinking was always done with my buddies during high school, except for one occasion. Putnam Porter liked to have a drink, and when he took some of us boys to Birmingham to nice restaurants he'd always have wine with his meals. Once when we were seniors he took Joe, Kenneth, Milton, and me to Joe's Steak House, a private club in Birmingham, and he ordered all of us a Manhattan. I don't know if I had ever heard of a rite of passage, but in retrospect I know I was going through one at that time.

When I went off to Auburn for the summer quarter of 1952, my distaste for overdrinking evaporated. Since we didn't have a car, I hitched a ride down to Auburn with my high school classmate Bobby Hawkins, with whom I would be rooming. Bobby and I were assigned to Magnolia Hall, and we arrived on a Sunday afternoon in early June and immediately found our room, selected our beds, and unpacked our gear. We both had meal tickets and would take our meals in the Magnolia cafeteria, which we found quite convenient.

Among the other residents at Magnolia were some Korean War veterans who were naturally much older than Bobby and me and who impressed me immediately with their knowledge of the world. One of the things they taught me was that a man proved himself by how much beer he could drink, and I set out that summer to prove I was a man. The feeling of newly found freedom was profound. I had drunk a good bit of beer in Montevallo, but

*Opposite ends of the scale. On the left, Ed Givhan was the leader in the proper rules of social drinking. His philosophy, "No matter what time it is or what the drink is, try it, you might like it." On the right, Bobby Hawkins, the teetotaler. "Always say no whatever the occasion."*

acquiring it was always difficult. Here at Auburn it flowed freely. I quickly learned the places in town that would serve you regardless of age, and I frequented those establishments.

Bobby did not develop a taste for beer the way I did, and he was much more serious about his studies. It never occurred to me that there was a correlation between the two, but I quickly found out there was. I was majoring in engineering, and I flunked the two five-hour courses I had enrolled in. But I must say that I did have a wonderful time, joining the ROTC, playing in the band, seeking out the company of any and all girls available. At the end of the summer quarter, I was naturally sad to return home, where the beer was not so free-flowing and the girls not so plentiful.

Bobby and I went back for the fall quarter, and we found that we were really incompatible as roommates. His priority was education and mine was beer. A certain tension developed, and in the end I drew a line down the middle of the room indicating my side and his. We tolerated each other for that quarter, but after that we parted ways.

Taylor Davis, an older Montevallo friend, had joined Delta Tau Delta, and he asked me to go out for rush. I did and wound up pledging that fraternity. At my first pledge party, I met Brian Johnson, a Korean War veteran who became a lifelong friend. He and some other Delt brothers got me a blind date for a rush party with a beautiful Tri-Delt, and when we arrived the Tri-Delt and I made our way down some steep concrete steps to the basement, where the bar was located. A big red blinking light hung from the ceiling, and someone was playing 45 RPM records so loud that the room was pulsing with rock and roll. I especially remember "Blue Suede Shoes" and "Shake, Rattle, and Roll." But another sight really captured my attention. There next to the bar was the first keg of beer I ever saw. My mouth watered as I gazed on this sixteen-gallon stainless steel container from which people were drawing plastic cups of foamy golden brew. This was heaven, as far as I was concerned. The Tri-Delt and I filled our glasses and introduced ourselves to the others hovering near the keg. I slugged down my first beer, and I noticed that the Tri-Delt's was almost full still. So I drew another cup, drank it quickly, and drew another. Then I suggested we go upstairs where there was a live band playing.

*The older brothers of Delta Tau Delta, all eager to share their knowledge of alcohol with their young pledge brothers. Left to right, Grady Hicks, a Shelby Street man and brother of Laura Ann, Brian Johnson, my drinking mentor, and Johnny Litton, a Wilton resident experienced in all the ways of consuming the "nectar of the gods."*

I asked the Tri-Delt to dance. Sister had taught me well, and I could tell how impressed she was with my jitterbugging and bopping. I thought others were watching in admiration as well. I was getting a nice buzz from the beer, but I wanted more than a buzz so I excused myself and went down to the basement for another beer. As I left the room, I noticed that the Tri-Delt's glass was still almost full, and I was shocked to realize an indisputable fact: that silver keg downstairs had a greater hold on me than this gorgeous beauty did.

During rush, everything ran on a schedule, and at eleven o'clock we were to take our dates home. Brian Johnson eased up to me and said in a hushed voice, "Mike, my boy, I think you are in no condition to escort a young lady home. So I'll take her for you."

As my legs were not working the way they should, I agreed. Even though I had only recently met him, I trusted Brian implicitly.

"And one more thing," Brian said. "You need to sober up, and this is how to do it. Go down to the bar and tell the brother bartender to give you a jigger of straight whiskey. Drink it down in one gulp, and in two or three minutes you will be stone sober."

Brian was a man of honor, I thought, and he certainly knew way more about these things than I did, so I did exactly as he instructed. That is the last thing I remember. I woke up the next morning on the concrete steps leading to the basement. The beautiful Tri-Delt was never seen again, but Brian became my friend forever.

For the most part, I was moderate in my drinking after that. When I joined the Auburn Knights of Rhythm, we had gigs in Phenix City at places like the Hawaii Club and the Fox Club, and booze was flowing everywhere. But if I were going to play, I had to limit my intake.

I broke my rule about moderation when working one memorable time. One New Year's, some of my friends and I got a great job playing at the Tally Ho in Selma. I had had no experience with champagne before, and it was flowing that night. The owner brought a bottle over for the band to share, and we drank it right down. Very good stuff. At midnight he returned with a bottle for each member of the band, and I drank mine straight from the bottle. I was feeling no pain, but suddenly the nausea hit. I tried to ignore it, but there was no way. It was obvious to my fellow players that I was going to throw up, and as I abandoned my bass and ran toward the men's room, Brian Johnson, who had come along for the fun that night, called out to me, "If you feel something fuzzy coming up, swallow, because it's your asshole." I got to the commode just in time. It seemed I threw up everything except my asshole.

I felt awful on the trip back to Auburn. I began to have a hangover. Brian asked if I knew how to handle a hangover. When I said no, he told me I should drink a quart of water. When I got home, I did what he said and got drunk all over again.

I now knew that I could be done in by champagne, but I had no fears about martinis. The Auburn Honor Band traveled to Atlantic City and Washington, D.C. At the hotel bar in D.C., the band director and some others were having martinis. I was late arriving, so my buddies said I needed to order double martinis to catch up. I took their suggestion and quickly drank three doubles. We were to go over to the Capitol steps to hear the Marine Band, so we started the trek over. Halfway, I lost my ability to walk, so I had to sit down on the curb. My friend, Art Sclater, a Korean War Merchant Marine veteran, flagged down a taxi and sent me back to the hotel.

Sam Parrish, a friend who was skipping the Marine Band, was in the lobby, and when he saw me, he said, "You're drunk as a lord. Come on with me." We went up to his room, and Sam drew a tub of water and told me to get in it. I pulled off my shoes, then stepped fully clothed into the water. No sooner than I sat down did I begin puking, and as I passed out I could see the chunky vomit floating around on the water's surface. I woke up hours later, very embarrassed and greatly chastened. I went to my room

*The Auburn Honor Band practicing on the front lawn of Thomas Jefferson's Monticello a few days before my infamous martini episode in D.C. This image received national coverage and infuriated our university president. The trombone player at far right, Ben Gregory of Demopolis, was caught in an awkward pose and seems to have had a serious case of "crotch crickets."*

and showered and dressed. I was waiting on the others when they returned from the concert. I decided not to join them in the bar and hoped that Sam Parrish would keep his mouth shut.

A more alcoholically pleasant evening occurred in 1953 when the Auburn Honor Band went to Starkville to play at the half-time show. We were all thrilled when Auburn beat Mississippi State by one point. Mississippi State was pissed. Auburn fans even tore the goal post down, and the anger increased. To help bring Auburn fans under control, the API Honor Band began playing the National Anthem, but that did little good. We then played the alma mater, which seemed to do the trick. The field was cleared, and we broke ranks and ran to the bus. We had to pass the main male dorm, and we were pelted by beer cans and bottles. Finally on the bus, we were still alarmed as a mob of guys continued to throw stuff at the bus. The driver said that he was afraid to drive back by the dorm, so we took off in the opposite direction and parked away from the action. Some guys had stashed two cases of beer in the back of the bus, and we got it out and began to party. The cheerleaders were on the bus too, and some of us started dancing in the aisles with them. We continued drinking and dancing and singing as the bus began the trip back to Auburn. There was no restroom on board, and some of the girls did what I would have thought impossible: they peed in empty beer cans. This college life was quite educational, I thought.

22

# Girls

There comes a time when a boy gets his first whiff of girls and gasoline, and that is a mighty powerful combination. When it hit me, I was grossly unprepared for the effect. I had no real systematic understanding of the mechanics and science of sex, though I had heard quite a bit of talk. Dad had never given me the story, though I once heard Mama telling him that he needed to take me aside and instruct me, that I was coming to the age that I needed to know about the birds and bees. I was embarrassed hearing her telling him that, as I knew he was reluctant to approach me. So I remained in abject ignorance on the subject.

Dad did at least advise me about my appearance. When I was in my teens and was getting interested in girls, Dad told me I should start paying more attention to how I looked. He taught me to use Old Spice deodorant and how to shave. He wanted me to use the straight razor, as he did, but sharpening the razor on the leather strop, using the shaving brush and cup to work up the lather, and completing the shave itself was just too much for me, and I was happy when Sister presented me with a Ronson electric razor that her husband Bobby had cast off. On some occasions, however, Dad would shave me in his shop, and I was amazed at how gentle his hand was. Once finished, he would apply a Rose oil aftershave that smelled wonderful, but burned like hell, and I left that shop smelling like a rose garden. No other boy in Montevallo was as lucky as I was, I thought, and I felt ready to go out and slay me a few girls.

The first girl I really noticed for her beauty and sensuous qualities, Laura Ann Hicks, moved into the Craig House across the street when I was in junior high school. After Mrs. Craig sold the house, the house had gone down, down, down. The spectacular flowerbeds went to weeds, the rose garden was abandoned. There were no more petunias and pansies. Mother

*The girl across the street, Laura Ann Hicks, whom I silently longed for and whose friendship has lasted to this day. Photograph made in her front yard about 1951 with the Hartley house in the background.*

had wanted to buy the house, but Dad convinced her that it would be far too expensive to heat. No one else seemed to want such a big house, or, if they did, they couldn't afford it. And soldiers returning from World War II wanted small ranch houses with picket fences. Then along came Roy and Laura Hicks. Mrs. Hicks, an absolutely beautiful woman, ran the five and dime, and Mr. Hicks was a telegrapher for the railroad. Their daughter's name was Laura Ann. She was one year younger than me, and I noticed her immediately.

Now when I went to the Craig House, no butler met me at the door, and there was no longer the fine furniture and the nice refreshments. The place was strewn with toys and other clutter, but little did I mind. I could, finally, slide down the banisters to my heart's content.

Laura Ann was very good looking, and all the boys on Shelby Street fell for her. The boys on other streets fell for her too, but we Shelby Street boys were jealous of our turf and we fully intended to protect our progesterone. Laura Ann became good friends with Martha Ann and Mary Katherine Cox,

Jane Russell, and Beverly (Bird Legs) Doyle, who lived next door to me on Shelby Street. We were in our early teens, but already we played games like spin the bottle. And we all hoped it would land on Laura Ann. I was so smitten with her that even though I was a Methodist I joined the Royal Ambassadors at the First Baptist Church, which the Hickses belonged to.

We boys obsessively monitored the growth of breasts on Shelby Street, and Martha Ann Cox took the laurels here. I liked Martha Ann very much. She lived with her aunt, Mrs. Rogan, a powerhouse of a woman who ran a very tight ship, even telling her husband, according to rumor, when he could tend to personal toiletries. She took in Martha Ann, her sister Mary Katherine (whom we called Kacky), and their brother Charles, and she was damned sure that nothing untoward was going to happen to them. I spent a lot of the time on the phone with Martha

*Left: Martha Ann Cox, queen of Middle Street. Above: Mary Katherine "Kacky" Cox, Martha Ann's baby sister and head majorette of Vicious Tiger's band.*

Ann. Although Mrs. Rogan would make her get off the phone soon after she had answered it, we worked out a deal where I would go out on the porch with my trumpet and give a bugle call signal for Martha Ann to call me. In that way we could talk as long as we wanted because Mrs. Rogan was less likely to be aware of the call.

Just off Shelby Street lived a red-headed girl named Dolly Jo with whom the other girls wouldn't associate. They said she was fast, and we guys thought she was a tease. She lived next door to Joe and Jack McGaughy, and she especially liked to put on a show for them. Her shorts were so tight that her front and back clefts were clearly visible in outline. She was also fond of tying her blouse at her midriff, like Betty Grable, and showing off her navel. She could get us boys panting, but we were hardly more comfortable with her than with the other girls. We were not used to aggressive girls.

When I was in the tenth grade, I fell for a girl out in the Spring Creek community. That area produced some lovely girls. One was Joann "Demps" Butler, who stole the hearts of Dudley Pendleton, Pat Kelly, and Dolan Small, although Demps said she never dated any of them. But the one I fell for was Beverly Taft, a majorette. There was something about that majorette uniform that turned me on. When we traveled to out-of-town football games we would sit together, trying to be discreet with our petting. After all, we didn't want to be caught by Vicious Tiger or the parent chaperones, who watched us closely and were only too eager to go back and tell what they saw to the members of Beverly's church, Spring Creek Cumberland Presbyterian.

I didn't have a car when I was in the tenth grade and had to double-date with Jack "Shug" McGaughy, who had a thing for Ann Ingram and, as a fine athlete with a good academic record, was well-received by Ann's family. I was neither an athlete nor a scholar, and I do not think that Mr. Everette Taft would have received me like that. Actually, I never ventured past the front porch of her house, and I never got the idea that Beverly wanted me to. Nevertheless, our romance intensified until it sadly flamed out after six months or so.

The double dates were great fun while they lasted, and the four of us would go to eat in Calera or Jemison, always ending the evening at one of our favorite parking places. We did that, of course, to save on gas, which

*Three of the Montevallo Bulldog majorettes, left to right, Beverly Taft, Eleanor Mitchell, and Wanda Faye Richardson.*

was a serious matter when I was making four or five dollars a week at Western Auto.

Later my friend Dudley Pendleton acquired a wonderful Model A two-door coupe with a gear shift on the floor. It also had a twin exhaust system and a muffler we had taken from another car. He let Beverly and me double date with him, the two of us packed into the rumble seat, which suited me just fine. Dudley was especially fond of Pearl's Restaurant in Calera, and when we went there we would marvel at the waiter who hopped curbs and could take orders from eight or ten cars without writing a thing down.

One night we all were aching for some excitement, so we decided that we would raid a watermelon patch, and we knew just which one to raid. Mr. Sam Knowles had the best patch around, sitting high on a hill above his house near Spring Creek Presbyterian Church.

Dudley's mufflers on his four-cylinder, split-manifold, twin-exhaust Model-A rumbled loudly as we approached the melon field, but we were not much worried. On our minds was the pint of vodka we would pour into a melon, which after we had plugged it we would take to Big Springs to cool.

Once we got to the patch, we jumped from the car and began thumping melons, listening for the deep thud that meant the melon was good and ripe. We got a little greedy and tossed seven or eight melons in the trunk, even whooping and hollering a little as we got back in the car as Dudley eased off in low gear. As we moved down the bumpy hill, suddenly off in the distance there loomed before us in our car lights the formidable person of Mr. Sam Knowles, who was the big poo-bah on the Board of Elders at Spring Creek Presbyterian. Whatever he said was the law. On this night he was dressed in overalls with no shirt, holding a double-barreled shotgun across his chest. We saw him lift the gun and fire into the air, frightening Dudley so bad that he steered off the path to the left and crashed right into a small pine tree. The tree bent forward, lifting the front end of the Model A in the air, and we sat there with the front tires spinning uselessly. Mr. Sam approached us, gun and a flashlight in hand.

Shining the flashlight into the rumble seat, Mr. Sam first spoke loudly to Beverly. "I can't believe that a good girl like you would fall in with such sorry thieves as these. What would your parents think?" He indicated that he intended to tell them and to announce it in church the next Sunday. He was even going to ask the minister to take as his text the commandment about stealing.

Then Mr. Sam moved on to Dudley, a sneer coming to his lips. "And just what the dickens did you think you were doing?" Dudley didn't answer. "Stealing, that's what. You are no better than a common thief serving time over there in the Columbiana jail. And that's where you'll be if I bring charges."

We all sat there speechless. As Mr. Knowles talked he got more agitated, and suddenly something awful but very funny happened. Mr. Sam's upper dentures fell out of his mouth, and he quickly dropped to the ground to retrieve the plate. That gave us a chance for escape, and Dudley took it. He put the car in reverse and backed off the pine tree, then shifting into low and tearing away from the crime scene. We drove back into Montevallo, wondering what to do. We drove down to Big Springs, but none of us had an appetite for watermelon, even if it were laced with eighty-proof vodka. We decided that we had no choice but to go back out Spring Creek Road to take Beverly home, and we worried that Mr. Sam might be waiting for us or

*Dudley Pendleton and his four-cylinder, split manifold, twin-exhaust Model-A, the car that climbed a tree at Spring Creek.*

perhaps Beverly's parents would be if he had told them about the escapade. We could not believe that everything was quiet and dark in Spring Creek, and we felt extremely lucky. I guess Mr. Sam thought he had taught us a lesson, and he never said a word to any of our parents, although he knew them all.

Another girlfriend of mine was the daughter of the minister at the First Methodist Church, where we attended, and I must say that my interest in church increased greatly because of her. Every Sunday, Mother and Dad and I walked down past Rat Scott's Chevrolet place, by the Fire Department on the left side of Shelby Street, past the building supply and hardware store owned by a sober pair we called Smiley and Giggles Frost, and on past the historic Negro quarters, where the crippled man Charlie, who delivered mail at the college, and the Deviners lived. Then we were at the Methodist Church, where I was greatly influenced by persons like my Sunday School teacher Mrs. Maggie Kelly, the organist Charles Mahaffey, Dean Napier from the college, Charlotte Peterson, the elementary school principal, and Victor Talmadge Young, the band director. But as important as the church was for me for all these reasons, there came about an even more important one. I met my first true love there.

*Above: Jane Triplett, the preacher's daughter and my first true love. Right: Jane, right, and Frances Klotzman, my buddy Harry's sister, are fetchingly posed at a Methodist Church swim and picnic outing at Jane's uncle's lake property near Sylacauga.*

When Reverend Triplett came to us after the war, he brought with him a wife and one daughter. The daughter's name was Jane, and never had I seen anyone so appealing. She was a stunning redhead, and, as we boys tritely put it, she was built like a brick outhouse. She had the finest butt I had ever seen. One year younger than me, she played the clarinet and the piano. And she was chosen as a majorette. I was not the only one attracted to her, and a guy from Pea Ridge first claimed her. It took a while, but I managed to steal her away.

Jane and I had marvelous times, primarily because Reverend Triplett, whose name was Minor, and his wife Marie were, by the standards of that day, quite permissive. I liked Reverend Triplett immediately. He smoked, and I am sure he took a drink, too. But best of all, he understood young people. The first time Jane and I left on a Saturday night date in Dad's car, he pulled me aside and delivered Minor's Rule: "Do not park. Come home. The living room is yours and you'll not be disturbed. If I have to come into the living room, I'll give you a signal before entering."

I thought that was a great thing for a father to say to his daughter's date. But I must say that we were slightly inhibited in that living room. Because the church was not locked in those days, we took to going into the sanctuary in the afternoons to neck. With light filtering in from the back-lit rose window, we engaged in petting that took us as close to heaven as I had ever been.

I began to hang around the parsonage all the time, and I was invited to go with the family several times to an uncle's lake house in Sylacauga. I had gotten an Argus C-4 camera with my earnings from my job at Western Auto, and I began to take cheesecake pictures of Jane in her bathing suit or in shorts with bare midriff. Her parents made no objection, though the shots were quite sensual.

I continued to date Jane until after I went to college. But after she spent a year at Alabama College, she transferred to Huntingdon College in Montgomery, and that ended my first great romance.

The Methodist Church played an important role in my maturation. But church was more than that. In fact, I tended to accept without question most of what I was taught there right on up into high school. I did, however, have some nagging questions. Why, I wondered, were the pictures of the Devil so much more detailed than those of Jesus, and why did he look so much more interesting? And how did they know he looked like that? When I looked at depictions of Jesus, I would get to wondering how we knew he was not colored. I even asked Mrs. Kelly about that and she said not to worry, he was from Jerusalem, and there weren't any colored people over there. So that settled that.

Harder to settle in my mind was the question of how heaven and hell could hold all the succeeding generations. I just couldn't imagine how there could possibly be room. And what about meeting up with your loved ones after you died? Wasn't that going to be next to impossible, I asked Mrs. Kelly. She said that through God all things were possible, but I continued to worry about heaven giving out of room.

In the eleventh and twelfth grades, however, Ed Givhan and I began reading philosophy. We were especially enamored of Neitzsche's *Thus Spake Zarathustra*, and thereafter we began to question some of the teachings of the church. Heaven and Hell bothered me a great deal, and, with the help of Putnam Porter, I began to believe that heaven was not a physical place but peace of mind after the storms of life. That was a comforting thought to me. He also straightened me out on the Bible not literally being written by God and that it was the result of many writers. In Sunday School we were told God dictated it, but that gave rise to even more questions.

Conversations with Putnam and others moved me to a more liberal interpretation of church doctrine. At my most extreme, I decided that the mystery of the holy trinity was hogwash, and I said so openly. I was chastised by several members of the church, chiefly by my mother. But these theological issues did not weigh nearly so heavily on my mind as did Jane Triplett's pretty butt and the heated sessions in the First Methodist sanctuary.

23

# The Military

My first encounter with war was World War II, though I was just a boy during it. My patriotism was stoked by the war, and I was proud that Mahans had been involved in earlier wars. According to family records, we had at least one ancestor in the Revolutionary War, John Mahan.

In the War of 1812, John's sons—Edward, James, John, and Archimedes—who lived in northeast Tennessee, had three-month deployments to fight in the long-rifle army of Andrew Jackson at Fort Jackson, which was located near Wetumpka. Later, they were in the battle at New Orleans.

During the Civil War the Mahans were, for the most part, Unionists. They fought against secession, and they fought for reunification after the war. They had forges and blacksmith shops, and, despite their ultimate allegiances, they and their slaves worked in the Brierfield ironworks supporting the Confederacy's war efforts. But Jesse, my great-grandfather, who was elected to the Alabama Senate in 1868 and 1870, fought hard for the reunification of the Union.

During World War I, Dad's brother Cary and his sister Kate served their country in Europe. Cary was drafted and served in France. He earned no medals, he told no stories, but he returned with his life. Kate, who had been trained as a nurse at St. Vincent's Hospital, enlisted in the Army Nurses' Corps and served on the front lines in Europe.

Although I was a young boy, I have some clear memories of World War II. On December 7, 1941, as we were sitting around the dining table having lunch with music playing on the radio in the background, the program was interrupted by a news bulletin. "Be quiet, Mike," Dad said, "The president is speaking." That was when we heard about the bombing at Pearl Harbor. I was only seven years old, but I had heard my parents speak of Germany

*Dad's oldest brother, Cary Mahan, served in France during World War I as a railroad engineer and was one of many soldiers gassed by the Germans. After the war, he moved to Fairfield and worked for TCI.*

and Hitler, and I knew something really bad had happened. Maggie came running in with wide eyes, and I then was stunned to see tears coming from Dad's eyes. "We'll be declaring war soon," he said. "We just have to, and I guess I'll have to go." Draft age ended at thirty-five at that time, but he didn't think that would last long.

I did not want my Daddy to go to war. I had seen my Uncle Cary Mahan when we visited him in Fairfield. He had been gassed in World War I, and everybody knew that he had never been the same after that. In his later years, he forsook the active, wild life of the Mahan brothers, got religion, and became an old man. He worked in the railroad yards at TCI, but after work he sat in a chair and did nothing except read. I didn't want my Dad to turn into an Uncle Cary.

As Dad had predicted, draft age was bumped up to forty after Pearl Harbor, and it even went higher than that. Dad was drafted, but luckily he was able to do industrial work in support of the war rather than going overseas. Because he had been a railroad man, he was assigned to work on the trains at the powder plant in Childersburg. For four years, he commuted on Wyman Brown's buses along with many others, but he was always home on the weekends cutting hair. And when his shift permitted, he cut during the week. Mother kept the beauty shop open, and Dad hired a young guy

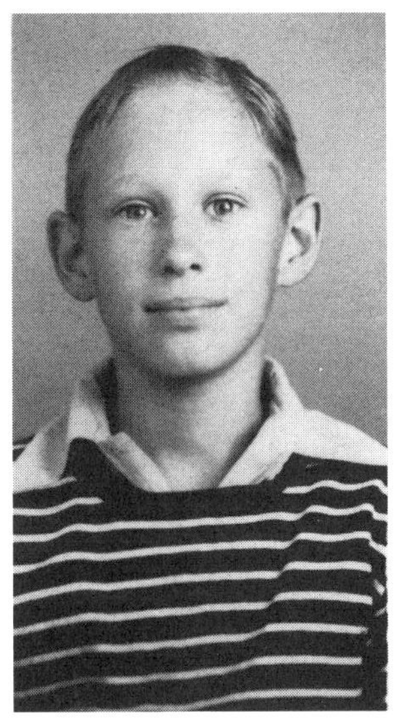

*Dolan Small was small in stature but large in creativity and actions and led the Shelby Street and Frog Holler gang into many adventures.*

to fill in for him. Working at Childersburg had one big plus. Every week Dad brought home a $25 war bond, which he promptly put in Merchants and Planters Bank. At school, I did my part by purchasing ten-cent red stamps to support the war.

I think I felt the effects of the war primarily by having to postpone getting a bicycle and having to do without candy and other sweets. But once during the war I had all the sweets I wanted. Dolan Small came to town during the war when his dad bought the ice plant. And wonder of wonders, though they had lots of money, they decided to live near me in Frog Holler. They could have easily lived on Highland Avenue.

Dolan was a little guy, but he was a big man in Frog Holler. He had a shiny Western Flyer bicycle, and he always had money in his pocket. He was a high roller. Near the end of the war he appeared at my door with a whole box of Hershey bars. Joe McGaughy and Milton Jeter were with me, and our eyes widened as we looked at the box of candy. We hadn't seen any Hersheys in months. We carried them over to the Presbyterian Church and, lying on the terrace, we stuffed ourselves—six Hershey bars apiece. I have never felt so affluent in my life, and part of my joy was to know that even the boys on Highland Avenue didn't have a whole box of Hershey bars.

My awareness of the war was also heightened every day when we hoisted the flag out in front of the elementary school, which was housed in the Boyd Building on Oak Street. We were a little band of patriots, and we performed our duties very solemnly. Eventually, the flag became rotten and tattered, and we had the crematory ceremony prescribed by the government. Charlotte Peterson, the principal, was in charge, and all the children performed. It was an impressive and proper tribute.

So we were keenly interested in the war, and we were always impressed by any soldier who returned. Mr. W. L. Wooley came back from his tour of duty with an amazing souvenir—an ear he had sliced off a Jap. Now, as twelve-year-old boys, we hated Japs with a passion, and this pleased us no end. Mr. Wooley hung out on Main Street in front of Jeter's Mercantile, and several times a day you could see him reach in his pocket and pull out that ear, a war hero standing in front of an awe-struck boy.

Cousin Leslie Hubbard joined the Navy during World War II. He had a medical degree from Hillman Medical School in Birmingham, and he served on a destroyer as a physician. And Bobby Lacey, son of Aunt Kate's husband by his first wife, was very young when he enlisted, serving in an armored division of the army. I knew Bobby, and I recall being at Aunt Kate's house when they would receive letters from him explaining what was happening on the front. Young and impressionable, I was set on fire by the high romanticism of his letters. I wanted to be in those tanks racing across Europe. Bobby also fought in Korea, where he was killed in 1950.

My sense of the war was most heightened because my Aunt Ween was married to an officer, Colonel William B. Morrell, whom we called Bill. Bill, a dashing young Boston native, came to Birmingham to play for the Birmingham Barons, a farm team for the Boston Red Sox. He spoke with an aristocratic Boston accent, speaking of cars as "cahs" and tomatoes as "tomahtoes." Ween was a beautiful, sensuous woman, and she fell for William and he fell for her. The family was not so sure it was a good match. After all, he was from up north.

Bill had been in a reserve unit in WWI, after which he remained in the reserves. He played two years for the Birmingham Barons, then went up to the big leagues, pitching for Boston for one year. But he threw his arm out and his ball playing ended. He returned to Birmingham for a while, then became a coach in the Georgia-Florida League, a class D organization that fielded small town baseball teams in these two states. The teams were supported by local industry, particularly cotton mills, paying the players (most of whom had full-time jobs in addition to playing ball) as well as the management. He was first in Valdosta, and later he joined a team in Cordele. In time, he and some others bought the Cordele team.

By 1939 there were rumblings of war in Europe. By 1940, Hitler had invaded Poland, France had fallen, and Rommel had invaded Africa. In 1942, Bill went to Africa as a second lieutenant, experiencing combat under General Patton. Subsequently, he went to Sicily and Italy and was involved in the campaigns there. He was moved from the regular army to the Army Air Corps and went to France, where he fought in Patton's operation. When the war ended, he had made the rank of Captain.

***Uncle Bill Morrell, far left, and me with a teammate a few years before World War II while he was playing in the minor leagues for Panama City, Florida.***

Bill was next assigned to the post-war trials at Nuremberg. While there, he developed a heart condition and was in the hospital for a good while. Ween went to Germany to take care of him. She was said to be the first army wife allowed to come over after the war.

Because Bill was so polished and well-educated and because Ween, though a little girl from Carbon Hill, was so socially adept, they were set up as good will ambassadors in a large palace with a heavy iron fence around it (said to have belonged to Goering), entertaining dignitaries who came in for the trials at Nuremberg. The palace was full of fine furniture, and massive oil paintings hung on the walls. Bill and Ween were driven around Nuremberg in a limousine that had been owned by the Nazi higher-ups who had lived in the house. Assigned to them was a couple called Mom and Pop, who had been servants to Goering.

Bill and Ween had chamber music every Sunday afternoon and various other entertainments. The guest book I now possess contains notes from many guests. Bill and Ween remained there about a year.

After the war, Bill remained in the Army Reserve until he retired as a colonel in the 1960s. We were told that he was the oldest reserve officer in the military. Moving back to Birmingham to be near Ween's family, they were full of stories of their experiences, and we all delighted in hearing them. One story had to do with their packing up and leaving Nuremberg. Ween and Bill always wanted to have fine things—silver, furniture, art—and it pained Ween especially that they were allowed to bring only one container back to the states. There was so much silver and china and other fine things that they decided, against army regulations, to pack up several barrels. As they transported their riches to the ship in a deuce-and-a-half truck, they were stopped at the French border and were found to have more containers than allowed. The inspectors removed the barrels from the truck and rolled them down the hill. Only one was rescued, and some of its contents had been destroyed. Some silver pieces embossed with the swastika were saved. They were marked with the words, *Das Gasthaus*, which Ween says was a small house behind the palace they had occupied. Ween always blamed Bill for having lost all the treasure.

Returning to the U.S., they were stationed in Baton Rouge. From there they would come to Birmingham to visit Momma, always driving down to Montevallo to see us. One summer they took me in their 1941 Chevrolet four-door sedan back to Baton Rouge for a few weeks' visit. Bill always meticulously cleaned and maintained his Chevrolets, which he always bought from Edwards Chevrolet, a company he much admired. He prided himself as being an excellent driver. As we drove to Baton Rouge in the deep of night, he would explain to me how best to take a curve: slow down as you approached it and accelerate as you went around the curve. I was impressed, but Ween, who I thought was quite often verbally abusive of Bill, was not so impressed. She would complain about his speed, especially on the curves. He never raised his voice back to her, at least when I was around.

Ween entertained the other officers' wives on Sunday afternoon at the Officers Club, and once I went there with her. She often played bingo while there, and she loved the slot machines too. She gave me a roll of nickels so I could play the one-armed bandits myself. I didn't win anything that day, nor have I since.

Another passion of Ween's was cats, and she had them throughout her life, even though it was not always easy to transport them when they moved around from place to place in the military. But she even had them in Nuremberg. Once she asked us to keep a cat for her when they were transferred, and we agreed, but the cat ran away, causing quite a crisis in the family.

Ween and Bill had no children—no one knew why. The family seemed to think it was Bill's fault. I was, in some ways, like an adopted son—a favorite nephew.

After their time in Baton Rouge, they went to England, where he was an instructor for the Strategic Air Command. There Ween bought linens, woolens, and fine clothes, and she looked like a fashion plate when they returned to Birmingham. They bought a small house in what is now the Hoover area. During the latter part of the war, Ween had lived in Berkely Apartments on Highland Avenue, not far from Five Points South, and her great aim was to open a tea house in an exclusive district of Five Points. But she never realized it.

In retirement, Bill took to writing letters to coaches, giving advice on how to improve their teams. He wrote many letters to coaches in the Big Leagues, and he even wrote some to Bear Bryant.

All told, Ween and Bill were a wonderful couple, and they gave me many experiences I wouldn't have had without them.

I was keenly aware of the war in one other way. After the war, when soldiers were disinterred from their battlefield graves at the request of their families, I became thoroughly sensitive to the cost of the war. There were so many funerals the government could not handle them, and the local American Legion had to step in. They lined up Teddy Ziolkowski or Johnny Ziolkowski and me to play echoing bugles for the ceremonies. Wearing starched khaki pants and neat white shirts, one of us would go up on the hill and the other would stay near the grave. Slowly and solemnly, we played taps. We must have performed at twenty or twenty-five of these ceremonies at Montevallo Cemetery and at little churches in the surrounding communities. Once we even went to Calera. We also played for veterans who died after returning from the war.

One of those veterans was Deacon Gregg, who had been a big football idol. He owned a service station and tire store in town and was a very popular figure. He was tragically killed in an automobile accident, and it seemed the whole town turned out for his funeral. It was quite an impressive ceremony. There were seven guys with rifles who did a twenty-one gun salute. Johnny Z and I were the buglers, and we stood next to the rifle squad. We watched the flag from the coffin being carefully folded and presented to the weeping widow.

Johnny Z and I took our places to play taps, with me standing at the foot of the casket and Johnny stationed on a nearby hill. For the first time ever at one of these ceremonies, I felt overcome with emotion. I had known

*Johnny Ziolkowski, far right, my bugle playing partner, with Dudley Pendleton and Emily Vest (soon to be Pendleton) at the Museum of Natural History in Chicago.*

Deacon when I worked at the Gulf Station and at Western Auto. He was just down the street. As I pulled the bugle up, I made the mistake of looking over at Deacon's beautiful wife, who had broken down in tears. I blew on the bugle but nothing came out. I tried again, summoning all the grit I could, and I blew for all I was worth. The sound came from the bugle, and Johnny echoed it. We got through it, though it wasn't as good as it should have been. I went directly home and told my mother that I couldn't play at any more funerals. "I understand," she said, and I loved her for understanding. And I never did play for another military funeral.

I never served in the military. Dad had not had to fight in World War II, nor had any of the other Shelby Street dads, so all and all the war seemed rather distant to me. My cousin Philip Lacey served in Korea, and my cousin John Mahan went to Annapolis and was full-time military for life. But somehow none of this registered very clearly with me at the time. I saw one-star and two-star banners hanging in people's windows and understood what it meant, but I gave it little thought. My friend Gene Baldwin went to Gordon Military Academy in Georgia, and some guys in town went to Marion Military Institute; I suppose the war must have been less abstract for them. I knew, of course, that I would be required to register for the draft when I was eighteen, but even that caused me very little worry.

On June 21, 1952, I drove to the county seat in Columbiana in Dad's 1947 Chevrolet and presented myself to the draft board personnel. I signed my name to an official document and was told because of my age and apparent good health I would receive my 1-A draft card soon. But still the chance of being involved in war seemed distant to me.

When I went to Auburn later in 1952, the chance of being drafted became a much greater possibility. It seemed advisable to join the ROTC program, so I joined the Air Force ROTC, donning a blue uniform and playing in the ROTC band. In my military classes I learned a lot of basic military terminology and procedures, and of course I learned to march, which was quite easy because of my experience in marching bands. I also began to hear much more about what was going on in Korea, and the idea that I might be sent there became much more real. That my friend Gene Baldwin was already in the Air Force and flying jets also made the war seem less abstract.

*Learning to protect the country in the Auburn Air Force ROTC.*

In my junior year at Auburn, the Korean conflict ceased, and the draft board announced that you could be deferred if you were in the upper twenty percent of your college class. Since I fit this new ruling, I dropped out of ROTC. After graduating in the summer of 1956, I notified the draft board I intended to further my education, but I felt sure that they would call me if they needed me.

In my last year at Auburn I began dating Carol Clark and fell in love. We hoped to get married as soon as I could get myself set up financially. The music education and performance degree I had just received didn't offer many prospects for making a living sufficient for starting a family.

In the spring of my senior year, the Cincinnati Symphony Orchestra came to Auburn for a concert. My string bass teacher, Mr. Edward Glyde, arranged for me to audition with the symphony's principal bass player, who taught at the Cincinnati Conservatory of Music. He liked what he heard and offered me a fellowship at the conservatory as well as a job in a church orchestra. I accepted, and before my marriage I made the two-day trip to the Cincinnati Conservatory of Music with the possibility of enrolling for one or two years, but the trip revealed that that was not a good avenue for a career. I found there were about forty bass players, all as good as I was, and I couldn't imagine enough orchestras in America to hire all of them. My future as a bassist looking so dim, I loaded my bass in my 1940 Plymouth and after less than twenty-four hours in Cincinnati, I was headed home to

Alabama. I decided to go back to school at Alabama College in Montevallo and study biology and chemistry. I took a job working for my friend Ralph Sears in the public relations office. I now felt I could afford to get married, and I did. I reported my new status to the draft board and was told that they could still draft me—married or unmarried, student or non-student.

Shortly after our marriage, Carol got pregnant. About the same time we discovered this, I got a 1-A draft notice to report to Montgomery and get examined. I thought to myself that this was it, but I happily discovered that there was a new loophole in the draft law. If you were drafted and a volunteer presented himself to the draft board, he could take your place if the draft board approved. I was in Montgomery ready to go when I learned that there was a volunteer in Shelby County, and I was set free. I immediately packed up and hitchhiked home. Sometimes I look back on the event and wonder if my Dad's political influence in Shelby County government had any connection with the sequence of events that were so much in my favor.

I never really tried hard to "beat the draft," as it was termed by those who didn't have to go. I just assumed that Uncle Sam did not need my services. And that was quite all right with me.

*With my dreams of an orchestral life dashed, I took a job with the Alabama College Public Relations Department as a photographer. My most memorable photograph, picked up by the national wire services and printed in newspapers across the country, was of outgoing college president, Dr. Franz Lund, right, and Dr. Howard Phillips, the incoming president, seemingly sharing a rather intimate moment.*

24

# Masonry

Shortly after World War II ended, a great change came into our lives. Dad became a Mason, as his forebears had been for 150 years. His great-grandfather Edward and his grandfather Jesse had both sat in the east as masters of their lodges, and Jesse and Dad's photographs still hang at Central Lodge 70 in Montevallo. For some reason, Dad waited until middle age to join, but his life was never the same afterwards. As a young man, Dad had been a rounder, and church for him never mattered a great deal, although he attended to please my mother. Masonry became the center of his spiritual life. Perhaps it was the pageantry and the archaic language that attracted him at first, but its intrinsic teachings rapidly took hold in him, and he seemed to gain greater reverence for life after joining the order.

Dad took on an almost missionary spirit about Masonry, though the Masons never actively set out to recruit members. At our house he began to tutor those who were interested in becoming Masons, and he traveled around to lodges in Boothton, Siluria, Randolph, Calera, and even to the state headquarters in Montgomery as a lecturer. The Montevallo lodge purchased a slide projector for him to use in what were primitive Power Point presentations. That projector is in the lodge to this day.

Nothing pleased Dad more than to bring a Mason up through the ranks, and he spent much of his off-time on Masonic activities. There is no telling how much time he devoted to committing the lectures to memory. Masonic publications recorded the prescribed rituals and teachings, but the transfer of this information was largely oral, as it had been since the time of King Solomon. I could hear him in the living room going over and over the lectures until he had them firmly in his mind. There were quite a number of these lectures, each taking thirty to forty minutes to deliver, so it was no light matter to take on this job.

To some extent Masonry also became an important component of his social life. This fraternity of Masons—made up of prominent educators, including presidents at Alabama College, and successful businessmen—met monthly, and Dad valued his association with the other Masons. Especially close to him were Reggie Lawley and Mr. John Cunningham because they, like him, were interested in teaching and lecturing.

Wherever Dad traveled, he sought out Masonic lodges and attended meetings. Once I was with him when we visited Tootsie in Poughkeepsie, New York, and it was vital for him to go to a lodge meeting there. He loved the consistency of Masonic teaching worldwide, and he always knew he would find brothers wherever he went.

But Masonry was in some ways rather disruptive to our family. Mother clearly was not altogether happy with how obsessed he had become and the time he spent with it, but I think she made her peace with it, knowing that it was preferable to a lot of other things he could have become obsessed with. Dad wanted Mother to join the Eastern Star, but she never wanted to learn the lessons and move up through the ranks. In fact, Dad was far more interested in the Eastern Star than she was, and I think it disappointed him that it never became an important part of her life.

Dad's interest in Masonry was disruptive to me because when he had a student locked in the living room I was unable to listen to the radio, and though the telephone was in the hall I was not allowed to use it, as it could be heard in the living room. For a boy in his early teens, this seemed unfair. If I complained, he would only shake his head and say, "Son, you just don't understand. I hope you will some day."

It would be a few years before I got serious about the Masons. I had heard here and there that you couldn't get a Mason drunk enough to reveal Masonic secrets, and that always puzzled me. Later, when I learned that he would have his tongue pulled out by the roots if he did so, that idea suddenly made a great deal of sense to me. I also knew that the Masons had a secret handshake, and when I was working in the barbershop I observed Dad practicing it. In fact, he shook everyone's hand that way, but non-Masons were unaware that he was using this secret grip. I did on occasion notice that a stranger would come to the shop, and when Dad shook his hand a look of recognition would come over his face and they would talk generally about Masonic matters.

As I progressed through my teens, I found myself a bit more curious about the Masons, particularly their secrecy. And I began to want one of those rings with the square and compass on it. Dad seemed to be aware of this growing interest, which pleased him to no end, and when I finished college and returned to Montevallo he asked if I would like to begin the process of becoming a Mason. I said yes, and I joined the local lodge at the lowest order, pledging my allegiance to the Masonic order and beginning my preparation to move up through the ranks. For some weeks Dad and I regularly went into the living room and had our lessons. At first I was dismayed at how much I was expected to memorize, but as time moved along it became more and more natural and easier. Finally, he thought I was ready to climb the stairs to the lodge, up above Times Printing, to be inducted. I had seen the sign above the entrance door for years, as I always gazed up to the second floor wondering what in the world was going on in secret up there.

Although I knew pretty much what to expect, I was a little worried. After all, I had been kidded a number of times by the Masons I knew about whether I was ready to "ride the goat." No amount of pleading for an explanation would avail, so I walked down the street preoccupied with an image of myself astride a demonic goat doing its best to throw me. I was twenty-six at the time, but I felt like an adolescent. I was a little shocked to find myself trembling a bit as we climbed the stairs. A man Dad said was a *tyler* stood guard at the door, making sure no unauthorized people entered the lodge, but because I was with Dad I was able to enter without being quizzed. But almost immediately one of the officers of the lodge came over and whispered a question in my ear to test my knowledge of the Masonic order, and I was relieved that Dad had taught me so well that I knew the answer. But I was so nervous I mispronounced the word I had to give in reply. The officer snickered slightly, but didn't turn me back.

Dad then motioned to the wall where the Masonic white leather aprons were hanging. He took his down and then handed me mine quite solemnly, showing me how it was to be put on properly. I did just as he said, and then we were dressed to enter the lodge. The lights were relatively weak, and there were no windows in the room. In fact, Dad worried about the room being a fire hazard, and the order eventually installed a fire escape that remains on the building today. On the west end of the room I saw two large columns. They looked immense to me then but have shrunk considerably over the years. I gazed at the Masonic brethren, many of whom I knew well, sitting on the old red-leather theater seats along each wall. In the center of the room was an altar surrounded by three candelabras higher than the altar. On the raised altar, which was really a small white table with a cabinet under it, rested a large black book, which I later learned to be the lodge's Bible. On a raised platform to the side, I especially noted the brother who sat in the east, the big honcho for the meeting. He sat magisterially on a large pulpit chair upholstered in red. Those sitting in the west and south also sat in similar chairs on raised platforms. I was struck by the solemnity of the group. The brothers were not demonstrative at all. They did not take you by the hand, hug you, or greet you. A couple seemed to smirk a bit, and I immediately thought of the goat. When would it appear?

I was then given my initiation robes and was ordered to take off my regular clothes and put them on. The ritual ceremony was conducted by various members from different stations in the lodge. When the Worthy Master quizzed me orally, I answered every question correctly. In fact, it all went like clockwork. Dad had prepared me well, and when I glanced at him I could see a pride on his face that gave me a very warm feeling.

The ritual was concluded with my expressing my faith in a prayer, which could be done silently or aloud. Dad insisted that I do it out loud, so I presented the Mason's prayer, after which I was welcomed into the brotherhood. All of my anxiety melted, and I was elated as I demonstrated the Masonic grip when I shook the hands of my new brothers.

I learned quickly that the brotherhood of the order was treasured by Masons above all things. I learned, however, that black Masons had their own lodges, and much later I learned that Catholics were not allowed in the order, as they were not free agents but were dictated to by the Pope. Besides, the Catholics had their own secret order, the Knights of Columbus.

Although respect for fellow man was a high ideal of the Masons, respect for one's brother Mason was the most important aspect of that ideal. Masons were taught not to commit adultery, but the most significant breach of the prohibition was committing adultery with a fellow Mason's wife or female relative. No one seemed to think it at all strange that the emphasis fell that way.

Dad held high hopes that I would proceed quickly through the various stages of Masonry, but I never really applied myself the way he did, nor, for all of its value, did it take as central a place in my life.

In 1987, Dad was becoming a little feeble, and he took a fall and broke his collarbone. He was put in the Shelby County Hospital in Alabaster, where he remained until his death. The very last night of his life I stayed in the room with him, and I listened as he mumbled the Masonic lectures he had learned in that locked living room on Shelby Street all those years ago. I could make out familiar words at times, and I felt tears welling up in my eyes. His last words were not for family, but the words of a brotherhood that had defined his life.

## 25

# My First Jobs

From when I was a small boy, I wanted the feeling of independence that having money jingling in your pockets gives you. I earned a little doing yard work for a few people around town, but my first real job was shining shoes at my dad's shop. Dad said if I would work for him shining shoes on Friday after school and all day Saturday, he would give me a nickel for each shine, which was half of the cost. He said I could keep all the tips, but even with that I couldn't make over a dollar and a half a day—and that was a good day. So when I was thirteen, I went over to Mr. Eddie Mahaffey, who owned the Gulf Service Station on Main Street, and asked him for a job. Mr. Eddie didn't hesitate. He just said okay, and called out, "Hey, Taft, get over here. I want you to teach Mike everything you know about this station."

Taft Hill, a tall black man who worked for Mr. Eddie, was always Mr. Taft to me. He had no fingers on his right hand, just a thumb, but that didn't keep him from performing any job around the station. In fact, it didn't take me long to realize that, although Mr. Eddie was supposed to be in charge, it was Mr. Taft who kept everything going. Mr. Eddie mainly gave orders and occasionally pumped a little gas, but Mr. Taft could do anything. It seemed a shame, but I never saw him get much credit. Although Mr. Eddie treated Mr. Taft respectfully and often deferred to his judgment, he never complimented him on a job well done or gave him any credit for the success of the station. I sort of thought Mr. Eddie acted like a colonel who has a buck private doing the real work. And Mr. Taft might have made five dollars a day, probably less.

The station, which was built almost up to the sidewalk, was small, with one big room and a couple of small rooms on the back and side. The gas pumps were on city property between the sidewalk and the street, and customers could gas up sitting in the street or in the space next to the station that included the sidewalk. Oftentimes, pedestrians would walk around cars being serviced, but no one seemed to think that was strange.

There were separate restrooms inside the building for white women and white men, but there was only one colored restroom out behind the building. One of my jobs was cleaning the white restrooms, but Mr. Taft had to handle the colored facilities.

There was also a Coca-Cola drink box, where six-and-a-half-ounce bottles sat vertically in cold water. As the box lacked an electrical cooling component, the water was cooled with blocks of ice delivered daily to the station by Mr. J. A. Brown's delivery man from the icehouse across the little red bridge on Shelby Street and later by an employee of Dolan Small's dad.

One of my routine jobs was to drain the old water from the box, then go out to a little room in the back and get out wooden cases of twenty-four bottles to restock the drink box. After the ice had been delivered, I would chip it up with an ice pick. Mr. Eddie told me that I needed to make the pieces small enough to fit between the bottles, but not a bit smaller, as he didn't want the ice to melt too quickly. Just about everyone who traded with Mr. Eddie bought a nickel sweet drink—Cokes, Grapicos, Orange Crushes, root beers, and even bottles of chocolate milk.

Mr. Eddie's wife, Miss Mary Lee, sat all day on a stool behind the only showcase, where she kept cigarettes, bags of tobacco and cigarette papers for those who rolled their own, cigars, chewing tobacco, and snuff. She also had penny boxes of matches as well as inner tubes and tire patches, valve stems, and valve stem covers. When it came to tobacco, Miss Mary Lee must have been her own best customer, as you seldom ever saw her that she didn't have a cigarette hanging out of her mouth. Her job was to collect the money and place it in the huge cash register, which was an antique even then. She must have opened that register a thousand times a day. I always called her Miss Mary Lee, but Mr. Taft always referred to her as Miss Haffey.

In those days there was no such thing as a credit card, but in addition to cash Miss Mary Lee would accept checks drawn on Merchants and Planters Bank. The only credit I remember them extending was to some of Mr. Eddie's friends or to Alabama Power Company. Each of these accounts had

*Miss Mary Lee and Mr. Eddie Mahaffey, the couple who gave me my first jobs, instilled a work ethic, and helped inspire my music career. They were both big-band musicians and played with the Bama Skippers.*

their own little book about 3 x 6 inches in size with carbon paper so the customer always could have a receipt. These little books were very important because they were the only records of accounts payable. Occasionally Miss Mary Lee would ask someone to sign the book after a purchase, but generally the credit system was based on trust. Most folks settled up their accounts on Friday, but some had monthly accounts. Miss Mary Lee watched these charge accounts like a hawk, and if they ran on too long she would tell Mr. Eddie he had to call somebody to remind them a payment was due. But overall there was no problem. After all, Mr. Eddie knew all these people very well. He knew where they lived, and he knew their reputations.

At Mr. Eddie's service station, the work was long and hard, and you got very dirty. I worked right alongside Mr. Taft, and by lunch my hands were as black as his. There was no OSHA in those days, and personal safely was left up to workers for the most part. And in that regard, Mr. Taft really took me under his wing. He not only taught me what I needed to know; he looked out for me. One day I went home and told Dad that Mr. Taft

Hill was safety officer, production manager, and quality control man at the service station. And it was really true.

On the left side of the building there was a grease pit with a sharply raked ramp on which cars and trucks would be driven over the pit. Mr. Taft and I could get under the vehicle, take a wrench and remove the plug out of the oil pan, drain out the old engine oil, replace the plug, and put new oil in the engine. The oil we drained was black and strong-smelling as it drained into a small barrel on the floor of the grease pit. Few people worried about the environment in those days, so there was no recycling. The used oil was dumped in a big hole out behind the station. We also checked and changed the oil in the transmissions, which were manual and usually under the front seats.

In the grease pit there was a long red hose from the air compressor out behind the station. On the end of the heavy stiff hose was a silver Alemite gun, as Mr. Taft called it. On its barrel end was a little opening that you pushed over the grease fittings under the car, near the wheels, brakes, springs, steering gear, and so forth. You would pull the trigger and the air pressure pushed the dark, thick grease into the fittings. I had to learn all brands of cars, as the fittings varied from make to make. I remember how Mr. Taft would say, "Any grease you see coming out between them fittings ain't doin' no good. It's the grease you don't see that does the good."

Mr. Eddie had the only hydraulic lift in town, which was used only for cars and light trucks. One of us would drive the vehicle over long parallel I-beams at ground level and let the axles rest there. Then we pushed a lever to raise the car or truck. Once the hydraulic lift was up, as a safety precaution we would take a piece of 4 x 4 lumber and stand it under one of the high beams. We didn't intend to let a car fall on Mr. Taft or me. Not only could we change oil and do grease jobs here, we also could repair brakes, replace mufflers, and do other small jobs. I was responsible for changing batteries and replacing headlight and taillight bulbs, and I was proud to be trusted to do those jobs correctly.

We also fixed flat tires on cars, trucks, and bicycles. If it was flat, we could fix it. As usual, Mr. Taft was my teacher. First I had to learn how to get the lug nuts loose. We had a big silver wrench in the shape of a cross, with each of its four arms ending in a different size socket. You had to find the socket that fit the lug nuts on the vehicle being worked on and with hand pressure twist the lug wrench to the left to loosen and right to tighten. I can hear Mr. Taft now saying, "Lefty loosy, righty tighty." This was graduate education that I received from Dr. Taft Hill. Occasionally I was not strong enough to loosen the lug nuts, and I'd have to call Mr. Taft. Invariably, I would hear a loud squeak, and the lug was freed. Mr. Taft said, "Now when it comes to tightening the lugs, you gotta tighten 'til it squeaks. Then you know it's done tight enough."

The most difficult job in the station was changing tires on the big trucks from Alabama Power. Removing the tire from a twenty-one inch rim was tough and really dangerous. You had to take the valve core out of the valve stem with a special wrench, which Mr. Taft always kept in his pocket. When all the air was out, the tire would be placed on the ground and, using a special tire iron, you broke the seal between the rim and the tire. On a tire this size, Mr. Taft would use a five-pound sledgehammer, after which he would remove a heavy metal ring and the inner tube. If you could, you patched the tube, but often you had to replace the tire and the tube. Then you would take the big metal ring and, using the sledgehammer, mount it where the tire meets the rim. Now you were ready to take the air hose and inflate the tire.

I was never allowed to be around when Mr. Taft was putting the air in truck tires. You had to be very careful to be in just the right position because if the air pressure went in too quickly, the heavy ring could be pushed off the wheel and fly out into the air. "If that ring blows off, Mike," Mr. Taft told me, "you could get hit in the head and get killed. Or you could get an arm cut off. You just stay back when I'm putting air in a truck tire."

I never saw a rim ring blow, but I was quite concerned that Mr. Taft was in harm's way every time he aired up a big truck tire. And I appreciated that he would look out for me as he did. Among the many things he taught me, I gained my lifelong habit of keeping my tools organized and in their proper places.

Our hours were long, from seven in the morning until six at night. And there was little idle time. Most of my time was spent waiting on customers at the pumps. Mr. Eddie wanted this done properly, which meant I was to go to the driver's window and ask what I could do for him or her. Most often it was gas they wanted—the better-off would get a fill-up and the not-so-well-off a dollar or two's worth. I'd also lift the hood and check the oil. I always had a rag in my pocket to wipe off the dipstick. Cars burned a lot of oil in those days, and I opened many a quart metal can of oil with the beer can opener (or church key, as we called it) I kept for that purpose. Then I would wash the windshield, clean headlight lenses, and check the air in all the tires. I quickly learned you could take a big-handled screwdriver and rap the tire, and from the thud or the sharp sound you could tell if a tire needed air. If the customer had gone inside the station, I would take a whiskbroom and sweep the floorboard in front of the driver's seat. At Mr. Eddie's Gulf station we were proud to live up to the words, "Complete Service."

Mr. Eddie said we were always to keep busy. If we weren't waiting on customers or doing some other task, we were to sweep the sidewalk and wash the concrete around the station. But he didn't mind us having a cold drink a couple of times a day. I preferred Grapicos, and I have never enjoyed any drink more than those at Mr. Eddie's. When I finished my lips and tongue would be purple, and Mr. Taft would laugh when I would stick out my tongue at him.

The most memorable moment I ever had at Mr. Eddie's Gulf Station involved Miss Ethel Reisener, an interesting character around town. Miss Reisener, who lived with her companion Dr. Ann Eastman in a little duplex on Highland Avenue, ran The Little Shop on Main Street, which sold very fine ladies' clothes. In those days we called them roommates; today we would probably call them gay or lesbian. Miss Reisener was a large, mannish woman—obviously the dominant one in her relationship with Dr. Eastman. She wore men's suits and smoked cigarettes incessantly, holding them between her thumb and index finger like a man would. She walked with a male gait and cussed like a sailor, and every two weeks, when she came to my parents' shop, she did not go back to the beauty shop, but took her seat in one of the barber's chairs for Dad to cut her close-cropped hair.

Miss Reisener brought her black Chevrolet sedan of pre-war vintage to the station every Saturday and left it to have it washed. The first time I washed it, she picked it up and left, but in no time I saw her coming back, driving like a hot-rod speedster. As she got out of the car I could see a distinct scowl on her face. She walked up to Mr. Eddie, who was standing by the gas pumps.

"Eddie, who washed my car?" she asked sternly.

"Taft," Mr. Eddie said, "who washed Miss Reisener's car?"

At that point I decided I should speak. "I did, sir."

"Did you wash my car, Mike Mahan?" Miss Reisener asked.

"Yes, ma'am."

"You didn't wash under the fenders," she said scornfully.

"No, ma'am," I said weakly, "but you couldn't see under there."

"I wash my ass every night even though no one can see it. Now, get this car in there and finish washing it."

As I obeyed, I saw Mr. Eddie walk inside shaking his head, and Mr. Taft, I could have sworn, turned white. But Miss Reisener had taught me a lesson, and I have never forgotten it.

One day Mr. Eddie announced that he was closing the Gulf Station and would be opening a Western Auto Store. He rented a building half a block away on the corner of Main and Boundary, where Whaley Furniture Company had been. This building had two floors, the second of which was an apartment occupied by the Albright sisters.

When I was told he was closing the Gulf Service Station, I was broken up. I thought I had lost my job, but Miss Mary Lee informed me if I wanted to I could move to the Western Auto and work some after school and on Saturdays. This made me very happy because I didn't want to go back to shining shoes at Dad's barbershop. But I was shocked when he told Mr. Taft there was no place for him. It seemed so callous to let Mr. Taft go after all those years he had given to making the station a success. But I knew, of course, that in those days a black clerk was unheard of. Luckily, because of his work ethic and his talents, Mr. Taft was quickly hired by Smiley and Giggles Frost at the Montevallo Lumber Company, where he served until he got old enough that he could no longer do heavy work.

I don't know how well Mr. Taft was treated by Smiley and Giggles. Many times I would be walking down the street and hear one of them yelling loudly, "Damnit, Taft, get in here." And I would think to myself that Mr. Taft Hill deserved more respect than that.

The whole town was excited about the arrival of Western Auto, its first national chain store, which would handle auto parts, fishing tackle, guns, kitchen appliances, radios, and later household goods. We all watched excitedly as Western Auto headquarters sent in workers to remodel the old store. They brought in showcases, display counters, and tables, and they stocked the shelves and cabinets with Western Auto merchandise. And practically everybody in town attended the grand opening.

***Once a "grunt, grease monkey, and hey boy" at Mr. Eddie's Gulf Service Station, now a clean, well-dressed sales associate (the only one) at the Montevallo Western Auto, 1952.***

Miss Mary Lee was again in charge of the cash register, which rested on a showcase in the middle of the store. I think she carried her stool from the service station there, and she still used the old manual register. I feel sure her fingerprints were permanently etched into the handle that opened the cash drawer. One other duty Miss Mary Lee took on seems rather quaint today. She waited on all the lady customers.

I was amazed as I watched Mr. Eddie become an expert on car parts. Someone would want a water pump for a 1949 Hudson, and he could pull it from the shelf without even consulting a parts list he kept on the counter. Although I was hired as a gopher for both Mr. Eddie and Miss Mary Lee, as time went on I too began to sell parts and whatever else the store carried. Because of my extensive auto repair experience at the service station, I quickly moved up to changing batteries and light bulbs of all descriptions. And I was the number one assembly person in the store. Whatever was ordered from Western Auto warehouse and delivered by a big truck on Wednesdays or Thursdays, I was assigned to put it together on Saturdays or after school during the week.

I was very proud of the trust Mr. Eddie and Miss Mary Lee put in me after opening Western Auto. Very quickly they even trusted me to make change out of Miss Mary Lee's cash register if she was busy with a customer. On occasion, I took money to Merchants and Planters Bank for deposit. I was also trusted to add charges to the charge account ledger. I was proud of my work with the Mahaffeys, but in time I left them to begin working for H. H. Tchakarian and Sons Organ Builders. Even then, when I was home I would help out at Western Auto if I was needed. And I was happy to find that my friend, Teeny Mahaffey—a nephew of Mr. Eddie, would be taking my place.

# 26

# The Organ Business

When I was fifteen, something happened that changed the direction of my life. Walking back to Western Auto from lunch, I noticed an immense 1939 black LaSalle parked in front of the First Baptist Church. Stenciled on its side in what I thought might be Gothic letters was:

H. H. Tchakarian and Sons
Oakland, Florida

I walked over and peered in the window, looking first at the strange gear shift, not knowing that it was the first automatic transmission I had ever laid eyes on. Then I looked up and saw the door to the church was open, and since I didn't have to be back at work for twenty minutes, I decided to look inside and see what was happening. There I saw a portly man with a giant belly standing next to the organ, the front of which had been removed. The man looked at me without speaking a word, so I said, "I'm Mike Mahan, and I just wonder what y'all are doing."

In a thick foreign sounding voice, he asked, "What's it to you, son?"

"Just curious," I said, a little taken aback by his gruffness.

"Well. For your information, my nephew and I—he's over behind that partition—are here to rebuild the leatherworks in this goddamn organ."

Hearing *goddamn* in a church further shocked me, though I was to learn that this man could hardly make a sentence without some form of the word.

"How often does the leather have to rebuilt and how do you do it?" I asked, and I thought he seemed a little surprised at my question.

"Hey, Sam," he called out, "come out here. I want you to meet a boy named Michel. He has more goddamn questions than the police."

While I was wondering why he called me what sounded like "Michelle," a younger man—also somewhat portly and short, with a mustache and long

*"Uncle" H. H. Tchakarian, always eating, cussing, working, and searching for perfection. Tallahassee, Florida, 1953.*

hair—walked out.

"Sam, tell this boy how to rebuild leatherworks."

Sam looked me over, a little confused, and began telling me about the job they were working on. At some point he turned to the older man and said something in a foreign language, which I would later learn was Armenian. As he spoke, I unconsciously picked up a broom and started sweeping the floor. Later on the old man, Chick Tchakarian, told me that had impressed him about me. "Too many boys are lazy." He was also impressed that I had a job at Western Auto.

After my initial visit, I stopped by regularly to watch them work and to ask questions and help straighten up. Finally, one day when I had picked up a broom and was sweeping the floor, Sam turned to me and said, "Well, if you are going to hang out down here, we may as well hire you," and that began employment that lasted for over six years.

To begin with, I was sort of the handyman, and they paid me a dollar or two. I quickly learned that the two were tough taskmasters. They did things right, and they meant for me to do them right, too. Both had tempers that would rise on occasion, and it took me a bit to get used to that. I soon discovered, however, that there was no malice in it. Neither man approved of carrying tools in your back pocket, and if they caught me doing it they would administer a swift kick. Despite that, I came to respect and love both men. Chick, especially, liked me very much. He said to call him Uncle. When he and Sam got ready to leave town, they asked my parents if they could take me on their late summer tuning tour, and they agreed. That was really when my apprenticeship began.

We took off for Georgia in Sam's LaSalle, tuning organs in Hawkinsville, Savannah, and other towns. When it was time for me to return to school in September, Sam put me on a bus and sent me home. From then on, I worked for Uncle and Sam during Christmas holidays and during the summers. And I was paid big money—$100 per month, plus food, lodging, and laundry. In those days that was quite a fine salary for a boy, plus I was learning the pipe organ business inside and out.

I also became Uncle's driver, and I was thrilled, not only for the chance

*Sam Hovsepian and son, Johnny, at a church in Hawkinsville, Georgia, where we did the annual maintenance on the organ. My success as a dentist I owe to Sam for expecting from me the best of my ability.*

to make money, but to have adventures. He always had the biggest, fanciest cars. I loved the idea of a Shelby Street boy tooling down the highway behind the wheel of a shiny two-tone Cadillac. When I returned home every fall I had a fine set of bragging rights. I was seeing the world and learning its ways. I took many a trip, both literally and figuratively, with this amazing man, Chick. He might have been five feet, six inches tall and weighed in at over 200 pounds, but he was one tough customer. He was as hard as a rock.

I learned just how hard he was one day when he and I had to go to Young and Van Hardware in Birmingham to pick up supplies. As we walked in, three black guys in their late teens started snickering and pointing at Uncle's voluminous stomach. When Uncle walked over to them, I wondered what would happen. These were big strong young men who, I supposed, could be pretty dangerous if riled up. Uncle began talking to them in some language other than English, and they got sort of quiet. Then Uncle said, "I know. You are looking at my belly. You are right. It is big, but let me tell you it's no laughing matter. I tell you what. You hit me in the stomach as hard as you can, and if you hurt me I give you a dollar. Then I hit you on the shoulder, and if I hurt you, you give me a dollar. Then we see who is grinning." I looked at the well-built guys and thought that any one of them could destroy Uncle.

"Naw sir," one of them said.

"Me neither," the second boy said.

Uncle turned to the last boy and said, "Come on, or I think you a coward."

With that the boy half-heartedly drew back his fist and delivered a glancing blow. Uncle did not flinch.

"Hit me again," Uncle said. "Harder. Draw back more. Give me your best shot."

I thought oh my God as the fellow drew his arm far back and punched with all his might. Again Uncle was unfazed.

"My time now," Uncle said, drawing back his fist and landing a blow so powerful that the fellow staggered four feet at least across the floor before landing. As he got up, I felt anxious, but Uncle was laughing. "Just keep your dollar," he said, "but be careful who you laugh at." He then walked

***The Hovsepian family, left to right, Lucille, Sam, Eva Jane, a nephew, and Johnny. Johnny is leaning on the Cadillac and the famous DeSoto 4-door Woodie is behind the group.***

slowly over to the counter to put in his order. The clerk's eyes were very wide, I thought.

When Uncle wasn't sleeping, which he did regularly on the road, he was talking, always sprinkling his heavily accented speech liberally with colorful profanity. Slowly I pieced together his remarkable story. When the Turks took over Armenia, Uncle escaped with his mother and three siblings. The family was transported across a border river by his father, who returned to Armenia to get a last child. He was never seen again, and the mother took the family to Athens. From there, Chick went back to Turkey to study electricity in Istanbul, where he distinguished himself as a scholar and an athlete. After graduation, he moved to Edinburgh, Scotland, to study further, and while there he represented Scotland in the Olympics in the shot put and javelin competitions. In Edinburgh, he was also hired by an organ company and began his career of building and repairing organs.

From Scotland, the family moved to Canada, where Uncle took a job with the Hope-Jones Organ Company. That company was bought by the Wurlitzer Company, but Uncle didn't stay with them. He had a terrible temper and almost immediately couldn't get along with the new people at Wurlitzer. That is when he became an original member of the E. M. Skinner Organ Manufacturing team. He was one of the designers of the Pittman Chest, which helped establish Skinner as the premiere builder of organs in the U.S.

Eventually Uncle moved to Miami, Florida, where his sister and her husband, Mr. Hovsepian, had moved to work in the citrus groves. He began installing organs throughout the South. Uncle married a woman we called Auntie, and they had a daughter and a son. When the son showed no interest in the organ business, Uncle took on his nephew as his number one man, and in time Sam became a full partner. In 1928 and 1929, Uncle built and installed the large Skinner organ at Alabama College in Montevallo, a sister organ to one they built at the University of Florida in Gainesville. During the late twenties they installed Skinner organs in major cities throughout the south. But shortly after that, Sam and Uncle had a falling out and separated for some time. Uncle tried to get his son interested in the organ business, but to no avail. Sam went on to wire the world's largest organ at the Atlantic City Music Hall. Luckily, Uncle and Sam went back together and continued to service and install organs together in the Carolinas, Georgia, Florida, and Alabama for many years.

My employment with H. H. Tchakarian and Sons was a liberal education in itself. Not only did I learn about organs, I learned about life. I saw places I would not have otherwise seen, and I learned more than I ever thought I would about women. From my bed in one corner of the room, I would listen to Sam, lying in his own bed, spin out tales about various amorous adventures. He could be very literal about his sexual experience, and in his long tales, the romance of love loomed as large as the mechanics of sex. I had never experienced anything like this.

I developed a great affection for Uncle, who was almost a surrogate father to me. I was truly astounded at his encyclopedic knowledge. Especially impressive was his mastery of languages. He still spoke Armenian with Sam and

*Sam and Lucille Hovsepian, Tallahassee, Florida, 1953. She lived a married life dominated by overpowering Armenian customs, quite a change for a simple Georgia girl. But she made a great mother, wife, and co-worker in the organ business.*

other family members, but he also spoke English, French, German, Greek, Italian, and Turkish. Maybe more. He claimed to be the only person in the world who could speak Latin. When we went to a university town, as we often did, he would strike out for the student gathering place and look for foreign students to engage in conversation. As a young man, I was impressed by his amazing ability.

The biggest leap I made with Uncle in the ways of the world, however, was my experiences with unfamiliar food. You could look at Uncle and Sam and tell that they enjoyed food. Uncle got up from the table thinking about the next meal. Like many people with European backgrounds, they were extremely fond of lamb, and I ate my first lamb when I traveled with them. I was not squeamish about food, and that was a good thing, as I had some strange things put before me.

Uncle and Sam also taught me a few things about drinking. Once, at the Shamrock Hotel in Fort Pierce, Florida, Chick and Sam ordered me a beer, and I felt a bit funny drinking it in front of all the adults in there. But I liked the feeling. After the meal, Sam decided that we should have an after-dinner drink, and he ordered us all a Drambuie. They brought it out in a tiny glass no bigger than a thumb, and I thought that the drinks looked awfully chintzy. Sam knew what I was thinking. "Don't slug it down, Michel. Smell it first, then taste it with your tongue." The peppery drink burned my tongue at first, but by the end of the drink I thought I had never tasted any drink that was better.

One time we were working at Florida State University in Tallahassee, and I was staying with Sam and his wife, Lucille, a cracker girl from Georgia, in the house they had rented for the summer. One day I was working with Uncle in a large auditorium when he called me over. He told me to come go with him somewhere, and we got into his huge DeSoto Suburban he used to haul organ parts. He drove to the stockyard, told me to stay in the Suburban, and disappeared. When he came back out he had a sheep's head. "Michel," he said, "We gonna have the best goddamn thing you ever ate. You just wait." I stared over at the sheep's head, covered with matted hair and one of its eyes all blood shot. I wondered how that could be made edible.

Back home, we put the head in a huge pot and boiled it, hair and all. Then Uncle took it to a table in the backyard, and instructed me on how to remove the hair with a stone. He turned the job over to me, and when I finished the sheep's head was a smooth, milky white. Then Sam's wife, Lucille, brought out a pan of stuffing, and Uncle popped the sheep's mouth open and started poking the stuffing in. It was then cooked over slow heat for a very long time. When it was finally served, I could see why they thought it was a delicacy. I stopped short of eating an eye—Uncle got both of those—but I did eat some of what I was told was the brain, and it was quite tasty.

The sheep's head was tame compared to the pickled maggots we had one time or some kind of insects that resembled limousine roaches. I would try anything, and to this day I will eat what is put before me and eaten by others, no questions asked.

I loved visiting Sam in Oakland, not far from Tampa, Florida, where he had his permanent home. Uncle was often there, even when his wife was still alive and staying in Miami to be near her children. After her death early in my tenure with Uncle and Sam, Uncle lived primarily at Sam's home. In Oakland, I would often help with chores related to food preparation. They loved to make guava jelly, and I would help them cook it and put it up in pint jars. When I went there at Christmas, I was pressed into service harvesting oranges and grapefruit in their large backyard. We would put them in crates and ship them to family members, friends, and organ customers.

Uncle would send me up the ladder to pick the fruit, and he would sit in a metal glider below the tree and have me toss the fruit down to him. He would throw up his hands and catch the fruit as deftly as a professional baseball player. One day I picked a rotten grapefruit from the tree, and I can't say why but I was suddenly possessed by the devil. Rather than throw it away, I threw it with more force than necessary down to Uncle, and when he caught it, it exploded all over him. I immediately was sorry I had done it, knowing that Uncle could have a terrible temper. I held my breath for his reaction. He said, "Goddamnit, Michel, if I had been in the tree and you on the ground, I'd have done the same thing." Now, there is one prince of a man, I thought.

Both Uncle and Sam loved great restaurants, and they spared no expense in getting the best food, especially in large cities like Savannah, Atlanta, and Gainesville. In the early fifties when I was driving for Uncle, we left Montevallo about mid-afternoon headed for Tallahassee, Florida. We hadn't gone but a few miles past Montgomery when Uncle crossed his arms over his massive stomach and promptly went to sleep. After a bit he fell into his usual rhythm of sleep sounds, blowing air out of his mouth with a *poof, puff, puh . . . poof, puff, puh.* At sundown, just as we were going across the ridge into Troy, Alabama, Uncle woke up. As usual he rubbed his eyes and asked, "Goddamnit, Michel, where are we?"

"Troy," I answered.

"Have you ever eaten at Antoine's in New Orleans?" he asked abruptly.

"No, sir," I answered, knowing what he had in mind. He was willing to drive way out of his way for a good meal, and I had heard him sing the praises of Antoine's many times.

"Get out the map," he said.

"But, Uncle Chick," I said, "that's a long way and we have to meet Sam in Tallahassee tomorrow."

"Goddamnit, Michel, I don't need to be reminded of that. But we've got time. We can make it. Turn this car toward New Orleans. We gonna eat at Antoine's."

And I obeyed, getting us into the Crescent City about 3:00 in the morning. We checked into the Monteleone, and I fell out exhausted. We pulled ourselves out of bed in time to go to lunch, and what a lunch: oysters Rockefeller, trout marguerie, bread pudding with whiskey sauce, the whole works. It was worth the effort. Then it was off again to Tallahassee. We arrived almost a day late, but Sam had taken care of whatever needed to be done there.

Sam and Uncle did not mind spending big bucks on food, but the rule of the road was order anything you want but you have to eat all of it. Once at the Floridian Hotel in Gainesville we ordered jumbo fried shrimp and all the extras, and try all I could, I could not eat the final shrimp on my plate. The next day I left with Sam for a job in Savannah, and when we checked into the DeSoto Hotel I had a package waiting for me. Uncle had packaged up that uneaten shrimp and sent it with the message, "Goddamnit, Michel, eat your shrimp." I wrapped it right back up and mailed it back to him. That began the mailing back and forth of that shrimp for the entire summer. But it was never mentioned afterwards.

For over six years, I worked for Uncle and Sam, often living with Sam and his family. I became so proficient in the organ business that I thought I'd make it my profession, and I became Sam's bound apprentice. When I started to Auburn, Uncle suggested that I major in engineering, which would be quite useful to me in the organ business. After struggling two quarters with the math courses, I shifted to music, and Uncle said he reckoned that would have to do. I enjoyed my time in the music department, holding a band/work fellowship that paid tuition in exchange for work for band director Dave Herbert, along with other duties. I also played with the Auburn marching band, the concert band, and the ROTC band. As I neared graduation, Sam came to me and offered me the entire territory north of Dothan, Alabama, but I had become so intrigued with the idea of being a concert bass player that I turned him down. It made him very angry, and for several years he did not speak to me.

After my ill-fated trip to Cincinnati and my conclusion that my career would not be in music, I had to face the same thing about the organ business. By then Uncle had died and Sam had retired, and large organs at theaters and other public places were a passing thing. The work was just not going to be there. But I must say that I have never regretted that time I spent with

Uncle and Sam. My interest in the organ has certainly remained. In 1967, I was reading ads in the *Birmingham News* when I saw an ad for a used pipe organ in Selma at the Presbyterian church. I called about it and found it was an original E. M. Skinner installed in 1923, and when I saw this jewel I knew that it would be perfect for my church, the First Methodist Church of Montevallo. The church bought it. It needed a great deal of work, and with my growing dental practice I did not have time to restore it. Although Sam and I had been estranged since I turned down his job offer, I decided to call him to see if we could get him to restore the organ. Without hesitation, he said yes, and he came to Montevallo and did the job, staying with Linda and me on and off for over a year. After that, he returned to Montevallo for an annual visit. Sam died around 2000, but I still communicate with his son Johnny about once a year. Some tie to these vital people in my life has seemed necessary to me.

The demands of my profession of dentistry have not allowed me to use much the skills Chick and Sam taught me. But since I worked those years with them, very few days have passed that I have not thought of one or the other of them, and I am convinced that the skills and values they taught me can be seen in how I respect my tools, in how I attend to minute details in order to achieve quality work, and in the respect I have for those I serve. All of that came from Uncle and Sam.

# Afterword

After receiving my bachelor's degree in music education in 1956 and having realized that the two career avenues I had expected to follow, one music and the other organ building, were no longer realistic choices, I faced the challenge of deciding what course my life would take. In August of that year I married Carol Clark, a fellow Auburn band member, and we returned to Montevallo, moving into an apartment in the basement of my parents' home on Shelby Street. In 1957, my daughter Miki was conceived and born. Unfortunately, the marriage to Carol didn't last, and Mother and I took on the responsibility of helping to raise Miki.

Ralph Sears, who gave me a job in the Public Relations Department at Alabama College, generously allowed me to take courses while working, and I found myself moving away from the arts, filling in science courses I had not taken at Auburn. I was especially encouraged by Dr. Paul Bailey, head of the biology department, and I received a second B.S. degree in biology and chemistry. Later, Dr. Bailey, who headed the College's summer science institute, arranged for me to take master's degree courses in those summer institutes, and I received my master's in biology and chemistry in 1961. I was now ready, I thought, to go job hunting.

Dr. L. C. "Foots" Parnell, an OB/GYN who had grown up in Montevallo, suggested that I consider a career in drug sales, and later he recommended me to Upjohn Drug Company. I applied, and they flew me to Atlanta for an interview—my first time to fly. They offered me a job, which I readily accepted, and I moved to Columbus, Georgia, calling on drug stores, doctors, and dentists in western Georgia and eastern Alabama. I worked very hard at the job and won awards for my sales. Among those I called on was a successful older dentist in the small town of Roanoke, Alabama. For the first time I found myself greatly attracted to dentistry as a vocation.

Arriving in Columbus, Georgia, I immediately joined the Columbus Symphony, and at the first fall rehearsal I found myself sitting across from a beautiful brunette who played violin. This was Linda.

The year of 1962 would hands-down be the most important of my life, both professionally and personally. On February 20, 1962, I had an epiphany. I was riding down the highway toward Opelika, Alabama, listening excitedly to the big news of that day: John Glenn was orbiting the Earth. I stopped on a hill and listened to every word about this important event. What an achievement, I thought, and it came to me that I too could do something greater with my life. I knew without a doubt I did not want a career as a drug representative, and with equal clarity I knew that I *did* want a life as a dentist. I turned the car around immediately and drove back to a pay phone at the Dairy Queen in Opelika. I got the number of the University of Alabama Dental School in Birmingham from information and excitedly deposited my coins and dialed. I was directed to the registrar, Mrs. Bridges, and I asked if I could come and talk to her about going to dental school. She agreed, and I told her I'd be there in three hours.

***Carol Clark Mahan in 1956. A majorette at Auburn, my first wife, and Miki's mother.***

On arrival, I was directed to Mrs. Bridges's office. She asked about my background and said that I seemed to have the proper pre-dental studies. Then she asked if I had taken the National Dental Aptitude

Exam, which I had not. I asked when it would be given, and she said the following Saturday. I said I wanted to sign up, and she said that it was too late, that the forms had been submitted for all applicants along with a $25 exam fee. I asked if she could call and see if I could be added to the list. She replied that she had never done it before, but she would give it a shot. She called them and they said, "Yes, sign him up," and I sent the fee.

Mrs. Bridges suggested that I also might go see the head of the admissions committee, who I later found out was called "Happy Jack" Clapper, as he never smiled. He was not at all impressed with me. In fact, he told me that he didn't think I had what it took to go to dental school or to be a dentist. I told him that I didn't know whether I would go to the dental school at the University of Alabama, but I was determined to go somewhere. Later Mrs. Bridges gave me a list of dental schools in the country, and Linda helped me get out application letters to a number of schools, including Harvard, Tufts, Tennessee, Emory, and Meharry. In those days, all applications required a photo, and I received a very nice letter from the admissions officer at Meharry saying perhaps I was not familiar with the fact that they were a black dental school.

I took the exam on a Saturday morning and was told to expect results in two weeks. After a week Mrs. Bridges called and asked if I could meet with the admissions committee on the following Wednesday afternoon. I took that to be a good sign. I arrived dressed very professionally and was escorted to a very sterile room. I sat down before at least ten committee members. After asking generally about why I wanted to be a dentist, they asked me about my job at Upjohn. One person asked me to talk about one drug that I was now detailing, and I chose to speak about a new drug called Monase because I had just read up on it and had memorized the information for my sales spiel. Without a shred of a note, I detailed the drug fully for the group, and I must say they seemed impressed. The only other question they had was about how I would pay for my dental studies. Without knowing for sure, I said confidently that I would borrow the money for the first year from Central State Bank in Calera, which in the end I actually did.

The confidence I felt on leaving that meeting was soon validated when I received a letter from the Alabama School of Dentistry. I was very nervous

*In the living room of Linda's parents' Sylvania, Georgia, home, on September 1, 1962, when Linda Chambers and I were married, witnessed by Sandra Lowe as matron of honor and my dad as best man. Reverend Jim Summerford performed the ceremony.*

about opening the letter so I waited for Linda to get home from teaching music in the public schools of Columbus. She opened it and found I was admitted to the program. I told Upjohn I would be leaving, and they generously let me continue to work that summer.

The other reason 1962 was a pivotal year for me was that Linda, although she didn't literally ask me to marry her, said that if our relationship was to continue it must include a marriage ceremony. That summer she was working at Brevard Music Center, and I went up early in the summer and agreed to her proposal. The next thing I knew the wedding date was set. I returned to Brevard several times that summer, including three days before camp ended and five days before our wedding. We packed up Linda's Simca and headed back to Sylvania, Georgia, where her parents, a public school principal and a librarian, lived. The car broke down on the way to her home, and we had to spend the night on the road. When Linda called her mother, she said it was okay but added, "I hope you have separate rooms."

After the "I do's" were over on September 1, 1962, we spent our honeymoon night at the Holiday Inn in Macon, Georgia. On Sunday, September 2, we stopped in Columbus and loaded all of our possessions in *Miki II*, a boat I owned. We arrived in Birmingham that night in the Upjohn company car, pulling the loaded boat. We moved our things into a new student housing unit on the UAB campus that would be our home for four years. Monday, September 3, was Labor Day, and on Tuesday, September 4, I entered dental school.

That summer Linda had gotten a job teaching strings for the Jefferson County school system making $261 a month. Our rent was $70 a month so we had to learn quickly how to live very frugally. If it hadn't been for my mother, dad, and sister, we probably would have starved. Each Sunday afternoon we picked up or they delivered manna from Mother.

In 1964, while I was in my junior year of dental school, we bought Montebrier from Ruby Lee Latham, but it was not suitable to live in until we finished renovating it in August of 1966. It needed lots of work, and I obtained a loan from Merchants and Planters Bank in 1965 to begin restoring and renovating. We lived on Shelby Street with my parents for a month before the work was completed.

In 1966, I began my dental practice in the Medical Arts Building on Salem Road in Montevallo. Birmingham Trust was known for lending money to doctors and dentists getting established, and I borrowed my start-up money from them. I remained in this office for years, though my dream was to have an office on the banks of Mahan Creek. I finally began building there in 1976. Along with a friend, Ward Tishler, I went to Tennessee to scout out log cabins to incorporate into the new building. Near Sneedville, I found the Mahan cabin, which was built in the 1700s by my great-great-great uncle. That became the center of the Mahan Creek Dental Arts Building in Brierfield. I continued to practice half-time in Montevallo and half-time in Brierfield for a number of years, finally moving full-time to Brierfield. On March 3, 2006, the office caught fire, but luckily much of the log cabin was not destroyed.

In establishing myself as a dentist in my hometown, I had several objec-

***Dentistry in the Yucatan. First came the kids, then the women and mothers, and if they did o.k., the men and fathers gathered their courage and walked up. Linda is on the left wearing a white coat, and I am kneeling in the center.***

tives. Most importantly, I wanted to provide state-of-the-art dentistry to my patients. To do that I knew that I would need to keep up with changes in the profession. Although I joined a number of professional organizations, two were the most important. Delta Sigma Delta International Dental Fraternity offered numerous opportunities for learning and serving, and in 1984 I was designated as Supreme Grand Master, the chief executive officer of the international organization. There, I co-founded the special projects committee, which sent undergraduates to work with Mayan Indians in Mexico. I myself did dental work with the Mayans in Yucatan from 1976–84.

The other organization that has provided me many opportunities for professional development has been the Pankey Institute, founded forty years ago. I have served in its mentor program since 1998.

As a dentist in Montevallo, I did not wish to limit myself to my professional endeavors. I wanted to be a fully participating member of the community, just as my father had been. Like him, I focused on working in fire suppression and prevention. I became a volunteer fireman in 1956, and I served as fire chief 1971–91. As with dentistry, I joined firemen's local and national associations to learn all I could to help protect lives and property in our town. For most of my life, I have also been an active member of the First United Methodist Church, serving on the administrative council and working with the music program.

Music has in many ways always been my greatest love. When Linda and I came to Birmingham, we both played in the Birmingham Symphony. Later, Linda was a founding member of the Red Mountain Chamber Orchestra, and subsequently I joined it. We were members until 2011. Much of my musical activity, however, has related to Dixieland, ragtime, and jazz, and I have played with several groups, most recently with Chuck King and Friends. I feel fortunate to have been able to support many worthy causes in the area through my music.

Another great passion has been history. I have served on the boards of local, state, and national organizations and was particularly active as a member of the Alabama Historical Commission from 1984–2004, serving as its chairman in 1992. I received a gubernatorial appointment to the Alabama Historic Ironworks Commission, which manages the Brierfield and Tannehill Ironworks Historical State Parks. I have also served on the Cahaba Trace Commission. Since 1968, I have participated in Civil War reenactment activities. Linda and I were named charter co-chairmen of the Live-in-a-Landmark Council of Alabama in 1975. My love of old houses led me to participate in national work with the National Trust for Historical Preservation and the Historic House Association of America.

I have also been an active alumnus of the University of Montevallo. In 1980, I was named Alumnus of the Year. For many years I taught Elderhostel classes on the history of the South at UM, sharing these classes with outstanding historians, including the late Kathryn Tucker Windham, with musician Jim Connor, and with writer Bill Cobb. I also helped organize and conduct University of Montevallo's Alabama Heritage tours for a number of years.

The only significant thing I wanted to do in my life that did not work out was in the realm of politics. When Representative Curtis Smith decided not to run for his seat in the Alabama Legislature, some people came to me asking if I would run. I was thrilled by the idea, and even more thrilled when money was pledged to my campaign. Excitedly I rushed home to tell Linda, who responded unequivocally: "You can be a legislator or my husband. Just pick the one you want." That ended my short flirtation with Alabama politics. I was made quite happy and proud when in 2000 our daughter Stann was elected to the Montevallo City Council, as her grandfather had been so many years ago.

So, here I am at seventy-nine, still practicing dentistry, still playing music, still trying to serve my community. Recently my staff and I promoted a national program known as "Dentistry from the Heart." For one day a year, I call on my fellow dentists, professional hygienists, and assistants as well as many community volunteers to participate in an effort to provide extractions at no cost to those less fortunate. In one day, we extracted 444 teeth and relieved the suffering and pain of 243 patients. When I think of that accomplishment, I feel proud.

For some reason my Dad's old saying keeps coming back to me, "There ain't no hill too high for a stepper." My life in Montevallo and Brierfield has been filled with opportunities and challenges, and I have tried to face them with optimism and self-confidence.

~

# Index

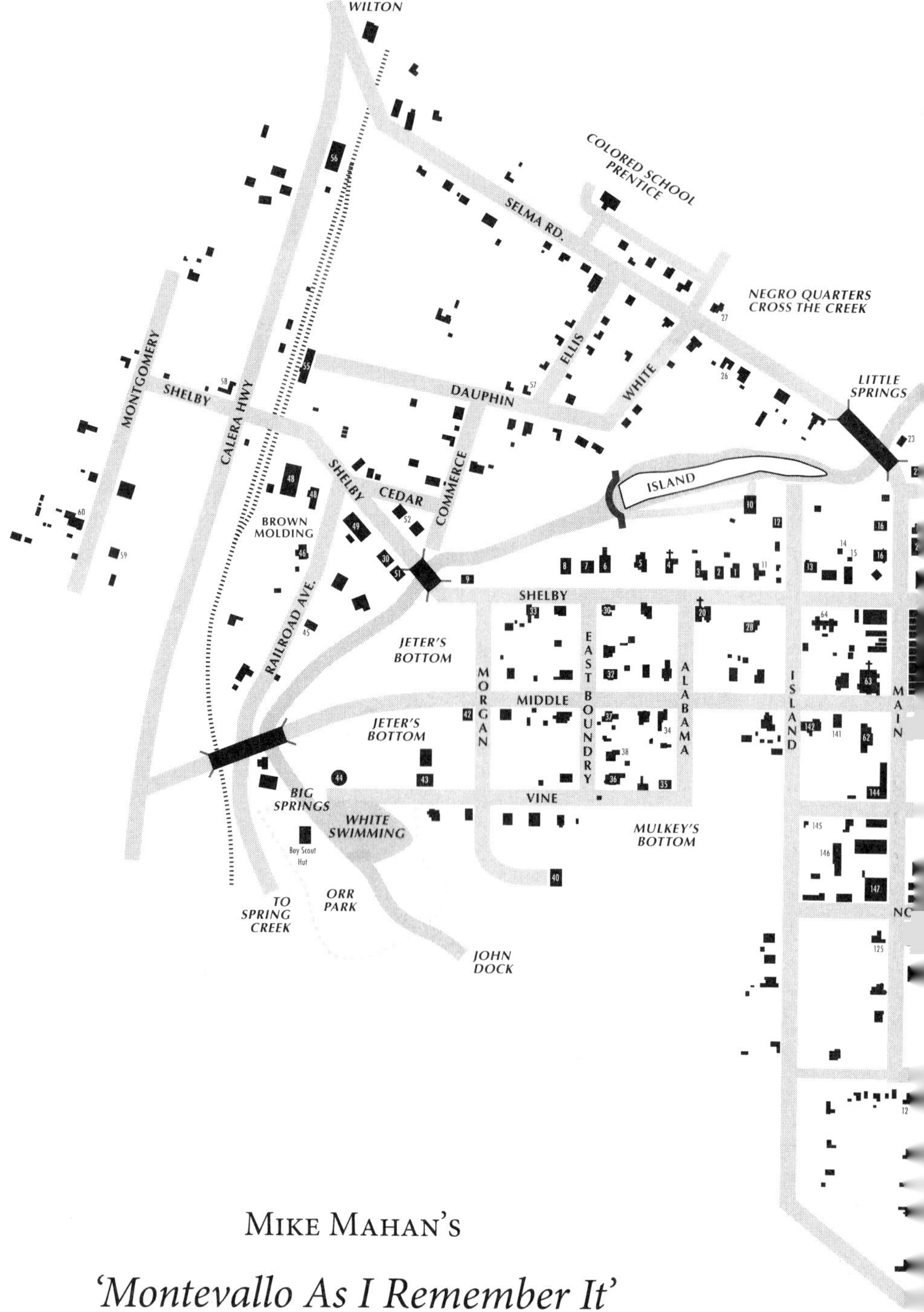


Mike Mahan's

# 'Montevallo As I Remember It'

Drawn by Hal Huber, after a 1933 Sanborn Company map.

*(see larger map with legend at www.newsouthbooks.com/stepper/map)*